Study Guide

Juvenile Delinquency
The Core
THIRD EDITION

Larry J. Siegel
University of Massachusetts, Lowell

Brandon C. Welsh
University of Massachusetts, Lowell

Prepared by

Michael Fischer
Norfolk State University

THOMSON
✱
WADSWORTH

Australia • Brazil • Canada • Mexico • Singapore • Spain • United Kingdom • United States

ISBN-13: 978-0-495-38281-2
ISBN-10: 0-495-38281-7

Thomson Higher Education
10 Davis Drive
Belmont, CA 94002-3098
USA

For more information about our products,
contact us at:
Thomson Learning Academic Resource Center
1-800-423-0563

For permission to use material from this text or
product, submit a request online at
http://www.thomsonrights.com.
Any additional questions about permissions can be
submitted by email to **thomsonrights@thomson.com.**

Juvenile Delinquency: The Core

Table of Contents

CHAPTER ONE
CHILDHOOD AND DELINQUENCY

LEARNING OBJECTIVES

- Be familiar with the problems of youth in American culture.
- Be able to discuss the concept of adolescence and risk taking.
- Develop an understanding of the history of childhood.
- Be familiar with the concept of *parens patriae*.
- Be able to discuss development of a special status of minor offenders.
- Know what is meant by the terms juvenile delinquent and status offender.
- Be able to describe the differences between delinquency and status offending.
- Be able to discuss what is meant by parental responsibility laws.
- Be familiar with juvenile curfew laws.
- Identify the efforts being made to reform status offense laws.

CHAPTER OUTLINE

I.   Introduction
    A.   Aaliyah Parker
        1. runaway
        2. addict
        3. Arrested and diverted to therapy where she does well
        4. When she turns 18, must advocate for herself to avoid being homeless.
    B.   70 million children under age 18 in the United States
        1.   juveniles are 25 percent of the population
        2.   expected to reach 24 percent of the population in 2020
        3.   by age 18 they have spent more time in front of a TV set than in the classroom

II. Adolescent Dilemma
    A.   Adolescence is a time of trial and uncertainty
        1.   youths experience anxiety, humiliation, and mood swings
        2.   juveniles are maturing at an earlier age
        3.   youths may experience ego identity and role diffusion
    B.   Youth in crisis
        1.   youths considered at risk are those who engage in dangerous conduct
        2.   dangerous conduct includes drug abuse, alcohol use, and precocious sexuality
        3.   estimates 25 percent of the population under age seventeen are at risk
    C.   Children and poverty
        1.   studies documented the association between family poverty and children's health, achievement, and behavior impairments

      a.   issues such as chronic health problems

      b.   children in poverty receive inadequate health care

      c.   more than 9 million children have no health insurance

D.   Family problems

      1.   divorce strikes about half of all new marriages

E.   Substandard living conditions

      1.   many children live in substandard housing

      2.   create negative influence on their long-term psychological health

      3.   one third of U.S. households with children had one or more of the following three housing problems:

            a.   physically inadequate housing

            b.   crowded housing

            c.   housing that cost more than 30% of the household income

F.   Inadequate education

      1.   education seems to be failing many young people

      2.   US lagging behind other developed nations in critical areas

      3.   retention rates are associated with dropping out

G.   Is there reason for hope?

      1.   teenage birthrates have declined substantially

      2.   abortion rate was down 39% in this age group

III.   Study of Juvenile Delinquency

A.   Juvenile delinquency defined as criminal behavior engaged in by minors

      1.   important because of the damage suffered by its victims

      2.   important also because of the problems faced by its perpetrators

B.   1.5 million youths under age 18 arrested each year

      1.   crimes range from loitering to murder

      2.   chronic juvenile offenders are a serious social problem

C.   Teen Risk Taking

      1. 18.5% have carried a weapon

      2. 20.2% had smoked marijuana

      3. 35.9% had been in a physical fight

      4. 37.2% of sexually active high school students had not used a condom at last sexual intercourse

      5. 13.1% were overweight

D.   Study of delinquency involves the analysis of the juvenile justice system

      1.   includes law enforcement, court, and correctional agencies

      2.   reaction to juvenile delinquency frequently divides the public

      3.   in Roper v Simmons (2005) the death penalty for anybody who committed a crime when he or she was less than 18 years of age was declared unconstitutional, as a violation of the 8th Amendment's provision against cruel and unusual punishment and the 14th amendment

IV.   The Development of Childhood

A.   Treating children as a distinct social group is a new concept

      1.   paternalistic family

2.   father exercised complete control over his wife and children
3.   children subject to severe physical punishment, even death

B.   Custom and practice in the Middle Ages
    1.   children of all classes were expected to take on adult roles
    2.   boys born to landholding families
        a.   sent to a monastery or cathedral school
        b.   serve as squires or assistants to experienced knights
    3.   Aries described the medieval child as a "miniature adult"

C.   Child rearing and discipline
    1.   impersonal relationship between parent and child common
    2.   traced to the high mortality rates of the day

V.   Development of Concern for Children

A.   Areas influenced
    1.   recognition of children's rights
    2.   changes in family style and child care
    3.   English Poor Laws
    4.   apprenticeship movement
    5.   role of the chancery court

B.   Changes in family structure
    1.   family structure began to change after the Middle Ages
    2.   grammar and boarding schools were established in large cities
    3.   teachers often ruled by fear

C.   Voltaire, Rousseau, and Locke launched a new age for childhood
    1.   produced a period known as the Enlightenment
    2.   children began to emerge as a distinct group
        a.   independent needs and interests

D.   Poor Laws
    1.   English passed statutes known as Poor Laws
    2.   allowed for the appointment of overseers
        a.   placed destitute or neglected children as servants for the affluent
        b.   trained in agricultural, trade, or domestic services

E.   Apprenticeship movement
    1.   children were placed in the care of adults
    2.   trained them in specific skills
    3.   voluntary apprentices were bound out by parents for a fee
        a.   legal authority over the child transferred to the apprentice's master
    4.   involuntary apprentices were abandoned or wayward youth
        a.   compelled by the legal authorities to serve a master until age 21

F.   Chancery Court
    1.   established to protect property rights
    2.   seek equitable solutions to disputes and conflicts

3.   authority extended to the welfare of children
       a.   cases involving the guardianship of orphans
       b.   safeguarding their property and inheritance rights

G.   *Parens patriae*
     1.   refers to the role of the king as the father of his country
     2.   created with 1827 case *Wellesley v. Wellesley*
     3.   chancery courts jurisdiction
       a.   did not extend to children charged with criminal conduct
       b.   law violations handled through the regular criminal court system

VI.   Childhood in America
     A.   American colonies were developing similar concepts
       1.   colonists had illegitimate, neglected, and delinquent children
       2.   legislation for apprenticeships passed
         a.   Virginia in 1646
         b.   Massachusetts and Connecticut in 1673
       3.   Maryland and Virginia developed an orphans' court
         a.   supervised the treatment of youths placed with guardians
       4.   apprenticeship system gave way to the factory system

     B.   Factory Act
       1.   limited the hours children were permitted to work
       2.   limited age at which they could begin to work
       3.   prescribed a minimum amount of schooling to be provided by factory owners

     C.   Controlling children
       1.   moral discipline was rigidly enforced
       2.   stubborn child laws were passed
         a.   required children to obey their parents
       3.   child protection laws were passed as early as 1639
       4.   few cases of child abuse brought before the courts
       5.   children were productive laborers

VI.   The Concept of Delinquency
     A.   Until the 20th century, little distinction was made between adult and juvenile offenders
       1.   society became sensitive to the special needs of children
       2.   child savers were formed to assist children

     B.   Delinquency and *parens patriae*
       1.   current treatment is by-product of national consciousness of children's needs
       2.   delinquents viewed as victims of improper care at home
       3.   state should act in the best interests of the child
       4.   children should not be punished for their misdeeds

C.   Legal status of delinquency
       1.   child savers fought for a legal status of juvenile delinquent
       2.   Early British jurisprudence held that children:
            a.   under the age of seven were legally incapable of committing crimes
            b.   between 7 and 14 were responsible for their actions
            c.   their age might excuse or lighten their punishment
       3.   juvenile delinquent refers to a minor child who has violated the penal code
       4.   states define minor child as an individual who falls under a statutory age limit
            a.   most commonly 17 or 18 years of age
       5.   juveniles are usually kept separate from adults
       6.   every state has some form of juvenile court
       7.   terminology is different
       8.   children have a unique legal status
D.   Legal responsibility of youths
       1.   actions of adults are controlled by two types of law: criminal law and civil law
       2.   criminal laws prohibit activities that are injurious to the well-being of society
       3.   civil laws control interpersonal or private activities
       4.   juvenile delinquency falls somewhere between criminal and civil law
       5.   delinquent acts are not considered criminal violations
       6.   delinquent behavior is treated more leniently than adult
E.   Adolescents are believed to
       1.   have a stronger preference for risk and novelty
       2.   be less accurate in assessing the potential consequences of risky conduct
       3.   more impulsive and more concerned with short-term consequences
       4.   have a different appreciation of time and self-control
       5.   more susceptible to peer pressure
F.   Juveniles are subject to arrest, trial, and incarceration
       1.   children have many of the same legal protections as adults
       2.   there are violent juvenile offenders
       3.   behavior requires a firmer response
       4.   some contend that hard-core offenders cannot be treated as children
       5.   prompted the policy of waiver
       6.   transfer legal jurisdiction to the adult court for criminal prosecution

VII. Status Offenders
    A. Actions that would not be considered illegal if committed by an adult
        1. terminology varies by state
            a. child in need of supervision
            b. unruly child
            c. incorrigible child
            d. minor in need of supervision
    B. Status Offense Law: Maryland
        1. child means an individual under the age of 18 years
        2. defines child in need of supervision
        3. is required by law to attend school and is habitually truant
        4. habitually disobedient and ungovernable
        5. deports himself so as to injure or endanger himself or others
        6. has committed an offense applicable only to children
    C. State control over a child's noncriminal behavior supports the *parens patriae* philosophy
        1. assumed to be in the best interests of the child
        2. historical basis exists for status offense statutes
        3. almost every state treated status offenders and juvenile delinquents alike until the 1960's/70's
        4. trend from 1960s resulted in the creation of separate status offense categories
            a. CHINS, MINS, PINS, YINS, or JINS
            b. shield noncriminal youths from the stigma attached to delinquent label
            c. signify that they have special needs and problems
        5. some noncriminal conduct may be included in the definition of delinquency
        6. less serious criminal offenses occasionally may be labeled as status offenses
    D. Status offender in the Juvenile Justice System
        1. may have little effect on treatment
    E. Aiding the status offender
        1. In 1974, the U.S. Congress passed the JJDPA
        2. provides major source of federal funding to improve states' JJS
        3. required to remove status offenders from secure detention and lockups
            a. insulate them from more serious delinquent offenders
        4. act created the OJJDP
        5. distribute grants to states that developed alternate procedural methods
        6. Runaway and Homeless Youth Act (RHYA) of 1974
        7. provides funds for nonsecure facilities
            a. status offenders receive safe shelter

8. act amended in 1987
   a. allows status offenders to be detained for violations of court orders

F. Changes in the treatment of status offenders
   1. reflect the current attitude toward children who violate the law
   2. movement to severely sanction youths who commit serious offenses
   3. effort made to remove nonserious cases from the official agencies of justice

G. Reforming status offense laws
   1. commissions have called for limiting control over status offenders
   2. National Advisory Commission on Criminal Justice Standards and Goals
   3. opted for the nonjudicial treatment of status offenders
   4. controlling five status offenses
      a. habitual truancy
      b. repeated disregard for parental authority
      c. repeated running away
      d. repeated use of intoxicating beverages
      e. delinquent acts by youths under the age of 10
   5. calls for reform prompted a number of changes
   6. serious debate over the liberalization of status offense laws
   7. some states have resisted weakening status offense laws

VIII. Increasing social control over juveniles and their parents
   A. Curfews
      1. since 1990 there has been an explosion in the passage of curfew
      2. 59 of 77 large cities have curfews
      3. each year 60,000 youths are arrested for curfew violations
      4. victimizations increased significantly during noncurfew hours
      5. many contend that curfews another misguided anticrime strategy
   B. Disciplining parents
      1. laws for contributing to the delinquency of a minor
      2. half of states enacted or strengthened existing parental liability statutes
      3. make parents criminally liable for the actions of their delinquent children
      4. parents sanctioned in juvenile court for child's misbehavior
      5. all states except New Hampshire have parental liability laws
   C. Parents may also be held civilly liable
      1. concept of vicarious liability
      2. responsible for damages caused by their child
      3. parents can also be charged with civil negligence
      4. critics charge laws contravene the right to due process
      5. unfairly used only against lower-class and minority parents
      6. imposing penalties on these parents may actually be detrimental

CHAPTER SUMMARY

The study of delinquency is concerned with the nature and extent of the criminal behavior of youths, the causes of youthful law violations, the legal rights of juveniles, and prevention and treatment. The problems of American youths have become an important subject of academic study. Many children live in poverty, have inadequate health care, and suffer family problems. Adolescence is a time of taking risks, which can get kids into trouble.

Our modern conception of a separate status for children is quite different than in the past. With the start of the seventeenth century came greater recognition of the needs of children. In Great Britain, the chancery court movement, Poor Laws, and apprenticeship programs helped reinforce the idea of children as a distinct social group. In colonial America, many of the characteristics of English family living were adopted. In the nineteenth century, delinquent and runaway children were treated no differently than criminal defendants.

The concept of delinquency was adopted in the early twentieth century. The child savers helped create a separate delinquency category to insulate juvenile offenders from the influence of adult criminals. The status of juvenile delinquency is based on the *parens patriae* philosophy. This philosophy holds that children have the right to care and custody and that if parents are not capable of providing that care, the state must step in to take control.

Juvenile courts also have jurisdiction over noncriminal status offenders. Status offenses such as truancy, running away, and sexual misconduct are illegal only because of their minority status of the juvenile offender. Some experts have called for an end to juvenile court control over status offenders. Some research indicates that status offenders are harmed by juvenile court processing. Other research indicates that status offenders and delinquents are quite similar. There has been a successful effort to separate status offenders from delinquents and to maintain separate facilities for those who need to be placed in a shelter care program. The treatment of juveniles is an ongoing dilemma. Still uncertain is whether young law violators respond better to harsh punishments or to benevolent treatment.

KEY TERMS

ego identity: According to Erik Erikson, ego identity is formed when persons develop a firm sense of who they are and what they stand for.

role diffusion: According to Erik Erikson, role diffusion occurs when youths spread themselves too thin, experience personal uncertainty, and place themselves at the mercy of leaders who promise to give them a sense of identity they cannot develop for themselves.

at-risk youths: Young people who are extremely vulnerable to the negative consequences of school failure, substance abuse, and/or early sexuality.

juvenile delinquency: Participation in illegal behavior by a minor who falls under a statutory age limit.

chronic juvenile offenders: youths who have been arrested four or more times during their minority and perpetuate a striking majority of serious criminal acts; this small group, known as the "chronic 6 percent," is believed to engage in a significant portion of all delinquent behavior; these youths do not age out of crime, but continue their criminal behavior into adulthood.

juvenile justice system: The segment of the justice system including law enforcement officers, the courts, and correctional agencies that is designed to treat youthful offenders.

paternalistic family: A family style wherein the father is the final authority on all family matters and exercises complete control over his wife and children.

Poor Laws: English statutes that allowed the courts to appoint overseers for destitute and neglected children, allowing placement of these children as servants in the homes of the affluent.

chancery courts: Court proceedings created in fifteenth-century England to oversee the lives of highborn minors who were orphaned or otherwise could not care for themselves.

parens patriae: The power of the state to act on behalf of the child and provide care and protection equivalent to that of a parent.

child savers: Nineteenth-century reformers who developed programs for troubled youth and influenced legislation creating the juvenile justice system; today some critics view them as being more concerned with control of the poor than with their welfare.

delinquent: Juvenile who has been adjudicated by a judicial officer of a juvenile court as having committed a delinquent act.

best interests of the child: A philosophical viewpoint that encourages the state to take control of wayward children and provide care, custody, and treatment to remedy delinquent behavior.

need for treatment: The criteria on which juvenile sentencing is based. Ideally, juveniles are treated according to their need for treatment and not for the seriousness of the delinquent act they committed.

waiver: Transferring legal jurisdiction over the most serious and experienced juvenile offenders to the adult court for criminal prosecution.

status offense: Conduct that is illegal only because the child is under age.

wayward minors: Early legal designation of youths who violate the law because of their minority status; now referred to as status offenders.

Office of Juvenile Justice and Delinquency Prevention (OJJDP): Branch of the U.S. Justice Department charged with shaping national juvenile justice policy through disbursement of federal aid and research funds.

SELF TEST QUESTIONS

MULTIPLE CHOICE

1. There are more than _____ children in the United States.
   - A. 20,000,000
   - B. 40,000,000
   - C. 70,000,000
   - D. 120,000,000

2. _____ is formed when youths develop a firm sense of who they are and what they stand for.
   - A. Alter ego
   - B. Ego identity
   - C. Role diffusion
   - D. Ego transformation

3. _____ occurs when youths experience uncertainty and place themselves at the mercy of leaders who promise to give them a sense of identity they cannot mold for themselves.
   - A. Ego identity
   - B. Identity transformation
   - C. Role diffusion
   - D. Identity indoctrination

4. The Hispanic-American high school dropout rate is almost _____ times that of European American high school students.
   - A. 2
   - B. 4
   - C. 5
   - D. 6

5. In the United States, what amount of deaths among youth are preventable?
   - A. one third
   - B. one half
   - C. two-thirds
   - D. three-quarters

6. Siegel and Welsh note that about _____ percent of high school students had driven a car or other vehicle after drinking alcohol.
   - A. 6.9
   - B. 9.9
   - C. 11.9
   - D. 13.9

7. Siegel and Welsh note that about _____ of sexually active high school students reported not using a condom at last sexual intercourse.
   - A. 17.2
   - B. 24.2
   - C. 37.2
   - D. 40.2

8. According to the text, more than _____ million children have no health insurance.
   - A. 5
   - B. 6
   - C. 8
   - D. 9

9. Transferring legal jurisdiction over the most serious and experienced juvenile offenders to the adult court for criminal prosecution is known as _____.
   - A. waiver
   - B. widening the net
   - C. diversion
   - D. *parens patriae*

10. Youths who have been arrested four or more times during their minority and perpetuate a striking majority of serious criminal acts are known as _____.
    A. really bad kids
    B. gang members
    C. chronic delinquents
    D. status offenders

11. A family style wherein the father is the final authority on all family matters and exercises complete control over his wife and children is _____.
    A. paternalistic
    B. maternalistic
    C. egalitarian
    D. matriarchal

12. Which of the following best describes the Poor Laws?
    A. In 1535, the King of England used them to outlaw poverty and raise the standard of living.
    B. They were laws that placed neglected and destitute children as servants for the rich in exchange for training.
    C. They were laws that provided social service assistance to the neediest families in the kingdom.
    D. They were really bad laws that were repealed shortly after being enacted.

13. Under the _____, children were placed in the care of adults who trained them in specific skills.
    A. binding over movement
    B. apprenticeship movement
    C. chancery courts
    D. primogeniture

14. Chancery courts were founded on the proposition that children were under the protective control of the king, or _____, which refers to the role of the king as father of his country.
    A. monastic privilege
    B. *lex talionis*
    C. *parens patriae*
    D. *stare decisis*

15. Why were children often required to attend public whippings and executions in Colonial America?
    A. These events were thought to be important forms of moral instruction.
    B. It was difficult to arrange childcare.
    C. It was viewed as a form of entertainment.
    D. It was designed to scare children straight.

16. Which of the following best describes the operating philosophy of the juvenile court under *parens patriae*?
    A. best interests of the child
    B. best interests of the government
    C. best interests of the community
    D. deterrence, retribution, and rehabilitation

17. While acting in the best interests of the child, youths should be _____.
    A. punished for their crimes to teach them a lesson
    B. punished for their crimes to deter other youths
    C. given the care necessary to control their misbehavior
    D. held accountable for their offenses just as adults

18. What types of matters are controlled by civil law?
- A. felonies
- B. misdemeanors
- C. interpersonal or private disputes
- D. all of the above

19. The waiver process is defined as _____.
- A. transferring legal jurisdiction of juvenile offenders to the adult court for criminal prosecution
- B. the court's decision to dismiss the case if the youth agrees to participate in a treatment program
- C. when a petition is not filed in juvenile court because the matter is deemed insignificant for formal action
- D. when the youth admits to the facts of the case and accepts the recommendation for treatment

20. Early British jurisprudence held that children under the age of _____ were legally incapable of committing crimes.
- A. two
- B. seven
- C. fourteen
- D. eighteen

21. CHINS, MINS, PINS, YINS, and JINS refer to _____.
- A. street names for various drugs
- B. legal classifications for status offenders
- C. another term for juvenile delinquents
- D. terms to refer to various criminal offenses

22. Created in 1974, the _____ is charged with shaping national juvenile justice policy through disbursement of federal aid and research funds.
- A. Office of Juvenile Justice and Delinquency Prevention (OJJDP)
- B. National Institute of Justice (NIJ)
- C. National Criminal Justice Reference Service (NCJRS)
- D. Federal Juvenile Delinquency Policy Center (FJDPC)

23. Youths considered _____ are those dabbling in various forms of dangerous conduct such as drug abuse, alcohol use, and precocious sexuality.
- A. at risk
- B. delinquent
- C. developmentally appropriate
- D. deviant

24. Who cared for medieval newborns?
- A. knights
- B. wet nurses
- C. serfs
- D. nobility

25. How would you characterize the relationship between Middle Ages parents and their children?
- A. impersonal
- B. attentive and caring
- C. much the same as an adult relationship
- D. protective in order to maintain primogeniture

26. The practice of early American childhood discipline was based on what premises?
   A. religion and moral discipline
   B. hard work and industriousness
   C. a recognition and protection of the newly-created constitutional rights of children
   D. respect for the working potential of young factory workers

27. What philosophical period stressed a humanistic view of life, freedom, family, reason and law?
   A. the Middle Ages   C. the Feudal period
   B. the dark ages   D. the Enlightenment

28. The National Advisory Commission on Criminal Justice Standards and Goals recommended that which of the following behaviors be considered a status offense?
   A. delinquent acts by children over the age of twelve
   B. loitering near and around establishments that serve alcoholic beverages
   C. excessive use of foul and lewd language
   D. habitual truancy

29. Recent contributing laws aimed at reducing status offenses have used what strategy?
   A. shock incarceration   C. sanctioning parents
   B. fining juveniles   D. shock treatment

30. According to the text, each year youth may see up to _____ rapes, murders, and assaults on TV,
   A. one hundred   C. one thousand
   B. five hundred   D. five thousand

TRUE/FALSE

1. Psychologists conclude that late adolescence is dominated by a desire for independence from parental control.
   A. True
   B. False

2. Siegel and Welsh note that the rates of both teenage pregnancy and infant mortality are increasing.
   A. True
   B. False

3. In medieval times, parents displayed much care, attention, and devotion for their children.
   A. True
   B. False

14

4. The concept of *parens patriae* was upheld in *Wellesley v Wellesley* in 1827, when a duke's children were taken away because of his scandalous behavior.
    A. True
    B. False

5. The Office of Juvenile Justice and Delinquency Prefention was mandated by the Supreme Court to remedy abuse of juvenile's rights.
    A. True
    B. False

6. Poor Laws were passed in Virginia in 1646 and in Massachusetts in 1673, and they were modeled after those laws passed in England.
    A. True
    B. False

7. Children were often required to attend public whippings and executions because these events were thought to be important forms of moral instruction.
    A. True
    B. False

8. Children were prohibited from attending public whippings and executions because it was feared that it would lead to greater depravity among young adults.
    A. True
    B. False

9. Early British law held that children under the age of eleven were legally incapable of committing crimes.
    A. True
    B. False

10. Early British law held that youths between the ages of seven and fourteen were responsible for their actions, but their age might be used to excuse or lighten the punishment.
    A. True
    B. False

11. Juvenile records are confidential, and juvenile proceedings are not open to the public; these practices are intended to shield the youth from the stigma of a criminal conviction and to prevent youthful misdeeds from becoming a lifelong burden.
    A. True
    B. False

12. Civil laws control interpersonal or private activities, and legal actions are usually initiated by those who have been harmed, injured or wronged by another.
    A. True
    B. False

13. Juveniles in the juvenile justice system have been granted many of the same rights enjoyed by adults in the criminal justice system.
    A. True
    B. False

14. The federal Office of Juvenile Justice and Delinquency Prevention (OJJDP) has advocated to remove status offenders from secure lockups, detention centers, and post-disposition treatment facilities that also house delinquent offenders.
    A. True
    B. False

15. While policies have been successful in keeping status offenders out of secure lockups, judges have held youths in detention on contempt of court charges related to failing to following the court's orders concerning status offenses.
    A. True
    B. False

16. According to Erik Erikson, role diffusion happens when juveniles experience personal uncertainty, spread themselves too thin, and look to others to gain identity they cannot mold for themselves.
    A. True
    B. False

17. Under *parens patriae*, delinquent acts are considered criminal violations.
    A. True
    B. False

18. Colorado was the first state to discipline parents for contributing to the delinquency of minors.
    A. True
    B. False

19. The concept of delinquency was developed in the early twentieth century; before that, criminal youths and adults were treated in almost the same fashion.
    A. True
    B. False

20. The separate status of juvenile delinquency is based on the *parens patriae* philosophy, which holds that children have the right to care and custody and that, if parents are not capable of providing that care, the state must step in to take control.
    A. True
    B. False

21. Siegel and Welsh note that all states have incorporated parental liability laws in their statutes.
    A. True
    B. False

22. Parents may also be held civilly liable, under the concept of vicarious liability, for the damages caused by their child.
    A. True
    B. False

23. At last count, about forty states were in compliance with the OJJDP mandate and were eligible for receiving federal funds.
    A. True
    B. False

24. Siegel and Welsh note that, compared with adults, adolescents are believed to have a stronger preference for risk and novelty, be less accurate in assessing the potential consequences of risky conduct, be more impulsive and more concerned with short-term consequences, have a different appreciation of time and self-control, and be more susceptible to peer pressure.
    A. True
    B. False

25. Juveniles have the right to consult an attorney, to be free from self-incrimination, and to be protected from illegal searches and seizures.
    A. True
    B. False

FILL IN

1. _____ are young people who are extremely vulnerable to the negative consequences of school failure, substance abuse, and early sexuality.

2. Divorce strikes about _____ of all new marriages.

3. The _____ movement helped shape our current conception of the child.

4. _____ is defined as the participation in illegal behavior by a minor who falls under a statutory age limit.

5. The segment of the justice system designed to treat youthful offenders, and including law enforcement officers, the courts, and correctional agencies, is known as the

_____ .

6. Under the _____, children were placed in the care of adults who trained them in specific skills.

7. Adults are tried in court; children are _____ in court.

8. Adults can be punished if found guilty; children are _____ by the court.

9. Juvenile records are _____, and juvenile trials are not open to the public.

10. Transferring legal jurisdiction over the most serious and experienced juvenile offenders to the adult court for criminal prosecution is called _____.

11. Conduct that is illegal only because the child is under age is known as a _____.

12. A youth is considered _____ if he or she habitually disobeys the reasonable and lawful demands of his or her parents, and is ungovernable and beyond their control.

13. Many states attempt to discipline parents for _____; these laws allow parents to be sanctioned in juvenile courts for behaviors associated with their child's misbehavior.

14. Parents may be held civilly liable, under the concept of _____, for the damages caused by their child.

15. The _____ is when youths are legally adults and may be independent of parental control.

ESSAY

1. Should status offenders be treated differently than juvenile delinquents? If a juvenile is a chronic truant, what should be done? To what degree should the youth's home life influence the decision?

2. What challenges and issues do adolescents face today?

3. At what age are juveniles truly capable of understanding the seriousness of their actions?

4. Identify and discuss the social, economic, and political reasons offered by Siegel and Welsh to explain adolescent risk taking.

5. Describe family relations in the Middle Ages.

ANSWER KEY

MULTIPLE CHOICE

1. C	11. A	21. B
2. B	12. B	22. A
3. C	13. B	23. A
4. C	14.C	24. B
5. D	15. A	25. A
6. B	16. A	26. A
7. C	17. C	27. D
8. D	18. C	28. D
9. A	19. A	29. C
10. C	20. B	30 C

TRUE FALSE

1. True	11. True	21. False
2. False	12. True	22. True
3. False	13. True	23. False
4. True	14. True	24. True
5. False	15. True	25. True
6. True	16. True	
7. True	17. False	
8. False	18. True	
9. False	19. True	
10. True	20. True	

FILL IN

1. at-risk youths	11. status offense
2. half	12. incorrigible
3. child savers	13. contributing to the delinquency of a minor
4. juvenile delinquency	14. vicarious liability
5. juvenile justice system	15. age of consent
6. apprenticeship movement	
7. adjudicated	
8. treated	
9. confidential	
10. waiver	

Multiple Choice
1. Adolescence
   A. in all societies has been a bridge between childhood and adulthood
   B. according to Erikson is a period of turbulence in which youths face the developmental task of ego identity or role diffusion
   C. seriously diminishes the importance of parents.
   D. all of the above.

2. The concept of the legal status of juvenile delinquency developed
   A. in ancient Roman
   B. from British Common Law
   C. was included in the US Constitution
   D. in the 19th century and was adopted in the early 20th century.

3. Chancery courts
   A. dealt with runaways in 17th century England
   B. helped find adoptive parents for abandoned youth in Virginia in the 18th century
   C. were created in the 15th century England to oversee the lives of highborn minors who were orphaned or otherwise could not care for themselves.
   D. were the first child protective agencies in England.

4. Poverty affects children in which of the following ways
   A. health problems
   B. substandard housing
   C. poor education
   D. all of the above

5. The right of the state to intervene in the best interests of the youth derives from
   A. *parens patriae*
   B. *stare decisis*
   C. *loco parenti*
   D. all of the above

6. Status offenders
   A. have committed crimes
   B. are legally culpable
   C. have committed an act which would be a crime if they were adults
   D. none of the above

7. The status of delinquency
   A. is the same as that of criminal
   B. is just another form of civil commitment
   C. lays somewhere between criminal and civil commitment
   D. is required by the US constitution

8. The following legislation called for transfer of juveniles to adult court
   A. The National Advisory Commission on Criminal Justice Standards and Goals.
   B. The Law Enforcement Assistance Act.
   C. Truth in Sentencing Laws.
   D. None of the above

9. Curfew laws
   A. Are unconstitutional for youth over 16 years of age.
   B. May only suppress crime at night and have it increase in the day
   C. Cannot be used by police as pretext stops.
   D. Apply only to status offenders.

10. Transfer of juveniles to adult court
   A. Violates the double jeopardy clause
   B. Teaches the youth responsibility
   C. Is automatic for certain offenses.
   D. Is one answer to the public's fear of serious juvenile crime.

True False
   1. It is clear that the Child Savers understood that coercive treatment can lead to harm as well as good. T F

   2. Juvenile crime has continued to rise in the last 10 years T F

   3. The text reports that curfew laws have been found to violate youth's 4th amendment right to freedom of movement. T F

   4. Status offenders do not always differ that much in their behavioral and other problems from juvenile delinquents. T F

   5. Chronic juvenile recidivists, who are arrested four or five times, are well overrepresented among juvenile offenders who commit serious crimes. T F

Multiple Choice
1. B
2. D
3. C
4. D
5. A
6. D
7. C
8. D
9. B
10. D

True False
1. F
2. F
3. F
4. T
5. T

CHAPTER TWO
THE NATURE AND EXTENT OF DELINQUENCY

LEARNING OBJECTIVES

- Know what is meant by the term official delinquency.
- Understand how the FBI's Uniform Crime Report (UCR) is compiled.
- Be familiar with recent trends in juvenile delinquency.
- Understand how self-report data are collected and what they say about juvenile crime.
- Recognize the factors that affect the juvenile crime rate.
- Be aware of gender patterns in delinquency.
- Appreciate the factors that cause racial differences in delinquency.
- Be able to debate the issue of class position and delinquency.
- Be aware of the debate over the role age plays in delinquency.
- Understand the concept of the chronic persistent offender.
- Be familiar with the relationship between childhood and victimization.

CHAPTER OUTLINE

I.   Adolescent Victims/Offenders
        A.   Jamesetta is poor and resides in an urban environment
                1. She was physically and sexually abused before age 5 and placed in
                foster care.
                2. By age 9 she was skipping school, shoplifting, and violating curfew.
                3. At age 13 she assaults her foster mother and enters the juvenile justice
                system with charges of disorderly conduct and habitual delinquency
                4. At age 14 she is pregnant and is enrolled in school designed to support
                pregnant teens.
                5. Jamesetta continues to have status offenses
                6. After her baby is born she begins to follow rules and understand that
                there are consequences to her actions.

II.   Official Statistics
        A.   U.S. Justice Department's Federal Bureau of Investigation (FBI)
                1.   information gathered by police departments
                2.   number of criminal acts reported by citizens
                3.   the number of persons arrested
                4.   published in the annual Uniform Crime Report (UCR)
                5.   most widely used source of national crime and delinquency statistics
        B.   UCR is compiled from 17,000 police departments
                1.   Part I offenses are also known as index crimes
                        a.   homicide and non-negligent manslaughter
                        b.   forcible rape
                        c.   robbery
                        d.   aggravated assault
                        e.   burglary

        f.   larceny

        g.   arson

        h.   motor vehicle theft

      2.   Part II offenses

          a.   all other criminal offenses

C.   UCR uses three methods to express crime data

      1.   expressed as raw figures

      2.   crime rates per 100,000 people are computed

      3.   computes changes in the number and rate of crime over time

D.   Crime trends in the United States

      1.   U.S. crime rate skyrocketed between 1960 and 1981

      2.   1991 the FBI was recording more than 14 million crimes annually

      3.   both the number and rate of crimes had been declining until 2005

III.   Measuring Official Delinquency

A.   UCR arrest statistics are disaggregated

      1.   juvenile arrest data must be interpreted with caution

      2.   arrests does not represent the actual number of delinquents

      3.   some offenders are never caught

      4.   others are counted more than once because of their multiple arrests

      5.   only the most serious one is reported in an episode including multiple crimes

      6.   more than 350,000 youth are arrested each year for serious crimes

      7.   nature of arrest data remains constant over time

B.   Official Delinquency

      1.   in 2005, about 14 million arrests were made

      2.   more than 2 million were for serious Part I crimes

      3.   12 million for less serious Part II crimes

      4.   in 2005 juveniles under 18 were responsible for about 26% of property crime arrests and 16% of Part I violent crime arrests

      5.   Juveniles aged 14-17 who account for almost all underage arrests are 6 percent of the population

C.   About 1.2 million juvenile arrests were made in 2002 for Part II offenses

      1.   90,000 arrests for running away from home

      2.   139,000 for disorderly conduct

      3.   133,000 for drug-abuse violations

      4.   103,000 for curfew violations.

D.   Juvenile crime trends

      1.   juvenile crime has a significant influence on the nation's overall crime statistics

      2.   juvenile arrest rate began to climb in the 1960s

      3.   peaked induring the mid-1990s

      4.   it has since been in decline

      5.   1,700 youths were arrested for murder in 1997

      6.   by 2005, the number of juveniles arrested for murder had declined by more than one half (to 900)

E.   Rise and fall of juvenile crime rates

1 nation's teenage population will increase by 15%
2. number in the high-risk ages of 15 to 17 will increase by 31%
3. juveniles' influence on the nation's total crime rate may be offset
  a. growing number of crime-free senior citizens

F. Are the UCR data valid?
  1. victim surveys show that less than half of all victims report the crime to police
  2. police departments make systematic errors in recording crime data
  3. victimless crimes such as drug and alcohol use are significantly undercounted
  4. arrest decision criteria vary among police agencies
  5. problems associated with collecting UCR data are consistent and stable over time
  6. absolute accuracy of the data can be questioned
  7. trends and patterns they show are probably reliable

G. National Incident-Based Reporting System (NIBRS)
  1. new program that collects data on each reported crime incident
  2. require local police agencies to provide at least a brief account of each arrest
  3. forty-six specific offenses

IV. Focus on Delinquency: Shaping Delinquency Trends
  Rise and Fall of Juvenile Crime Rates

A. Age
  1. change in the age distribution of the population influences delinquency rates
  2. juvenile males commit more crime than any other population segment
  3. general rule the crime rate follows the proportion of young males in the population

B. Economy
  1. a poor economy may actually help lower crime rates
  2. unemployed parents are at home to supervise children and guard their homes
  3. a poor economy means that there are actually fewer valuables worth stealing
  4. no relationship between unemployment and most crimes desperate kids might commit
  5. long-term periods of economic weakness and unemployment eventually lift crime rates
  6. perception of hopelessness that leads to crime and delinquency
  7. legitimate economic opportunities no longer exist
  8. low-skill manufacturing jobs have been dispersed to overseas plants
  9. most new jobs that don't require specialized skills are in the low-paying service area

      C.   Drugs
- 1. drug use linked to fluctuations in the crime and delinquency rate
- 2. abusers are particularly crime-prone
- 3. teenage substance abusers commit a significant portion of all serious crimes
- 4. alcohol-abusing kids engage in acts of senseless violence

      D.   Media
- 1. violent media can influence youth crime

      E.   Ongoing social problems
- 1. as the level of social problems increase so do crime and delinquency rates
- 2. child homicide rates are greatest in those nations with:
  - a. highest rates of children born out of wedlock and with teenage mothers
- 3. children living in single-parent homes
  - a. twice as likely to be impoverished than those in two-parent homes

      F.   Abortion
- 1. Donohue and Levitt study
- 2. drop in the crime rate can be attributed to the availability of legalized abortion
- 3. in 1991, first group of potential offenders affected by the abortion decision
- 4. crime rates and abortion is the result of two mechanisms:
- 5. selective abortion on the part of women most at risk to have delinquents
- 6. improved child-rearing or environmental circumstances

      G.   Guns
- 1. in 2002, twenty-five thousand kids were arrested on weapons-related charges
- 2. 60% of the homicides committed by juveniles involve firearms

      H.   Gangs
- 1. more than 750,000 gang members in the United States
- 2. about one-third of kids who are gang members carry a gun all or most of the time

      I.   Juvenile justice policy
- 1. new laws call for mandatory incarceration for juvenile offenders

V.   Self-Reported Delinquency
      A.   Self reported delinquency
- 1. designed to obtain information from youthful subjects about their violations of the law
- 2. self-report information can be collected in many ways
  - a. in one-to-one interviews
  - b. self-administered questionnaire
  - c. mass distribution of anonymous questionnaires
- 3. provide information on offenders who have never been
- 4. measures behavior that is rarely detected by police, such as drug abuse
- 5. information may be collected on
  - a. self-image, intelligence, personality, and attitudes
  - b. family background, social status, race, and sex.

6.   used self-report studies of delinquency for more than forty years

7.   dark figures of crime is those who have escaped official notice

B.   What self-report data show

    1.   number who break the law is far greater than official statistics

    2.   University of Michigan's Institute for Social Research (ISR)

        a.   conduct an annual national self-report survey (MTF)

    3.   surprising number of teenagers reported involvement in serious criminal behavior

    4.   12% reported hurting someone badly enough that the victim needed medical care

    5.   29% reported stealing something worth less than $50

    6.   some question about the accuracy of self-report data

V.   Correlates of Delinquency

A.   Gender and delinquency

    1.   males are significantly more delinquent than females

    2.   teenage gender ratio for serious violent crime is approximately 4 to 1

    3.   property crime approximately 2 to 1, male to female

    4.   girls are more likely than boys to be arrested as runaways

    5.   between 1993 and 2002 male arrests decreased about 16%

    6.   number of female delinquents arrested actually increased about 6%

    7.   males arrested for serious violent crime decreased by 33%

    8.   female violent crime arrests remained relatively stable

    9.   crimes committed by males are also the ones most female offenders commit

    10.   33 percent of boys and 25 percent of girls admit to shoplifting

    11.   girls have increased their self-reported delinquency

B.   Race and delinquency

    1.   minorities are disproportionately represented in the arrest

    2.   minority youths are more likely to be arrested for serious criminal behavior

    3.   some experts warn that African-American youths may underreport more serious crimes

    4.   one view is that it is a result of bias by the police and courts

    5.   African-American youths are more likely to get an official record.

    6.   correspondence between official and self-report data

        a.   conclude that racial differences in the crime rate are real

    7.   racial differentials tied to the social and economic disparity

    8.   lower-class African Americans are left out of the economic mainstream

C.   Social class and delinquency

    1.   key element in the study of delinquency

    2.   at first glance, the relationship between class and crime seems clear

    3.   relationship was challenged by pioneering self-report studies

D.   Age and delinquency

    1.   age is inversely related to criminality

    2.   aging-out process

    3.   increasing levels of responsibility result in lower levels of criminality

    4.   the age of onset of a delinquent career has an important effect on its length

5.   no question that people commit less crime as they grow older
6.   growing older means having to face the future
7.   with maturity comes the ability to resist the "quick fix" to their problems
8.   maturation coincides with increased levels of responsibility
9.   personalities can change with age
10.   young adults become more aware of the risks that accompany crime

VI.   Chronic Offending: Careers in Delinquency
    A.   Chronic offenders
        1.   relatively small number of youths begin to violate the law early in their lives
        2.   continue at a high rate well into adulthood
        3.   chronic offenders are responsible for a significant amount of all delinquency
        4.   chronic offenders can be distinguished from other delinquent youths
        5.   repeated delinquent activity is the best predictor of future adult criminality
    B.   Delinquency in a Birth Cohort
        1.   most closely associated with the research efforts of Marvin Wolfgang
        2.   delinquent careers of a cohort of 9,945 boys born in Philadelphia
        3.   about one-third of the boys (3,475) had some police contact
        4.   54% (1,862) of the sample's delinquent youths were repeat offenders
        5.   627 boys labeled chronic recidivists had been arrested five times or more
        6.   6 percent of the total sample and responsible for 52% of all offenses
        7.   two factors stood out as encouraging recidivism:
            a.   seriousness of the original offense
            b.   severity of the punishment
    C.   Stability in crime: From delinquent to criminal
        1.   chronic juvenile offenders had an 80% chance of becoming adult offenders and a 50 percent chance of being arrested 4 or more times as adults
        2.   severity of offending had the greatest impact on later adult criminality
    D.   What causes chronic offending?
        1.   chronic offenders suffer from a number of deficits
        2.   early antisocial behavior
        3.   family factors
        4.   peer factors
        5.   school and community factors
        6.   neighborhood disadvantage
    E.   Policy implications
        1.   identify persistent offenders at the beginning of their offending careers
        2.   provide early treatment

VI.   Juvenile Victimization
    A.   National Crime Victimization Survey (NCVS)
        1.   household survey of victims of criminal behavior
        2.   annual sample size of about forty thousand households
        3.   each group is interviewed twice a year

B.   Victimization in the United States
      1.   about twenty-three million criminal incidents occur each year
      2.   cost of crime is $450 billion or $1,800 for every person in the United States
      3.   less than half of all violent victimization reported to the police
      4.   only 40 percent of all property crimes were reported to the police
      5.   young people are much more likely to be the victims of crime

C.   Victims and their criminals
      1.   teens tend to be victimized by their peers
      2.   violent crime victims report a disproportionate number of attackers are young
      3.   victimization is intraracial
      4.   most teens are victimized by people with whom they are acquainted

CHAPTER SUMMARY

Official delinquency refers to youths who are arrested. Arrest data come from the FBI's Uniform Crime Report (UCR), an annual tally of crimes reported to police by citizens. The FBI gathers arrest statistics from local police departments. From these, it is possible to determine the number of youths who are arrested each year, along with their age, race, and gender. About two million youths are arrested annually. After a long increase in juvenile crime, there has been a decade decrease in the number of juveniles arrested for nonviolent and violent crimes.

Dissatisfaction with the UCR prompted criminologists to develop other means of measuring delinquent behavior. Self-reports are surveys in which subjects are asked to describe their misbehavior. Although self-reports indicate that many more crimes are committed than are known to the police, they also show that the delinquency rate is rather stable.

The factors that are believed to shape and control teen delinquency rates include gang activity, drug abuse, and teen gun ownership, abortion rates, economy, punishment, and social conditions. Delinquents are disproportionately male, although female delinquency rates are rising faster than those for males. Minority youth are overrepresented in the delinquency rate, especially for violent crime. Experts are split on the cause of racial differences. Some believe they are a function of system bias, others see them as representing actual differences in the delinquency rate.

Disagreement also exists over the relationship between class position and delinquency. Some hold that adolescent crime is a lower-class phenomenon, whereas others see it throughout the social structure. Problems in methodology have obscured the true class-crime relationship. However, official statistics indicate that lower-class youths are responsible for the most serious criminal acts. There is general agreement that delinquency rates decline with age. Some experts believe this phenomenon is universal, whereas others believe a small group of offenders persist in crime at a high rate. The age-crime relationship has spurred research on the nature of delinquency over the life course.

Delinquency data show the existence of a chronic persistent offender who begins his or her offending career early in life and persists as an adult. Wolfgang and his colleagues identified chronic offenders in a series of cohort studies conducted in Philadelphia. Ongoing research has identified the characteristics of persistent offenders as they mature, and both personality and social factors help us predict long-term offending patterns. The National Crime Victimization Survey (NCVS) is an annual national survey of the victims of crime that is conducted by agencies of the federal government. Teenagers are much more likely to become victims of crime than are people in other age groups.

KEY TERMS

Federal Bureau of Investigation (FBI): Arm of the U.S. Department of Justice that investigates violations of federal law, gathers crime statistics, runs a comprehensive crime laboratory, and helps train local law enforcement officers.

Uniform Crime Report (UCR): Compiled by the FBI, the UCR is the most widely used source of national crime and delinquency statistics.

Part I offenses (also known as index crimes): Offenses including homicide and nonnegligent manslaughter, forcible rape, robbery, aggravated assault, burglary, larceny, arson, and motor vehicle theft; recorded by local law enforcement officers, these crimes are tallied quarterly and sent to the FBI for inclusion in the UCR.

Part II offenses: All crimes other than Part I offenses; recorded by local law enforcement officers, arrests for these crimes are tallied quarterly and sent to the FBI for inclusion in the UCR.

disaggregated: Analyzing the relationship between two or more independent variables (such as murder convictions and death sentence) while controlling for the influence of a dependent variable (such as race).

self-reports: Questionnaire or survey technique that asks subjects to reveal their own participation in delinquent or criminal acts.

dark figure of crime: Incidents of crime and delinquency that go undetected by police.

aging-out process (also known as desistance or spontaneous remission): The tendency for youths to reduce the frequency of their offending behavior as they age; aging out is thought to occur among all groups of offenders.

age of onset: Age at which youths begin their delinquent careers; early onset is believed to be linked with chronic offending patterns.

chronic recidivists: According to Wolfgang, Figlio, Sellen and other researchers, chronic recidivists are youths who have been arrested five or more times during their minority and perpetuate a striking majority of serious criminal acts; this small group, known as the "chronic 6 percent," is believed to engage in a majority of all serious delinquent behavior; these youths do not age out of crime, but continue their criminal behavior into adulthood.

continuity of crime: The idea that chronic juvenile offenders are likely to continue violating the law as adults.

victimization: The number of people who are victims of criminal acts; young teens are fifteen times more likely than older adults (age sixty-five and over) to be victims of crimes.

SELF TEST QUESTIONS

MULTIPLE CHOICE

1. Each year the _____ compiles information gathered by police departments on the number of criminal acts reported by citizens and the number of persons arrested.
    A. FBI   C. CDC
    B. CIA   D. Attorney General

2. Compiled by the FBI, the _____ is the most widely used source of national crime and delinquency statistics reporting crimes known to the police and the number of persons arrested.
    A. Uniform Crime Report
    B. National Crime Victimization Survey
    C. National Annual Crime Data
    D. Who's Who among American Criminals

3. The Uniform Crime Report is viewed as _____ since the problems with collecting and verifying the official data are consistent and stable over time.
    A. valid   C. accurate
    B. reliable   D. untrustworthy

4. Which of the following is information *not* provided by the Uniform Crime Report?
    A. information on individuals arrested
    B. crimes reported to the police
    C. information on criminal convictions
    D. rates per 100,000 people

5. Which of the following was identified by Siegel and Welsh as a concern of the Uniform Crime Reports for estimating juvenile crime?
    A. Some juveniles are not caught by the police.
    B. Some juveniles are arrested more than once.
    C. Only the most serious crime is reported to the FBI when an offender is arrested after committing multiple crimes in one criminal episode.
    D. all of the above

6. _____ are questionnaire or survey techniques that ask subjects to reveal their own participation in delinquent or criminal acts.
    A. victim surveys   C. official records
    B. self reports   D. Uniform Crime Reports

7. Which of the following best describes the dark figures of crime?
    A. the amount of crime that cannot be explained by rational choice
    B. the number of arrests that do not lead to charges being filed
    C. incidents of crime that goes undetected by the police
    D. the crimes known to the police that cannot be solved

8. Researchers at the University of Michigan's Institute for Social Research (ISR) report that about _____ of teenagers reported hurting someone badly enough that the victim needed medical care.

        A. 1 percent   C. 12 percent

        B. 6 percent   D. 34 percent

9. Researchers at the University of Michigan's Institute for Social Research (ISR) report that about _____ of teenagers reported hitting a teacher or supervisor.

        A. 3 percent   C. 12 percent

        B. 6 percent   D. 34 percent

10. Researchers at the University of Michigan's Institute for Social Research (ISR) conduct an annual national self-report survey, called _____.

        A. Monitoring the Future

        B. Up with people

        C. Uniform Crime Report

        D. National Youth Risk Behavior Survey

11. Age is _____ related to criminality.

        A. directly   C. positively

        B. inversely   D. all of the above

12. What does "age of onset" refer to?

        A. when youths enter puberty

        B. when youths are influenced by criminogenic forces in the environment

        C. when youths begin their delinquent careers

        D. when youths begin to feel pressure from their peers

13. The tendency for youths to reduce the frequency of their offending behavior as they age is called _____.

        A. aging out   C. older and wiser hypothesis

        B. matriculation tendency   D. maturation tendency

14. Which of the following best describes why people commit fewer crimes as they get older?

        A. growing old means having to face the future

        B. increased levels of responsibility

        C. personalities change with age

        D. a person becomes more aware of the risks of crime

        E. all of the above

15. According to Siegel and Welsh, the financial cost of crime is equivalent to about _____.

        A. 900 million   C. 90 billion

        B. 30 billion   D. 450 billion

16. Siegel and Welsh note that juveniles
    A. are most victimized by people they are acquainted with
    B. are usually victimized by adults
    C. are usually victimized by youth from another race
    D. are most often victimized from 9:00-11:00 pm.

17. Monitoring the Future is a _____.
    A. official source of data
    B. victimization survey
    C. self administered questionnaire
    D. observational study

18. Research shows that some kids may turn to crime as a way to solve the problems of adolescence, loneliness, frustration, and fear of peer rejection, and as they mature, conventional means of problem solving become available. This best illustrates _____.
    A. with maturity comes the ability to resist the "quick fix" to their problems
    B. maturation coincides with increased levels of responsibility
    C. personalities can change with age
    D. young adults become more aware of the risks that accompany crime

19. Petty crimes are risky and exciting social activities that provide adventure in an otherwise boring world, and as youths grow older, they take on new responsibilities that are inconsistent with criminality. This best illustrates _____.
    A. with maturity comes the ability to resist the "quick fix" to their problems
    B. maturation coincides with increased levels of responsibility
    C. personalities can change with age
    D. young adults become more aware of the risks that accompany crime

20. As youths mature, rebellious youngsters may develop increased self-control and be able to resist antisocial behavior. This best illustrates _____.
    A. with maturity comes the ability to resist the "quick fix" to their problems
    B. maturation coincides with increased levels of responsibility
    C. personalities can change with age
    D. young adults become more aware of the risks that accompany crime

21. As adults, they are no longer protected by the relatively kindly arms of the juvenile justice system. This best illustrates _____.
    A. with maturity comes the ability to resist the "quick fix" to their problems
    B. maturation coincides with increased levels of responsibility
    C. personalities can change with age
    D. young adults become more aware of the risks that accompany crime

22. In what city was Wolfgang, Figlio, and Sellin's 1972 landmark study *Delinquency in a Birth Cohort* conducted?
    A. Panama City
    B. New York
    C. Philadelphia
    D. Chicago

23. In Wolfgang, Figlio, and Sellin's 1972 landmark study *Delinquency in a Birth Cohort*, about _____ of the boys had some police contact before his eighteenth birthday.

      A. one quarter   C. one half

      B. one-third   D. three quarters

24. The total annual sample size of the _____ has been about forty thousand households, containing about seventy-five thousand individuals.

      A. NCVS   C. MTF Survey

      B. UCR   D. DUF Survey

25. Surveys show that _____ percent of all high school students carry guns at least some of the time.

      A. 2-6   C. 9-11

      B. 6-10   D. 13-15

26. Youths aged 14 through 17 account for 6 percent of the US population, but account for ____ percent of arrests

      A. 10   C. 20

      B. 15   D. 25

27. The number of youth arrested for murder in 2005 was _____, compared to _____ arrested for muder in 1998:

      A. 900, 1700   C. 1700, 900

      B. 900, 1100   D. 1100, 900

28 Approximately how many gang members are there in our country?

      A. 25,000   C. 750,000

      B. 500,000   D. one million.

29. Which of the following does not refer to the same concept?

      A. aging-out process   C. spontaneous remission

      B. desistance from crime   D. age of onset

30. Less than half of all violent victimizations and _____ percent of all property crimes are reported to the police.

      A. 30   C. 75

      B. 40   D. 84

TRUE FALSE

1 Most offenders eventually become habitual offenders
    A. True
    B. False

2. Some experts, such as criminologist James Fox, predict a significant increase in teen violence if current population trends persist; the number of youths in the high-risk ages between fifteen and seventeen will increase by more than three million, or thirty-one percent.
    A. True
    B. False

3. Victim surveys show that more than half of all victims report the crime to police.
    A. True
    B. False

4. According to the Monitoring the Future survey, a surprising number of typical teenagers reported involvement in serious criminal behavior: about twelve percent reported hurting someone badly enough that the victim needed medical care; about nine percent stole something worth more than $50; and twenty-five percent reported shoplifting.
    A. True
    B. False

5. The teenage gender ratio for serious violent crime is approximately 4 to 1, and for property crime approximately 2 to 1, male to female.
    A. True
    B. False

6. Boys are more likely than girls to be arrested as runaways.
    A. True
    B. False

7. Self-report surveys ask respondents about their criminal activity; they are useful in measuring crimes, such as drug usage, that are rarely reported to police.
    A. True
    B. False

8. Donohue and Levitt contend that, if abortion were illegal, crime rates might be ten to twenty percent higher than they currently are with legal abortion.
    A. True
    B. False

9. The number of youths arrested for delinquent behavior has declined, including a significant decrease in those arrested for rape.
    A. True
    B. False

10. Age is inversely related to criminality; as youthful offenders mature, their offending rates decline.
    A. True
    B. False

11. In their study of 9,945 boys born in Philadelphia, Wolfgang, Figlio, and Sellin report that a chronic nine percent were responsible for 52 percent of all offenses, including 71 percent of the homicides, 82 percent of the robberies, and 64 percent of the aggravated assaults.
    A. True
    B. False

12. Adults age fifty and older, who make up slightly less than a third of the population, account for only about six percent of arrests.
    A. True
    B. False

13. Siegel and Welsh note a recent change in serious violent crime arrests that was striking: for males arrests decreased by thirty-three percent, while females' violent crime arrests decreased at the same rate.
    A. True
    B. False

14. Siegel and Welsh note that, if two million arrests of youths under eighteen years of age were reported in a given year on the UCR, we could not be sure if two million individuals had been arrested once or if five hundred thousand chronic offenders had been arrested four times each.
    A. True
    B. False

15. The nation's teenage population will increase by fifteen percent, or more than nine million, between now and 2010; Fox predicts a wave of youth violence even greater than that of the past ten years.
    A. True
    B. False

16. Siegel and Welsh note that although the reliability of the data of police crime reports can be questioned, the actual counts they show are probably accurate.
    A. True
    B. False

17. The FBI is in the process of moving to the Uniform Crime Report system of crime reporting as it moves away from the National Incident Based Reporting System.
    A. True
    B. False

18. Siegel and Welsh note that gun ownership affects delinquency trends.
    A. True
    B. False

19. The Uniform Crime Report is an annual tally of crime reported to researchers at the Institute for Social Research; it is considered the primary measure of crime in the United States.
    A. True
    B. False

20. Self-reports show us that a significant number of kids engage in criminal acts, far more than is measured by the arrest data.
    A. True
    B. False

21. African-American youths are arrested for a disproportionate number of murders, rapes, robberies, and assaults, while White youths are arrested for a disproportionate share of arsons.
    A. True
    B. False

22. Early researchers found that the relationship between race and self-reported delinquency was virtually nonexistent; this suggests that racial differences in the official crime data may reflect the fact that African-American youths have a much greater chance of being arrested and officially processed.
    A. True
    B. False

23. Youths ages fifteen to nineteen make up about seven percent of the total U.S. population, but they account for fifty percent of the index crime arrests and ninety percent of the arrests for all crimes.
    A. True
    B. False

24. Siegel and Welsh note that teens tend to be victimized by their peers.
    A. True
    B. False

25. Self-report data is most reliable with the most serious offenders
    A True
    B False

FILL IN

1. The _____ is an arm of the U.S. Department of Justice that investigates violations of federal law, gathers crime statistics, runs a comprehensive crime laboratory, and helps train local law enforcement officers.

2. The _____ is compiled by the FBI and is the most widely used source of national crime and delinquency statistics.

3. Siegel and Welsh note that teens tend to be victimized by their _____.

4. The _____ of crime is the idea that chronic juvenile offenders are likely to continue violating the law as adults.

5. Siegel and Welsh note that young teens are _____ times more likely than older adults (age sixty-five and over) to be victims of crimes.

6. Donohue and Levitt contend that if _____ were illegal, crime rates might be ten to twenty percent higher than they are currently.

7. The tendency for youths to reduce the frequency of their offending behavior as they age is called _____.

8. The total annual sample size of the _____ has been about forty thousand households, containing about seventy-five thousand individuals.

9. Siegel and Welsh note that the number of teenagers in the high-risk ages of fifteen to seventeen will increase by _____ percent.

10. It was noted that only _____ percent of all property crimes were reported to the police.

11. University of Michigan's Institute for Social Research (ISR) conducts an annual national self-report survey called Monitoring The _____.

12. The cost of crime is $450 billion, or _____ for every person in the United States.

13. The _____ view examines early onset and its connection to trajectories of crime and deviance.

14. Adults age fifty and older, who make up slightly less than a third of the population, account for only about _____ percent of arrests.

15. All crimes other than Part I offenses are called _____; arrests for these crimes are tallied quarterly and sent to the FBI for inclusion in the UCR.

ESSAY

1. Identify and describe five factors that influence juvenile crime rates.

2. Describe the findings of Wolfgang, Robert Figlio, and Thorsten Sellin's (1972) *Delinquency in a Birth Cohort*

3. To what extent do youths tell the truth on self-administered questionnaires? What can be done to improve honest responses?

4. What are some reasons offered by Siegel and Welsh to help explain and understand racial differences in juvenile offending patterns?

5. Contrast the Uniform Crime Reports to the National Crime Victimization Survey. What are the strengths and weaknesses of each approach?

ANSWER KEY

MULTIPLE CHOICE

1. A	11. B	21. D
2. A	12. C	22. C
3. B	13. A	23. B
4. C	14. E	24. A
5. D	15. D	25. B
6. B	16. A	26. B
7. C	17. C	27. A
8. C	18. A	28. C
9. A	19. B	29. D
10. A	20. C	30. B

TRUE FALSE

1. False	11. False	21. True
2. True	12. True	22. True
3. False	13. False	23. False
4. True	14. True	24. True
5. True	15. True	25 False
6. False	16. False	
7. True	17. False	
8. True	18. True	
9. True	19. False	
10. True	20. True	

FILL IN

1. Federal Bureau of Investigation
2. Uniform Crime Report
3. peers
4. continuity
5. fifteen
6. abortion
7. aging out
8. NCVS
9. 31
10. 40
11. Future
12. $1,800
13. developmental
14. 6
15. Part II offenses

Web Questions

Multiple Choice
1. Which of the following crimes is not part of Index Crimes of the UCR?
   A. rape
   B. robbery
   C. stalking
   D. assault

2. Which of the following crime trends is correct?
   A. crime skyrocketed between 1960 and 1981
   B. crime has continued to increase steadily since 1960
   C. crime decreased from 1960 until 1981 and has increased ever since
   D. crime stabilized in 1981.

3. Which of the following limitations of the UCR are true?
   A. only the most serious crimes in a criminal episode are reported by the police
   B. the UCR only records reported crime
   C. police departments vary in their recording crime data
   D. all of the above

4. Which of the following is true?
   A. the juvenile murder rate was almost reduced by one-half in 2005 from 1997
   B. the juvenile murder rate was reduced by one-quarter in 2005 as compared to 1997.
   C. the juvenile murder rate continues to climb
   D. the juvenile murder rate has stabilized since 1997.

5. The text mentions that
   A. the projected increase in the juvenile population will increase crime rates
   B. the projected increase in the juvenile population may be offset by the growth in the elderly population
   C. the projected increase in the juvenile population will have no affect on crime rates.
   D. the projected increase in the juvenile population will lead to more drug use.

6. The text presents what connection between drugs and juvenile delinquency?
   A. drugs cause crime
   B. drug use is linked to fluctuations in the crime and delinquency rates
   C. there is no relationship between drugs and crime
   D. they are one and the same.

7. Self-report data
   A. reveal significantly more crime than the UCR
   B. is not reliable or valid
   C. is obtained through annual national samples conducted by the FBI
   D. are more suited for serious offenders than middle class offenders

42

8. Between 1995–2005, during a period of rapidly declining crime rates, the number of arrests of male delinquents decreased about 28 percent, whereas the number of female delinquents arrested declined by
   A. 7 percent
   B. 14 percent
   C. 20 percent
   D. 22 percent

9. Chronic offenders
   A. usually become sex offenders
   B. start earlier than most delinquents, before adolescence, and do not desist
   C. usually start by taking hard drugs with their parents.
   D. start in adolescence and do not stop

10. The National Crime Victimization Survey shows that
    A. most crime occurs during school hours
    B. victimization levels as reported by the FBI's UCR are reliable and valid
    C. teens tend to be victimized by their peers
    D. homeless people suffer high levels of victimization

True False
1. The UCR gives us a pretty good picture of the total number of crimes committed in the US. T F

2. Research shows that the more kids watch TV, the more often they get into violent encounters.   T F

3. Juvenile crime rates significantly affect the overall UCR crime rate. T F

4. A poor economy almost always increases delinquency rates. T F

5. Self-reported delinquency allows for obtaining a greater depth of information about offenders than official statistics T F

Answer Key

Multiple Choice
1. C
2. A
3. D
4. A
5. B
6. B
7. A
8. B
9. B
10. C

True False
1. F
2. T
3. T
4. F
5. T

CHAPTER THREE
INDIVIDUAL VIEWS OF DELINQUENCY:
CHOICE AND TRAIT LEARNING OBJECTIVES

LEARNING OBJECTIVES

- Know the difference between choice and trait theories.
- Understand the concept of criminal choice.
- Be familiar with the concept of routine activities.
- Be able to discuss the pros and cons of general deterrence.
- Recognize what is meant by the term specific deterrence and how it differs from general deterrence.
- Understand the concept of situational crime prevention and be able to list the strategies now being used.
- Be familiar with Cesare Lombroso, the founder of biological criminology.
- Know the biochemical, neurological, and genetic factors linked to delinquency.
- Understand how the psychodynamic model of delinquency links antisocial behaviors to unconscious emotions and feelings.
- Understand why, according to the behavioral perspective, watching violent media causes violent behaviors.
- Know why some psychologists view delinquency as a function of improper information.
- Be familiar with the term psychopath.
- Recognize the issues linking intelligence to delinquency.

CHAPTER OUTLINE

I.   Introduction
        1. Eric Peterson lived in a home with domestic violence until his parents divorced when he was three years old. He was diagnosed by age 8 as having ADHD, reading and math deficiencies, and he suffers from learning disorders.
        2. Starting at age 15, Eric exhibited high levels of aggression at school, and at home was defiant and threatened his mother.
        3. Eric was referred by Family and Children's Services for group and family counseling to address his anger issues and to Adolescent Domestic Abuse program to address his abuse of his mother and girlfriend.
        4. Eric was been successful in this program and has graduated from high school and even started attending college.

II.   Choice Theory
A.   Choice
        1.   first formal explanations of crime based on choice
        2.   assumed that people had free will

3. those who violated the law were motivated by greed, revenge, survival, or hedonism
4. Beccaria and Bentham were utilitarian philosophers
5. people weigh the consequences of their actions before acting
6. classical criminology is now referred to as rational choice theory
7. most potential law violators would cease their actions if:
    a. the pain associated with a behavior outweighed the gain
8. crime seems attractive if rewards seem greater than the punishment
9. to prevent crime, the pain of punishment must outweigh the benefit

B. Rational delinquent
1. view that delinquents choose to violate the law remains popular

C. Choosing delinquent acts
1. the focus of choice theory is on the act, not on the offender
2. decision to forgo law-violating behavior may be based on the perception that the benefits are no longer good or the probability of successfully completing a crime is less than the chance of being caught

D. Lifestyle and delinquency
1. lifestyle also affects the decision to engage in delinquency
2. adolescent work experience may actually increase antisocial activity
3. qualities of work experience contribute to delinquency
    a. autonomy
    b. increased social status among peers
    c. increased income

E. Gangs and choice
1. cash in on a lucrative, albeit illegal, "business enterprise"
2. enormous risks to health, life, and freedom
3. study showed average gang members earned slightly more than the legitimate labor market
    a. about $6 to $11 per hour

F. Routine activities
1. attention must be paid to the opportunity to commit delinquent acts
2. routine activities theory was developed by Cohen and Felson
3. volume and distribution of predatory crimes influenced by the interaction of three variables:
    a. the availability of suitable targets
    b. the absence of capable guardians
    c. the presence of motivated offenders
4. crime levels are relatively low in neighborhoods where residents keep a watchful eye on their neighbors' property
5. delinquency rates trend upward as the number of adult caretakers (guardians) who are at home during the day decreases
6. more wealth a home contains the more likely it is to be a crime target
7. delinquents do not like to travel to commit crimes

8.   delinquency rates linked to the number of kids in the population who are highly motivated to commit crime

III.   Choice Theory and Delinquency Prevention

    A.   Penalties
        1.   punishing them so severely that they never again commit crimes
        2.   making it so difficult to commit crimes that the potential gain is not worth the risk

    B.   General deterrence
        1.   choice to commit delinquent acts can be controlled by the threat of punishment
        2.   guiding principle is certain, swift, and severe punishments
        3.   a mild sanction may deter crime if people believe punishment is certain

    C.   Deterrence and delinquency
        1.   juvenile justice authorities reluctant to incorporate deterrence-based punishments because they interfere with the *parens patriae* philosophy
        2.   shift from emphasis on treatment to emphasis on public safety
        3.   some juvenile court judges became more willing to waive youths to adult courts

    D.   Can delinquency be deterred?
        1.   punishment may not be effective when applied to young people
        2.   minors tend to be less capable of making mature judgments
        3.   the deterrent threat of formal sanctions may be irrelevant
        4.   many juvenile offenders are under the influence of drugs or alcohol
        5.   peer pressure can outweigh the deterrent effect of the law

    E.   Specific deterrence
        1.   if young offenders are punished severely the experience will convince them not to repeat their illegal acts
        2.   punished by state authorities with the understanding that their ordeal will deter future misbehavior
        3.   little evidence that punitive measures alone deter future delinquency
        4.   prior arrests, convictions, and punishments is the best predictor of rearrest
        5.   incarceration may also diminish chances for successful employment
        6.   punishment strategies may stigmatize kids
        7.   helps lock offenders into a delinquent career

    F.   Situational crime prevention
        1.   strategies are designed to make it so difficult to commit delinquent acts that would-be offenders will be convinced the risks are greater than the rewards
            a.   increasing the effort to commit delinquent acts
            b.   increasing the risks of delinquent activity

          c.   reducing the rewards attached to delinquent acts

          d.   increasing the shame of committing a delinquent act

    2.   increasing the effort of delinquency might involve target-hardening techniques

 G.   Hot spots and crackdowns

    1.   targets locales that are known to be the scene of repeated delinquent activity

    2.   seem to be an effective short-term strategy

    3.   combine aggressive problem solving with community improvement techniques

 H.   Do delinquents choose crime?

    1.   before we can accept the propositions of choice theory, several important questions must be addressed

          a.   Why do some poor kids choose to break the law while others in the same neighborhoods manage to abide by the law?

          b.   Why do affluent suburban youths choose to break the law when they have everything to lose and little to gain?

    2.   difficult to explain seeming irrational crimes such as vandalism, arson, and drug abuse

    3.   questions remain

IV.   Trait Theories: Biosocial and Psychological Views

 A.   Trait theory

    1.   argues that behavioral choices are a function of an individual's mental and physical makeup

    2.   views their decisions as a by-product of uncontrollable personal traits

 B.   Origins of trait theory

    1.   Cesare Lombroso (1835–1909) is known as the father of criminology; developed the theory of criminal atavism

    2.   Rafaele Garofalo (1851–1934) shared Lombroso's belief

    3.   Enrico Ferri (1856–1929) attempted to interweave social factors into Lombroso's explanation

    4.   Charles Goring (1870–1919) claimed delinquent behaviors bore a significant relationship to defective intelligence

 C.   Contemporary trait theory

    1.   sociobiology contends that behavior will adapt to the environment in which it evolved

    2.   specific traits may make a child more susceptible to the delinquency-producing factors

    3.   biosocial theory assumes that the cause of delinquency can be found in a child's physical or biological makeup

    4.   psychological traits and characteristics.

V.   Biosocial theories of delinquency

    1.   focuses on the association between biological makeup,

      2.   most research efforts are concentrated in three areas
          a.   biochemical factors
          b.   neurological dysfunction
          c.   genetic influences

A.   Biochemical factors
      1.   body chemistry can govern behavior and personality
      2.   exposure to lead in the environment
      3.   exposure to the now banned PCB
      4.   diet may impact body chemistry

B.   Diet and Delinquency: Recent study in Great Britain on the association between diet and delinquency found that people who have diets lacking in one or more combination of polyunsaturated fats, minerals, and vitamins, and/or contain too much saturated fat (or other elements, including sugar and a range of food and agricultural chemicals) seem to be at higher risk of developing
1. Attention-deficit/hyperactivity disorder (ADHD)
2. Schizophrenia,
3. Dementia, including Alzheimer's disease.
The study also found that eating too much saturated fat, sugar, and salt and not enough vitamins and minerals may contribute to higher levels of
1. mental illness
2. antisocial behavior.

C.   Hormonal levels
      1.   hormonal activity is at its greatest level during teen years
      2.   hormonal sensitivity may begin very early in life
      3.   fetus can be exposed to abnormally high levels of testosterone

D.   Neurological dysfunction
      1.   brain and nervous system structure of offenders
      2.   minimal brain dysfunction (MBD)
      3.   impairment in brain functioning may be present at birth
          a.   low birthweight
          b.   brain injury during pregnancy
          c.   birth complications
          d.   inherited abnormalities
      4.   brain injuries can also occur later in life
          a.   as a result of brutal beatings or sexual abuse by a parent
      5.   children who suffer from measurable neurological deficits at birth
          a.   are more likely to become criminals as adults

E.   Learning disabilities
      1.   relationship between learning disabilities and delinquency highlighted in studies
      2.   arrested and incarcerated children have a far higher LD rate than children in the general population
          a.   10% of all youths have some form of learning disorder

   b. estimates of LD among juvenile delinquents range from 26 to 73 %

  3. two possible explanations for link between LD and delinquency

   a. susceptibility rationale argues that the link is caused by side effects of LD, such as impulsiveness and inability to take social cues

   b. school failure rationale assumes frustration caused by poor school performance will lead to negative self-image and acting-out behavior

  4. Terrie Mofitt, psychologist, concludes there that learning disabilities are a significant correlate of persistent anti-social behavior

   a. neurological symptoms correlate highly with early onset of deviance, hyperactivity, and aggressiveness

  5. National Center on Addiction and Substance Abuse findings

   a. Risk factors for adolescent substance abuse similar to the Behavioral effects of LD

    i. reduced self-esteem

    ii. academic difficulty

    iii. loneliness

    iv. depression

    v. desire for social acceptance

   b. child with LD is twice as likely to suffer Attention Deficit Disorder (ADD) as a member of the general population

   c. children exposed to alcohol, tobacco, and drugs while in the womb are at higher risk for various developmental disorders, including LD

    i. mother who abuses drugs while pregnant may increase likelihood that the child will abuse drugs or alcohol

F. Arousal theory

  1. crimes offer the thrill of getting away with it

  2. we all seek to maintain an optimal level of arousal

  3. sensation seekers seek out stimulating activities including aggressive behavior

G. Attention Deficit Hyperactivity Disorder and Learning Disabilities (ADHD) -- condition in which a child shows a developmentally inappropriate traits:

   a. lack of attention

   b. distractibility

   c. impulsivity

   d. hyperactivity

  1. Symptoms of ADHD

   a. frequently fails to finish projects

   b. does not seem to pay attention

   c. does not sustain interest in play activities

   d. cannot sustain concentration on schoolwork or related tasks

  e. is easily distracted

  f. frequently acts without thinking

  g. often calls out in class

  h. does not want to wait his or her turn

  i. shifts from activity to activity

  j. cannot organize tasks or work

  k. requires constant supervision in school line or while playing games

  l. constantly runs around and climbs on things

  m. shows excessive motor activity while asleep

  n. cannot sit still and is constantly fidgeting

  o. does not remain in his or her seat in class

  p. has difficulty adjusting to social demands

2. Tied to dysfunction in the reticular activating system

  a. children from any background can develop ADHD

  b. five to seven times more common in boys than girls

  c. estimates of ADHD in the general population range from 3 to 12%

3. ADHD usually results in poor school performance

  a. high dropout rate

  b. bullying

  c. stubbornness

  d. mental disorder

  e. lack of response to discipline

4. Delinquency

  a. children with ADHD are more likely to:

    i. use illicit drugs

    ii. use alcohol

    iii. smoke cigarettes

  b. in adolescence

    i. more likely to be arrested

    ii. charged with a felony

    iii. multiple arrests

5. Learning disabilities

  a. arrested and incarcerated children

    i. higher LD rate than do children in the general population

  b. susceptibility rationale

    i. link is caused by side effects of learning disabilities

    ii. impulsiveness and inability to take social cues

  c. school failure rationale

    i. frustration caused by poor school performance

    ii. leads to a negative self-image and acting-out behavior

  d. correlate highly with early onset of deviance, hyperactivity, and aggressiveness

      e.   risk factors for adolescent substance abuse are similar
- i. reduced self-esteem
- ii. acedemic difficulty
- iii. loneliness
- iv. depression
- v. desire for social acceptance

      f.   exposure to alcohol, tobacco, and drugs in the womb
- i. increase risk for developmental disorders

      g.   link has always been artifact of bias
- i. way LD children are treated at school or by the police
- ii. record of school problems
- iii. does not want to wait his or her turn
- iv. shifts from activity to activity
- v. cannot organize tasks or work
- vi. requires constant supervision in school lines or while playing games

6.   Symptoms – hyperactivity
- a. constantly runs around and climbs on things
- b. shows excessive motor activity while asleep
- c. cannot sit still; constantly fidgeting
- d. does not remain in his or her seat in class
- e. is constantly on the "go"
- f. has difficulty regulating emotions
- g. has difficulty getting started
- h. has difficulty staying on track
- i. has difficulty adjusting to social demands

H.   Genetic influences
1. some youths inherit a genetic configuration that predisposes them to aggression
2. antisocial behavior characteristics and mental disorders may be passed down

I.   Parental deviance
1. data on parental deviance were gathered by West and Farrington
2. Cambridge Youth Survey
3. 8 percent of the sons of noncriminal fathers became chronic offenders
4. 37 percent of youths with criminal fathers were multiple offenders
5. Farrington found shoolyard aggression or bullying inter- and intragenerational
6. Farrington's findings are supported by some recent research data
   - a. Rochester Youth Development Study RYDS

J.   Twin studies
1. similarity in delinquency might be a function of environmental

influences
2.   compared the behavior of monozygotic twins with dizygotic twins
3.   significant relationship between the criminal activities of MZ twins
4.   lower association between those of DZ twins
5.   about 60 percent of MZ twins share criminal behavior patterns
6.   only 30 percent of DZ twins share criminal behavior patterns
7.   Minnesota Study of Twins Reared Apart
8.   compares the behavior of MZ and DZ twin pairs
   - a.   who were raised together with others who were separated at birth
   - b.   EEG is a measure of brain activity or brain waves
   - c.   used to monitor a person's state of arousal
   - d.   MZ twins tend to produce strikingly similar EEG spectra
   - e.   DZ twins show far less similarity.
   - f.   MZ twins are closer than DZ twins in such crime relevant measures as level of aggression and verbal skills

K.   Adoption studies
1.   generally supported link between genetics and behavior
2.   adoptees and their biological parents
   - a.   share many of the behavioral and intellectual characteristics
   - b.   despite the conditions found in their adoptive homes
3.   Mednick and Hutchings found that
   - a.   13% of the adoptive fathers of delinquent youths had criminal records
   - b.   31% of their biological fathers had criminal records

VI.   Psychological Theories of Delinquency
A.   Psychodynamic theory
1.   originated with Austrian physician Sigmund Freud (1856–1939)
2.   law violations are a product of an abnormal personality formed early in life
3.   the personality contains three major components:
   - a.   id is the unrestrained, pleasure-seeking component
   - b.   ego develops through the reality of living in the world
   - c.   superego represents the conscience and the moral rules
4.   suggests that an imbalance in personality traits
   - a.   caused by a traumatic early childhood
   - b.   can result in long-term psychological difficulties
5.   youth may demand immediate gratification
6.   lack sensitivity for the needs of others
7.   act aggressively and impulsively
8.   demonstrate psychotic symptoms
B.   Disorders and delinquency
1.   experience anxiety and fear they are losing control
2.   people who have lost control and are dominated by their id called psychotics

3. their behavior may be marked by hallucinations and inappropriate responses
4. psychosis takes many forms
    a. most common being schizophrenia
    b. contemporary psychologists no longer use the term neuroses
5. more common to refer to specific types of disorders
    a. anxiety disorder
    b. mood disorder
    c. sleep disorder
    d. bipolar disorder
6. Erikson coined identity crisis to denote this period of inner turmoil
    a. experience a life crisis
    b. feel emotional, impulsive, and uncertain of their role and purpose
7. delinquents are unable to control their impulsive drives
8. crime is a consequence of inability to cope with oppression or depression

C. The psychodynamic tradition and delinquency
1. Erikson speculated many adolescents experience a life crisis where they feel emotional, impulsive, uncertain about their role and purpose
2. some view youth crime as a result of unresolved internal conflict
3. delinquents unable to control their impulsive drives
4. in its most extreme form, delinquency may be viewed as a form of psychosis
5. antisocial behavior a consequence of inability to cope with feelings of oppression or depression
6. places heavy emphasis on the family's role
7. research shows a number of violent juvenile offenders suffer from some sort of personality disturbance
8. association between mental disturbance and delinquency is unresolved

D. Behavioral theory
1. argue that personality is learned throughout life during interaction with others
2. Watson (1878–1958) and Skinner (1904–1990)
3. concerns itself with measurable events rather than unobservable phenomena
4. individuals learn by observing how people react to their behavior
5. behavior is triggered initially by a stimulus or change in the environment

E. Social learning theory
1. learning and social experiences determine behavior
2. children model behavior to the reactions they receive from others
3. violence as a way of life may teach that such behavior is acceptable

        4.   more likely to heed what parents do than what they say

F.   Violent media/Violent behavior?
        1.   experts fear there is a link between sexual violence and viewing pornography
        2.   children are particularly susceptible to TV imagery

G.   TV and violence
        1.   watching violence on TV is correlated with aggressive behaviors
        2.   the relationship between TV viewing and violence is still uncertain
        3.   possible that violence-prone children like to watch violent TV shows

H.   Cognitive theory
        1.   focus on mental processes
        2.   concerned with how people morally represent and reason about the world
        3.   Piaget (1896–1980) founder of this approach
        4.   hypothesized that reasoning processes develop in an orderly fashion
        5.   Kohlberg suggested there are stages of moral development
        6.   serious offenders' moral orientation differs from law-abiding citizens
        7.   delinquents have a lack of respect for the law
        8.   delinquents have a personality marked by self-interest
        9.   nonoffenders viewed the law as something that benefits all of society
             a.   willing to honor the rights of others
        10.   nondelinquent youths displayed higher stages of moral

I.   Information processing
        1.   explain antisocial behavior in terms of perception and analysis of data
        2.   cognitive deficits and use information incorrectly when they make decisions
        3.   misperceive behavioral cues
             a.   decision making was shaped by traumatic life events
        4.   rely on mental "scripts" learned in early childhood
             a.   tell them how to interpret events
             b.   what to expect
             c.   how they should react
             d.   what the outcome of the interaction should be
        5.   violence becomes a stable behavior
        6.   scripts that emphasize aggressive responses are repeatedly rehearsed

J.   Cognitive treatment
        1.   acknowledges that people are more likely to respond aggressively
             a.   provocation stir feelings of anger
        2.   provocations as problems demanding a solution rather than as insults
        3.   programs teach problem-solving skills

K. Personality and delinquency
1. defined as the stable patterns of behavior distinguish one person from another
2. Sheldon and Eleanor Glueck key theorists
3. identified a number of personality traits that characterize delinquents
4. delinquents maintain a distinct personality
5. Eysenck's extraversion and neuroticism personality traits
6. Extraverts are impulsive individuals
   a. lack the ability to examine their own motives
7. those high in neuroticism are anxious and emotionally unstable
8. youths who are both neurotic and extraverted
   a. often lack insight and are highly impulsive
   b. they act self-destructively
L. Antisocial personality
1. no more than 3 percent of male offenders may be classified as antisocial, psychopathic, or sociopathic
2. exhibit low levels of guilt and anxiety
3. persistently violate the rights of others
4. they may exhibit charm and intelligence
5. incapable of forming enduring relationships
M. Origins of antisocial personality
1. family dysfunction and an emotionally disturbed parent
2. parental rejection during childhood
3. inconsistent or overly abusive discipline
4. psychopaths may have brain-related physical anomalies
   a. cause them to process emotional input differently than nonpsychopaths
5. antisocial youths suffer from lower levels of arousal than the general population
N. Intelligence and delinquency
1. correlation between IQ and crime by testing adjudicated juvenile delinquents
2. nature theory – Goddard found in 1920 that many institutionalized persons were "feebleminded"
3. concluded that at least half of all juvenile delinquents were mental defectives
4. more culturally sensitive explanations of behavior led to the nurture theory
5. nurture theorists discredit the IQ-crime link
6. low IQs result from an environment that also encourages delinquent behavior
O. Rethinking IQ and delinquency
1. Sutherland evaluated IQ studies of criminals
   a. evidence disputing the association between intelligence and criminality

2. Hirschi and Hindelang concluded
   a. IQ is more important than race and social class for delinquency
3. IQ s effect on school performance
   a. some believe IQ has an indirect influence on delinquency
   b. some experts believe IQ may have a direct influence on delinquency

VII. Critiquing Trait Theory Views
   A. Criticisms
      1. research methodologies they employ are invalid
      2. most research efforts use adjudicated or incarcerated offenders
      3. trait-theory research can be socially and politically damaging
   B. Defenses
      1. does not ignore environmental and social factors
      2. delinquency rate differences may then result from differential access to opportunities to either commit crime or to receive the treatment needed to correct developmental problems

CHAPTER SUMMARY

Criminological theories that focus on the individual can be classified in two groups: choice theories and trait theories. Choice theory holds that people have free will to control their actions. Delinquency is a product of weighing the risks of crime against its benefits. If the risk is greater than the gain, people will choose not to commit crimes. One way of creating a greater risk is to make sure that the punishments associated with delinquency are sufficiently severe, certain, and fast.

Routine activities theory maintains that a pool of motivated offenders exists and that these offenders will take advantage of suitable targets unless they are heavily guarded. General deterrence theory holds that if delinquents are rational, an inverse relationship should exist between punishment and crime. The harsher, more certain, and swifter the punishment, the more likely it will deter delinquency. General deterrence assumes that delinquents make a rational choice before committing delinquent acts. Research has not indicated that deterrent measures actually reduce the delinquency rate. Specific deterrence theory holds that the delinquency rate can be reduced if offenders are punished so severely that they never commit crimes again. There is little evidence that harsh punishments reduce the delinquency rate, perhaps because most delinquents are not severely punished. Choice theorists agree that if the punishment for delinquency could be increased, the delinquency rate might fall. One method is to transfer youths to the criminal courts or to grant the adult justice system jurisdiction over serious juvenile cases. Situational crime prevention strategies aim to reduce opportunities for crime to take place. By imposing obstacles that make it difficult to offend, such strategies strive to dissuade would-be offenders.

Trait theories hold that delinquents do not choose to commit crimes freely but are influenced by forces beyond their control. The two types of current trait theory are biosocial and psychological. One of the earliest branches of biosocial theory was biological theory, formulated by Cesare Lombroso, who linked delinquency to inborn traits. Following his lead were theories based on genetic inheritance and body build. Although biological theory was in disrepute for many years, it has recently reemerged. Biochemical factors linked to delinquency include diet, hormones, and blood chemistry. Neurological factors include brain damage and ADHD. Some experts believe that delinquent tendencies may be inherited. Studies use twins and adoptees to test this theory.

Psychological theories include the psychodynamic model, which links antisocial behaviors to unconscious emotions and feelings developed in early childhood. The behavioral perspective emphasizes that children imitate the behavior they observe personally or view on television or in movies. Children who are exposed to violence and see it rewarded may become violent as adults. Cognitive psychology is concerned with how people perceive the world. Criminality is viewed as a function of improper information processing or lack of moral development. Psychopaths are people with a total lack of concern for others. They may commit the most serious violent crimes. Intelligence has also been related to delinquency. Some studies claim to show that delinquents have lower IQs than nondelinquents. Many delinquency prevention efforts are based on psychological theory. Judges commonly order delinquent youths to receive counseling. Recently, some delinquent offenders have been given biochemical therapy.

KEY TERMS

choice theory: Holds that youths will engage in delinquent and criminal behavior after weighing the consequences and benefits of their actions; delinquent behavior is a rational choice made by a motivated offender who perceives that the chances of gain outweigh any possible punishment or loss.

trait theory: Holds that youths engage in delinquent or criminal behavior due to aberrant physical or psychological traits that govern behavioral choices; delinquent actions are impulsive or instinctual rather than rational choices.

free will: The view that youths are in charge of their own destinies and are free to make personal behavior choices unencumbered by environmental factors.

utilitarianism: Those who believe that people weigh the benefits and consequences of their future actions before deciding on a course of behavior.

classical criminology: Holds that decisions to violate the law are weighed against possible punishments and to deter crime the pain of punishment must outweigh the benefit of illegal gain; led to graduated punishments based on seriousness of the crime (let the punishment fit the crime).

routine activities theory: The view that crime is a "normal" function of the routine activities of modern living; offenses can be expected if there is a motivated offender and a suitable target that is not protected by capable guardians.

predatory crimes: Violent crimes against persons and crimes in which an offender attempts to steal an object directly from its holder.

general deterrence: Crime control policies that depend on the fear of criminal penalties, such as long prison sentences for violent crimes; the aim is to convince law violators that the pain outweighs the benefit of criminal activity.

co-offending: Committing criminal acts in groups.

specific deterrence: meting out severe punishments to offenders

situational crime prevention: A crime prevention method that relies on reducing the opportunity to commit criminal acts by making them more difficult to perform, reducing their reward, and increasing their risks.

hot spot: A particular location or address that is the site of repeated and frequent criminal activity.

crackdown: A law enforcement operation that is designed to reduce or eliminate a particular criminal activity through the application of aggressive police tactics, usually involving a larger than usual contingent of police officers.

criminal atavism: The idea that delinquents manifest physical anomalies that make them biologically and physiologically similar to our primitive ancestors, savage throwbacks to an earlier stage of human evolution.

biosocial theory: The view that both thought and behavior have biological and social bases.

minimal brain dysfunction (MBD): Damage to the brain itself that causes antisocial behavior injurious to the individual's lifestyle and social adjustment.

learning disabilities (LD): Neurological dysfunctions that prevent an individual from learning to his or her potential.

psychodynamic theory: Branch of psychology that holds that the human personality is controlled by unconscious mental processes developed early in childhood.

identity crisis: Psychological state, identified by Erikson, in which youth face inner turmoil and uncertainty about life roles.

behaviorism: Branch of psychology concerned with the study of observable behavior rather than unconscious processes; focuses on particular stimuli and responses to them.

social learning theory: The view that behavior is modeled through observation either directly through intimate contact with others or indirectly through media; interactions that are rewarded are copied, whereas those that are punished are avoided.

cognitive theory: The branch of psychology that studies the perception of reality and the mental processes required to understand the world we live in.

extraversion: Impulsive behavior without the ability to examine motives and behavior.

neuroticism: A personality trait marked by unfounded anxiety, tension, and emotional instability.

psychopathic personality/sociopathic personality/antisocial personality: A person lacking in warmth, exhibiting inappropriate behavior responses, and unable to learn from experience; the condition is defined by persistent violations of social norms, including lying, stealing, truancy, inconsistent work behavior, and traffic arrests.

nature theory: The view that intelligence is inherited and is a function of genetic makeup.

nurture theory: The view that intelligence is determined by environmental stimulation and socialization.

SELF TEST QUESTIONS

MULTIPLE CHOICE

1. Which of the following best describes the results of the adoption studies cited by Siegel and Welsh?
   A. The social environment is the sole determinant of criminality.
   B. The MZ twin is more likely to become delinquent than the DZ twin.
   C. The DZ twin is less likely to become delinquent than the non-twin child.
   D. There is a link between genetics and behavior.

2. Sigmund Freud is the pioneer theorist of which following psychological perspectives?
   A. gestalt therapy   C. psychodynamic theory
   B. behavioral theory   D. cognitive theory

3. Which theory suggests that youth offenders engage in delinquency because they believe that their actions will be profitable?
   A. trait theory   C. subculture theory
   B. choice theory   D. social disorganization theory

4. Modern trait theorists work under what assumption?
   A. Criminal behavior is predetermined by genetics at birth.
   B. Criminal behavior is a product of equipotentiality.
   C. A combination of personal traits and social environment combine to produce behavior.
   D. Reverse altruism negates criminogenic factors in the social environment.

5. Which theory draws attention to the effect of vicarious learning in drawing the connection between television violence and youth violence?
   A. Biosocial theory   C. Moral Development Theory
   B. Psychodynamic Theory   D. Social Learning Theory

6. Which type of theory links delinquency to biological, psychological, and environmental conditions?
   A. trait theory   C. subculture theory
   B. choice theory   D. social disorganization theory

7. What theoretical perspective do Cesare Beccaria and Jeremy Bentham best exemplify?
   A. biosocial criminologists   C. psychological criminologists
   B. psycho-social criminologists   D. utilitarian criminologists

8. Which of the following best describes deterrence theory?
   A. Rehabilitate the criminal for eventual reintegration into society.
   B. Let the punishment fit the criminal.
   C. Let the punishment fit the crime.
   D. Incarcerate to incapacitate.

9. From the classical view, why do youths become drug dealers?
   A. Biological factors push them toward crime.
   B. The rewards outweigh the potential costs.
   C. They are products of their neighborhood.
   D. They are psychologically disturbed.

10. Those who embrace the utility of punishment as a delinquency control mechanism consider the delinquent to be _____.
   A. a product of social forces
   B. redeemable and salvageable
   C. a rational person
   D. a consequence of overwhelming psychological urges

11. Which of the following best describes the focus of rational choice theory?
   A. the delinquent act
   B. the characteristics of the delinquent offender
   C. the criminogenic forces in the environment
   D. the impact of delinquent labels

12. Which of the following is the best criticism of general deterrence theory?
   A. It assumes that immature youths are rational.
   B. There is no way to implement it.
   C. It is racially biased.
   D. It doesn't explain gender differences in delinquency.

13. Sentencing a juvenile to secure incarceration is an example of what punishment strategy?
   A. cognitive treatment   C. primary prevention
   B. specific deterrence   D. reintegration therapy

14. Target-hardening techniques control crime by doing what?
   A. increasing the risks of crime by making the offender more likely to be detected
   B. increasing the effort needed to commit a crime
   C. reducing the rewards attached to crime by reducing the value of targets
   D. transferring the losses of crimes to insurance companies

15. What is the most basic premise of sociobiology?
   A. Criminal behavior is genetically predetermined.
   B. Human behavior is a the sole result of social interaction.
   C. Behavior is an adaptation to the environment in which it evolved.
   D. Delinquency is non-adaptive.

16. According to biosocial researchers, what two factors combine to produce individual behavior patterns?
    A. social interaction and social structure
    B. genetic traits and the environment
    C. cognitive learning and psychodynamic interrelations
    D. intellectual and moral development

17. Low birth weight and head injuries have been used as evidence to link criminality with what?
    A. neurological impairment
    B. somatotype body assessments
    C. environmental-biosocial constraints
    D. poor diet practices

18. The belief that delinquents require greater brain stimulation reflects which theory?
    A. minimal brain dysfunction   C. latent-trait
    B. arousal   D. social learning

19. Which component of human personality is unrestrained, primitive, and pleasure seeking?
    A. the ego   C. the superego
    B. the id   D. the jurisprudence

20. According to psychoanalytic theory, long-term psychological problems are caused by what?
    A. trauma during childhood life-stages
    B. adult life experiences
    C. adolescent labeling
    D. biochemical and dietary imbalances

21. The psychological clash between ego identity and role diffusion is precipitated by what?
    A. unresolved childhood trauma or conflict   C. an identity crisis
    B. stymied moral development   D. delinquency

22. Psychoanalysts view delinquents as being dominated by what component of human personality?
    A. the ego   C. the id
    B. the superego   D. the psychodynamic

23. According to the social learning approach, behavior is a result of what?
    A. social structure and childhood experiences
    B. diet and school performance
    C. learning and social experiences coupled with values and expectations
    D. individual response to environmental stimuli

24. According to _____ theory, developed by Cohen and Felson, the volume and distribution of predatory crimes in a particular area and at a particular time is influenced by the interaction of three variables: the availability of suitable targets, the absence of capable guardians, and the presence of motivated offenders.
    A. social learning
    B. psychodynamic
    C. routine activities
    D. choice

25. According to routine activities theory, which of the following best describes homeowners, police, security guards, and teachers?
    A. presence of motivated offenders
    B. suitable targets
    C. third party bystanders
    D. capable guardians

26. Juveniles often commit crimes in groups, a process called _____, and peer pressure can outweigh the deterrent effect of the law.
    A. cohort tendency
    B. co-offending
    C. group think
    D. reciprocity

27. _____ efforts are designed to reduce or redirect crime by making it more difficult to profit from illegal acts.
    A. situational crime prevention
    B. general deterrence
    C. specific deterrence
    D. routine activity theory

28. The trait perspective is generally believed to have originated with the Italian physician _____; he is known as the father of criminology.
    A. Larry Siegel
    B. Kevin Courtright
    C. Enrico Ferri
    D. Cesare Lombroso

29. Children from any background can develop ADHD, but it is _____ times more common in boys than girls.
    A. two
    B. five to seven
    C. ten
    D. fifty

30. An EEG is a measure of _____ that can be used to monitor a person's state of arousal.
    A. skin conductivity
    B. brain activity or brain waves
    C. intelligence
    D. honesty in verbal responses

TRUE FALSE

1. Children from any background can develop ADHD, but it is three times more common in girls than boys.
    A. True
    B. False

2. Kohlberg explains that delinquents' moral reasoning is likely to differ from that of law abiding youth
      A. True
      B. False

3. Delinquents do not like to travel to commit crimes, and look for suitable targets close to their homes; familiarity with an area gives kids a ready knowledge of escape routes referred to as their awareness space.
      A. True
      B. False

4. Delinquents who choose crime must evaluate the characteristics of a target to determine its suitability.
      A. True
      B. False

5. Studies conducted on twin behavior detected a significant relationship between the criminal activities of MZ twins and a much lower association between those of DZ twins; about sixty percent of MZ twins share criminal behavior patterns (if one twin was criminal, so was the other), whereas only thirty percent of DZ twins are similarly related.
      A. True
      B. False

6. The trait perspective is generally believed to have originated with the Italian physician Cesare Lombroso; he is known as the father of criminology.
      A. True
      B. False

7. Specific deterrence aims at reducing crime through the application of sufficiently severe punishments; once offenders experience these punishments they will be unwilling to repeat their delinquent activities.
      A. True
      B. False

8. Choice theory assumes that human behavior is determined by factors in the individual's psychological make-up.
      A. True
      B. False

9. The focus in choice theory is on the act, not the offender.
      A. True
      B. False

10. Youths may be more influenced by peer pressure than the economic rewards of crime.
      A. True
      B. False

11. Even a mild punishment may be sufficient to deter crime if people believe that the punishment is certain.
    A. True
    B. False

12. Lombroso believed that delinquents were atavistic throwbacks to an earlier stage of human evolution.
    A. True
    B. False

13. A chronically antisocial individual who possesses superficial charm and above-average intelligence describes someone with a sociopath or psychopath personality disorder.
    A. True
    B. False

14. The nurture theory of intelligence holds that intelligence is primarily sociological in nature.
    A. True
    B. False

15. Biological theories of crime and delinquency best explain rapid changes in crime rates among immigrant populations
    A. True
    B. False

16. Biosocial theories consider crime almost inevitable for some individuals.
    A. True
    B. False

17. The behavioral view contends that the development of the unconscious personality early in childhood influences behavior for the rest of a person's life; criminals have weak egos and damaged personalities.
    A. True
    B. False

18. Routine activities theory maintains that a pool of motivated offenders exists, and that these offenders will take advantage of suitable targets unless they are heavily guarded.
    A. True
    B. False

19. Henry Goddard found in 1920 that many institutionalized persons were "feebleminded" and concluded that at least half of all juvenile delinquents were mental defectives.
    A. True
    B. False

20. Siegel and Welsh note that evidence is inconclusive concerning high levels of violent TV viewing and rates of violent crime that are above the norm.
	A. True
	B. False

21. Social learning suggests that children who grow up in homes where violence is a way of life may learn to believe that such behavior is acceptable; even if parents tell children not to be violent and punish them if they are, the children will model their behavior on the observed violence.
	A. True
	B. False

22. The genetic perspective notes that criminal traits and predispositions are inherited; the criminality of parents can predict the delinquency of children.
	A. True
	B. False

23. The biochemical perspective notes that delinquents often suffer brain impairment, as measured by the EEG; ADHD and minimal brain dysfunction are related to antisocial behavior.
	A. True
	B. False

24. The biochemical perspective notes that delinquency, especially violence, is a function of diet, vitamin intake, hormonal imbalance, or food allergies.
	A. True
	B. False

25. An EEG is a measure of brain activity or brain waves that can be used to monitor a person's state of arousal; DZ twins tend to produce strikingly similar EEG spectra while MZ twins show far less similarity.
	A. True
	B. False

FILL IN

1. Cesare Beccaria and Jeremy Bentham's ideas are the core of _____ criminology.

2. Banning the sale of spray paint to minors would be a way of controlling the _____ of crime.

3. _____ holds that youths will engage in delinquent and criminal behavior after weighing the consequences and benefits of their actions; delinquent behavior is a rational choice made by a motivated offender who perceives that the chances of gain outweigh any possible punishment or loss.

4. _____ holds that youths engage in delinquent or criminal behavior due to aberrant physical or psychological traits that govern behavioral choices; delinquent actions are impulsive or instinctual rather than rational choices.

5. _____ is the view that youths are in charge of their own destinies and are free to make personal behavior choices unencumbered by environmental factors.

6. _____ are those who believe that people weigh the benefits and consequences of their future actions before deciding on a course of behavior.

7. _____ holds that decisions to violate the law are weighed against possible punishments and to deter crime the pain of punishment must outweigh the benefit of illegal gain.

8. Classical criminology led to graduated punishments based on seriousness of the crime and the saying "let the punishment fit the _____."

9. Routine activities theory is the view that crime is a "normal" function of the routine activities of modern living; offenses can be expected if there is a motivated offender and a suitable target that is not protected by _____.

10. _____crimes are violent crimes against persons and crimes in which an offender attempts to steal an object directly from its holder.

11. Juveniles often commit crimes in groups, a process called _____, and peer pressure can outweigh the deterrent effect of the law.

12. _____ is the idea that delinquents manifest physical anomalies that make them biologically and physiologically similar to our primitive ancestors, savage throwbacks to an earlier stage of human evolution.

13. _____ is the view that both thought and behavior have biological and social bases.

14. _____ is damage to the brain itself that causes antisocial behavior injurious to the individual's lifestyle and social adjustment.

15. _____ are neurological dysfunctions that prevent an individual from learning to his or her potential.

ESSAY

1. What types of juvenile justice policies would someone advocate using a biochemical perspective?

2. What are the juvenile justice policy implications of a genetic predisposition/link to crime?

3. Contrast general deterrence theory with specific deterrence theory.

4. What types of recommendations would someone make to reduce delinquency using situational crime prevention?

5. Discuss routine activity theory. How can school administrators apply routine activity theory to school crime?

ANSWER KEY

MULTIPLE CHOICE

1. D	11. A	21. C
2. C	12. A	22. C
3. B	13. B	23. C
4. C	14. B	24. C
5. D	15. C	25. D
6. A	16. B	26. B
7. D	17. A	27. A
8. C	18. B	28. D
9. B	19. B	29. B
10. C	20. A	30. B

TRUE FALSE

1. False	11. True	21. True
2. True	12. True	22. True
3. True	13. True	23. False
4. True	14. True	24. True
5. True	15. False	25. False
6. True	16. False	
7. True	17. False	
8. False	18. True	
9. True	19. True	
10. True	20. True	

FILL IN

1. classical	11. co-offending
2. facilitators	12. criminal atavism
3. choice theory	13. biosocial theory
4. trait theory	14. minimal brain dysfunction
5. free will	15. learning disabilities
6. utilitarians	
7. classical criminology	
8. crime	
9. capable guardians	
10. predatory	

Web Questions

Multiple Choice

1. Classical criminology
   A. assumes that people are driven by evil or good
   B. understand that many forces push and pull people to act which are virtually beyond their control
   C. examine social-economic correlates to crime
   D. assumes that people can rationally decide to obey the law or not based upon consequences.

2. General deterrence theory
   A. requires an analysis of a an individual offenders cognitive skills before determining sentence
   B. is concerned with rehabilitation of specific types of offenders
   C. is directed at convincing potential law violators that crime does not pay
   D. all of the above

3. In reference to specific deterrence, punitive measures rather then deter juvenile offenders can either have no effect or increase chances for recidivism because
   A. punishment may reduce changes for successful employment
   B. punishment may stigmatize youth and prevent them from leading prosocial lives reducing their stakes in conformity
   C. youthful offenders may be optimists and assume they won't get caught again
   D. all of the above

4. Lombrosso, the father of criminology, may have been influenced by his training. He was a
   A. physician
   B. lawyer
   C. judge
   D. lawyer

5. Biosocial theories of delinquency
   A. assert that some youth are born criminals
   B. stress biological determism.
   C. assert that if a person has certain compromised biological traits, if social conditions do not mitigate the weaknesses, the person is likely to adopt anti-social behaviors.
   D. are preeminent theories in the field

71

6. Which psychologist who has studied early onset of Life Course Persisters concluded that early onset of deviance, hyperactivity, and aggressiveness is associated with learning disorders
    A. Terrence Thornberry
    B. Charles Goring
    C. Albert Bandera
    D. Terrie Moffitt

7. Donald West and David Farrington's Cambridge Youth study found that
    A. school yard aggression or bullying was inter and intra generational
    B. criminal mothers were more criminogenic than criminal fathers.
    C. adolescent limited's committed most crimes
    D. all of the above

8. Social Learning theory
    A. stress rewards and punishments in a social milieu
    B. address delinquent egos and overactive ids
    C. consider faulty cognitive reasoning as responsible for delinquency
    D. believes that the first few years of life determine life trajectories

9. Kohlberg asserted that
    A. delinquents are equally found at all levels of moral reasoning
    B. delinquent behavior is related to moral development
    C. believed that psychodynamic development caused delinquency
    D. believed that cognitive scripts drove behavior

10. Eysenck proposed that
    A. Introverts and extraverts may commit relatively equal amounts of crime, but they commit different types of crimes
    B. extraverts are more likely to learn from their mistakes
    C. extraverts are more susceptible to cognitive behavioral therapy
    D. extraverts are impulsive individuals who lack the ability to examine their motives

True False

1. Those who have been diagnosed with antisocial personality characteristics will not be able to empathize with others T F

2. Hirschi and Hindelang found that low IQ almost always leads to delinquency. T F

3. Most research on trait theory reports using randomized subjects from the general population of high school students T F

4. Erikson coined the term identity crises to denote adolescent's period of inner turmoil. T F

5. Most researchers agree on the association between mental illness and delinquency T F.

Multiple Choice

1. d
2. c
3. d
4. a
5. c
6. d
7. a
8. a
9. b
10 d

True False

1. T
2. F
3. F
4. T
5. F

CHAPTER FOUR
SOCIOLOGICAL VIEWS OF DELINQUENCY

LEARNING OBJECTIVES

- Know what is meant by the term social disorganization.
- Understand the relationship between neighborhood fear, unemployment, social change, and lack of cohesion and delinquent behavior patterns.
- Be familiar with the concept of strain and anomie.
- Comprehend the elements of general strain theory and the concept of negative affective states.
- Understand how cultural deviance creates a breeding ground for gangs and law-violating groups.
- Know the social processes that have been linked to delinquency.
- Be able to differentiate between learning and control theories.
- Identify the elements of labeling and stigma that reinforce delinquency.
- Recognize the role that social conflict plays in creating an environment that breeds antisocial behaviors.
- Be familiar with the social programs that have been designed to improve neighborhood conditions, help children be properly socialized, and reduce conflict.

CHAPTER OUTLINE

Case Profile: Jay

        1. youngest of six children, in impoverished community
        2. although bright, regularly misses schools
        3. arrested on theft charges
        4. parents facing homelessness
        5. teacher becomes his foster mother
        6. misses appointments with probation officer
        7. follows court-ordered framework including community service, restitution, continued contact with biological family, contact with local human service agency, and retail theft group composed of other offenders, volunteers, store security and leader.
        8. Jay maintains close contact with family, works harder in school, and seriously considers college.

I   Introduction
      A.   No More Victims programs
          1.   kids often live in tough urban environments
          2.   key to understanding delinquent behavior lies in the social environment
      B.   Perspective
          1.   individual-level phenomenon fail to account for these consistent differences in delinquency rates

2. large cities have more crime problems than rural
C. Social factors and delinquency
1. interpersonal interactions
a. weakened family ties linked to delinquency
2. community ecological conditions and social change
3. political unrest and mistrust, economic stress, and family disintegration
4. socioeconomic status and lack of economic success

II. Social Factors and Delinquency
A. Critical social factors believed to cause or affect delinquent behaviors
1. interpersonal interactions – relationships with families, peers, schools, jobs, criminal justice agencies, and more may play an important role in creating or restraining delinquency
a. reduced influence of family in American society/increased emphasis on individuality, independence, and isolation
2. community ecological conditions – living in deteriorated inner-city areas marked by poverty, decay, fear, and despair influences delinquency
3. social change – political unrest and mistrust, economic stress, and family disintegration have been found to precede sharp increases in crime rates; stabilization of these traditional social institutions typically precede crime rate declines
4. socioeconomic status – may also affect delinquency. Logic finds that people on the lowest rung of the economic ladder will have the greatest incentive to commit crime. Delinquency may appear as an attractive alternative to a life of indigence.

III. Social Structure Theories
A. Culture of poverty – term coined by sociologist Oscar Lewis
1. describes the crushing burden faced by the urban poor
2. marked by apathy, cynicism, helplessness, and mistrust
3. permanent underclass whose members have little chance of upward mobility
4. hollowed out deteriorated inner core surrounded by less devastated communities
5. truly disadvantaged are members of the urban underclass
B. Economics
1. more than half of families in poverty are fatherless and husbandless
2. many are supported entirely by government aid
3. lack of employment opportunity also limits the authority of parents
4. poor children are more likely to suffer from health problems
5. children who live in extreme poverty exhibit the worst outcomes
6. tie delinquency rates to socioeconomic conditions, cultural values
7. frustrated by their inability to be part of the American Dream

75

IV. Social Disorganization
    A. Clifford Shaw and Henry McKay, sociologists
        1. first recognized concept of social disorganization
        2. delinquency rates were high in what they called transitional neighborhoods areas
        3. factories and commercial establishments were interspersed with residences
        4. cultural transmission passing on delinquent traditions
        5. distinct ecological areas had developed
        6. visualized as a series of concentric zones each with a stable delinquency rate
        7. data indicated a stable pattern of delinquency over a 65-year period
    B. Social control
        1. healthy, organized community has the ability to regulate itself
        2. common goals can be achieved
        3. social institutions cannot work effectively in climate of alienation and mistrust
    C. Social disorganization theory concepts
        1. relative deprivation
            a. where poor and wealthy live relatively close to one another
        2. community change
            a. some impoverished areas are being gentrified
            b. formerly affluent communities becoming rundown
            c. likely to experience increases in single-parent families
            d. changes in housing from owner- to renter-occupied units
            e. loss of semiskilled and unskilled jobs
            f. growth in the numbers of discouraged
            g. unemployed workers who are no longer seeking jobs
        3. community fear
            a. suffer social incivility, i.e., trash and litter, graffiti, burned-out buildings, drunks and vagabonds, loiterers, prostitutes, noise, congestion, and more
            b. residents become convinced neighborhood is dangerous and become fearful and weary, trying not to leave their homes at night
        5. collective cohesion
            a. high levels of social control and social integration, develop sense of collective efficacy or mutual trust and a willingness to intervene in the supervision of children

V. Anomie/Strain
    A. Strain
        1. feel isolated from the economic mainstream
        2. view crime as a direct result of lower-class frustration and anger
        3. Merton adopted the concept of strain to explain crime and delinquency

        4.   youths may either
              a.   use deviant methods to achieve their goals
              b.   reject socially accepted goals and substitute deviant

B.   General strain theory

        1.   Agnew argues there are more sources of strain than Merton realized

        2.   elements of general strain theory

              a.   strain caused by failure to achieve positively valued goals

              b.   strain as the removal of positively valued stimuli

              c.   strain as the presentation of negative stimuli

        3.   negative affective states

              a.   anger, frustration, and fear that derive from strain

C.   Cultural deviance

        1.   youths' desire to conform to lower-class neighborhood cultural values

        2.   lower class values conflict with those of the larger society

        3.   being tough, never showing fear, living for today, and disrespecting authority

        4.   experience a form of culture conflict

D.   The Code of the Streets

      1. Elijah Anderson asserts interrelationship of culture and behavior

      2. for the "ghetto poor" lack of jobs, stigma of race, drug use, alienation, and lack of hope puts youth at risk of deviant behavior and crime.

      3. oppositional culture which is opposed to mainstream and society competes with conventional culture

      4. the code demands that disrespect be confronted, often violently.

VI.   Social Process Theories: Socialization and Delinquency

A.   Socialization

        1.   root cause of delinquency traced to learning delinquent attitudes from peers

              a.   becoming detached from school

              b.   experiencing conflict in the home

        2.   process of guiding people into acceptable behavior patterns

              a.   through information, approval, rewards, and punishments

        3.   early socialization experiences have a lifelong

B.   Parental efficacy

        1.   primary influence is the family

        2.   children whose parents use severe discipline yet lack warmth and involvement are prone to antisocial behavior

        3.   family-crime relationship is significant across racial, ethnic, and gender lines

        5.   one of the most replicated findings in the criminological literature

C.   Socialization process affects delinquency in three different ways

        1.   learning – delinquency may be learned through interaction with other people

2.   control – delinquency may result when life circumstances weaken the attachment a child has to family, peers, school, and society

3.   reaction – some kids are stigmatized and find themselves locked out of conventional society and into a deviant or delinquent way of life

VII.   Social Learning Theories

     A.   Social learning theories

        1.   youths can resist crime if they have learned proper values and behaviors

        2.   learn the values and behaviors associated with crime

        3.   involves the techniques of crime and the psychological aspects

     B.   Sutherland's differential association theory

        1.   exposed to and learn pro-social and antisocial attitudes and behaviors

        2.   kids will be vulnerable to choosing criminal behaviors over conventional ones if

           a.   prodelinquency definitions outweigh the antidelinquency definitions

           b.   particularly influential if they come from significant others

VII.   Social Control Theories

     A.   Social control

        1.   strength of the relationships a child forms with conventional individuals

        2.   develop a positive self-image

        3.   develop a strong commitment to conformity

     B.   Hirschi developed the most prominent control theory, arguing that

        1.   all people have the potential to commit crimes

        2.   people are kept in check by their social bonds or attachments to society; if these social bonds are weakened, kids are able to engage in antisocial but personally desirable behaviors

     C.   Four main elements of the social bond

        1.   attachment to parents, peers, and schools

        2.   commitment to the pursuit of conventional

        3.   involvement in conventional activities such as school, sports, and religion

        4.   belief in values such as rights of others and respect for the legal code

     D.   Hirschi's vision of delinquency causation is one of the most influential of recent times and a significant amount of research evidence supports his ideas

        1.   positive social attachments help control delinquency

        2.   kids who are detached from the educational experience are at risk of criminality

        3.   kids who do well and are committed to school are less likely to engage in delinquent acts

          4.   kids who are attached to their families are less likely to get involved in a deviant peer group and consequently are less likely to engage in criminal activities

    E.   Criticism

          1.   social relations of delinquents

          2.   Hirschi portrays delinquents as lone wolves

IX.   Social Reaction Theories

    A.   Reaction

          1.   the way society reacts to individuals and

          2.   the way individuals react to society determines individual behavior

          3.   delinquents become stigmatized, or labeled, by agents of social control, i.e., the police and courts, parents, neighbors

    B.   Labeling theory

          1.   youths violate the law for a variety of reasons

          2.   if individuals' delinquent behaviors are detected

               a.   offenders given a negative label that follows them throughout life

          3.   degree to which youngsters are perceived as deviants may affect their treatment

               a.   neighbors may tell their children to avoid the troublemaker

          4.   youths will have an increasing commitment to delinquent careers

          5.   they accept that label as a personal identity

               a.   process called self-labeling

          6.   they may be given official labels, applied in ceremonies

          7.   process is a durable negative label and an accompanying loss of status

          8.   the label juvenile delinquent is conferred on offenders

          9.   their identities may be transformed

               a.   they become bad kids

         10.   labeling process helps create a self-fulfilling prophecy

         11.   self-fulfilling prophecy leads to a damaged self-image

X.   Critical/Social Conflict Theories

    A.   Social conflict theory

          1.   society is in a constant state of internal conflict

          2.   different groups strive to impose their will on others

          3.   those with power succeed in shaping the law to meet their needs

          4.   ruling class is a self-interested collective whose primary interest is self-gain

    B.   Law and justice

          1.   theorists view the law and justice system as vehicles for controlling the have-not members of society

          2.   law protects the property and physical safety of the haves from attack by the have-nots and helps control the behavior of those who might otherwise threaten the status quo

3.   consequently, deep-seated hostility is generated among members of the lower class toward a social order they may neither shape nor share in

    C.   The cause of delinquency
        1.   delinquency as a normal response to the conditions created by capitalism
        2.   child-saving movement's real goal was to maintain order and control
        3.   delinquency is a function of the capitalist system's inherent inequity
        4.   the values of capitalism are reinforced
        5.   schools prepare youths for placement in the capitalist system
            a.   class and delinquency – lower class youths form gangs which serve as a means of survival in a system that offers no reasonable alternative
            b.   controlling delinquents – theorists suggest that the justice system may help to sustain such behavior by failing to control them because it is in their best interest to maintain a large number of outcast deviant youths

XI.   Social Structure Theories and Delinquency Prevention
    A.   Social structure theories
        1.   1960s were the heyday of delinquency prevention programs based on social structure theory
        2.   seemed compatible with the policies of Kennedy and Johnson administrations
    B.   New York City–based Mobilization for Youth funded with $50 million
        1.   MOBY created employment opportunities in the community
        2.   coordinated social services
        3.   sponsored social action groups such as tenants' committees
    C.   Operation Weed and Seed
        1.   federal multilevel action plan for revitalizing communities
        2.   social service and law enforcement agencies must cooperate to be effective
        3.   four basic elements in this plan:
            a.   law enforcement
            b.   community policing
            c.   prevention, intervention, and treatment
            d.   neighborhood restoration
    D.   Socialization and delinquency prevention
        1.   one approach has been to help social institutions improve their outreach
        2.   educational programs have been improved
            a.   expanding preschool programs
            b.   develop curricula relevant to students' lives
            c.   stress teacher development
        3.   aimed at strengthening families in crisis

            4.   developing good family relations is an essential element

            5.   providing services for youngsters who have been identified as

E.   Labeling and delinquency prevention

            1.   divert youths from official processing at initial contact with police

            2.   others might be eligible for alternative sanctions

            3.   alternative community-based sanctions substituted for state training schools

            4.   anything producing stigma was to be avoided

            5.   removal of juveniles from adult jails

            6.   end housing status offenders and juvenile delinquents together

            7.   critics claimed that nonintervention movement created a new class of offenders

                  a.   phenomenon as widening the net

F.   Critical theories and delinquency prevention

            1.   conflict resolution may be the key to its demise

            2.   approach that relies on nonpunitive strategies for delinquency control

            3.   turns the justice system into a healing process

                  a.   rather than a distributor of retribution

            4.   restorative justice is based on a social rather than a legal view of delinquency

            5.   participation of community members in the adjudication process

            6.   balanced approach benefits victims, offender, and the community

                  a.   community protection and victims' rights

                  b.   offenders must take responsibility for their actions

G.   Principles of balanced and restorative justice

            1.   crime is fundamentally a violation of people and interpersonal relationships

            2.   victims and the community have been harmed and are in need of restoration

            3.   victims, offenders, and the affected communities are the key stakeholders

            4.   violations create obligations and liabilities

            5.   offenders have the obligation to make things right as much as possible

            6.   coercion is to be minimized

             7.   community's obligations are to both victims and offenders

CHAPTER SUMMARY

Social structure theories hold that delinquent behavior is an adaptation to conditions that predominate in lower-class environments. The social disorganization view suggests that economically deprived areas lose their ability to control the behavior of residents. Gangs flourish in these areas. Delinquency is a product of the socialization mechanisms in a neighborhood: unstable neighborhoods have the greatest chance of producing delinquents. Such factors as fear, unemployment, change, and lack of cohesion help produce delinquent behavior patterns.

Strain theories hold that lower-class youths may desire legitimate goals, but their unavailability causes frustration and deviant behavior. Merton linked strain to anomie, a condition caused when there is a disjunction between goals and means. In his general strain theory, Robert Agnew identifies two more sources of strain: the removal of positive reinforcements and the addition of negative ones. He shows how strain causes delinquent behavior by creating negative affective states, and he outlines the means adolescents employ to cope with strain.

Social process theories hold that improper socialization is the key to delinquency. Control theories suggest that kids are prone to delinquent behavior when they have not been properly socialized and lack a strong bond to society. Without a strong bond, they are free to succumb to the lure of delinquent behavior. Labeling and stigma may also reinforce delinquency. Kids who receive negative labels may internalize them and engage in self-labeling. This causes a self-fulfilling prophecy, which breeds even more deviant behaviors and locks kids into a delinquent way of life.

Critical, or social conflict theory, views delinquency as an inevitable result of the class and racial conflict that pervades society. Delinquents are members of the "have-not" class that is shut out of the mainstream. The law benefits the wealthy over the poor.

KEY TERMS

Critical, or social conflict theory, views delinquency as an inevitable result of the class and racial conflict that pervades society

culture of poverty: View that lower-class people form a separate culture with their own values and norms, which are sometimes in conflict with conventional society.

underclass: Group of urban poor whose members have little chance of upward mobility or improvement.

truly disadvantaged: According to William Julius Wilson, those people who are left out of the economic mainstream and reduced to living in the most deteriorated inner-city areas.

social disorganization: Neighborhood or area marked by culture conflict, lack of cohesiveness, a transient population, and insufficient social organizations; these problems are reflected in the problems at schools in these areas.

transitional neighborhood: Area undergoing a shift in population and structure, usually from middle-class residential to lower-class mixed use.

cultural transmission: The process of passing on deviant traditions and delinquent values from one from one generation to the next.

social control: Ability of social institutions to influence human behavior; the justice system is the primary agency of formal social control.

relative deprivation: Condition that exists when people of wealth and poverty live in close proximity to one another; the relatively deprived are apt to have feelings of anger and hostility, which may produce criminal behavior.

gentrified: The process of transforming a lower-class area into a middle-class enclave through property rehabilitation.

collective efficacy: A process in which mutual trust and a willingness to intervene in the supervision of children and help maintain public order creates a sense of well being in a neighborhood and helps control anti-social activities.

strain: A condition caused by the failure to achieve one's social goals.

anomie: Normlessness produced by rapidly shifting moral values; according to Merton, anomie occurs when personal goals cannot be achieved using available means.

general strain theory: Links delinquency to the strain of being locked out of the economic mainstream, which creates the anger and frustration that lead to delinquent acts.

negative affective states: Anger, depression, disappointment, fear, and other adverse emotions that derive from strain.

cultural deviance theory: Links delinquent acts to the formation of independent subcultures with a unique set of values that clash with the mainstream culture.

culture conflict: When the values of a subculture clash with those of the dominant culture.

socialization: The process of learning the values and norms of the society or the subculture to which the individual belongs.

parental efficacy: Parents are said to have parental efficacy when they are supportive and effectively control their children in a noncoercive fashion.

social learning theories: Posit that delinquency is learned through close relationships with others; assert that children are born "good" and learn to be "bad" from others.

differential association theory: Asserts that criminal behavior is learned primarily in interpersonal groups and that youths will become delinquent if definitions they learn in those groups that are favorable to violating the law exceed definitions favorable to obeying the law.

social control theories: Posit that delinquency results from a weakened commitment to the major social institutions (family, peers, and school); lack of such commitment allows youths to exercise antisocial behavioral choices.

social bond: Ties a person to the institutions and processes of society; elements of the bond include attachment, commitment, involvement, and belief.

stigmatized: People who have been negatively labeled because of their participation, or alleged participation, in deviant or outlawed behaviors.

labeling theory: Posits that society creates deviance through a system of social control agencies that designate (or label) certain individuals as delinquent, thereby stigmatizing them and encouraging them to accept this negative personal identity.

self-labeling: The process by which a person who has been negatively labeled accepts the label as a personal role or identity.

self-fulfilling prophecy: Deviant behavior patterns that are a response to an earlier labeling experience; youths act out these social roles even if they were falsely bestowed.

social conflict theories: The view that intergroup conflict, born out of the unequal distribution of wealth and power, is the root cause of delinquency.

deinstitutionalization: Removing juveniles from adult jails and placing them in community-based programs to avoid the stigma attached to these facilities.

restorative justice: Nonpunitive strategies for dealing with juvenile offenders that make the justice system a healing process rather than a punishment process.

MULTIPLE CHOICE

1. _____ is removing juveniles from adult jails and placing them in community-based programs to avoid the stigma attached to these facilities.
    A. Deinstitutionalization   C. *Parens patriae*
    B. Net widening   D. Collective efficacy

2. Diversion and deinstitutionalization may actually bring more youths into the system who previously would have avoided any type of formal action because of the availability of the program; this is referred to as _____.
    A. tentacles of justice   C. exponential factor
    B. widening the net   D. fallacy of limited control

3. According to the concept of _____, most neighborhood residents share the common goal of living in a crime-free area.
    A. collective efficacy   C. stewardship
    B. ombudsmen   D. *fearitis*

4. _____ justice attempts to address the issues that produced conflict between people rather than to treat one as a victim deserving sympathy and the other as a delinquent deserving punishment.
    A. Restorative   C. Vindictive
    B. Retributive   D. Hybrid

5. _____ theorists view delinquent behavior as a function of the capitalist system's inherent inequity; youths who are judged inferior as potential job prospects become known as losers and punks and wind up in delinquent roles.
    A. Reaction   C. Disorganization
    B. Process   D. Conflict

6. Control theory sees delinquency as the result of _____.
    A. the poor and the rich living in close physical proximity to one another
    B. living in an area with weakened community institutions
    C. a failure to achieve positive goals in life
    D. an individual having weakened bonds to family, school, and peers

7. Which of the following best describes social disorganization theory principles?
    A. Offenders choose to commit crimes because the benefits outweigh the costs.
    B. More individuals who have psychological and physical traits for crime live in areas with higher crime rates.
    C. Communities no longer have the capability of regulating the conduct of residents.
    D. Youths model the behavior of older residents who are seen committing crimes.

8. As noted by Siegel and Welsh, while mapping the crime rates in _____, Shaw and McKay noted that distinct ecological areas had developed that could be visualized as a series of concentric zones, each with a stable delinquency rate.

    A. Chicago   C. Phoenix

    B. Los Angeles   D. Milwaukee

9. According to Merton, when is strain more likely to occur?

    A. when acceptable means for success are blocked

    B. when neighborhood disorganization reaches transitional stages

    C. when drug abuse rates increase

    D. when cultural norms come in conflict with subcultural values

10. What does the concept of relative deprivation concept imply?

    A. If one is born poor, one will remain poor.

    B. Criminality is relative to the subculture in which the deviant resides.

    C. A sense of social injustice occurs where the poor and rich live in close proximity.

    D. Juveniles will emulate relatives when deprived of standard models of conventional values.

11. _____ refers to neighborhoods or areas marked by culture conflict, lack of cohesiveness, and a transient population.

    A. Social control   C. Social disorganization

    B. Cultural transmission   D. Social learning

12. According to Agnew's General Strain Theory, adolescents engage in delinquency as a result of _____, the anger, frustration, fear, and other adverse emotions that derive from strain.

    A. negative affective states   C. psychopathological anomalies

    B. relative deprivation   D. cognitive dissonance

13. _____ is the process of passing on deviant traditions and delinquent values from one from one generation to the next.

    A. social disorganization   C. social control

    B. social learning   D. cultural transmission

14. Residents of cohesive communities develop a sense of _____: people know one another; develop interpersonal ties, mutual trust and a willingness to intervene in the supervision of children; and help maintain public order.

    A. collective efficacy   C. community vigilantism

    B. collective control   D. community conscientiousness

15. _____ refers to the ability of social institutions to influence human behavior.

    A. Social control   C. Social disorganization

    B. Cultural transmission   D. Social learning

16. _____ theory holds that delinquency is a result of youths' desire to conform to lower-class neighborhood cultural values that conflict with those of the greater society; lower-class values include being tough, never showing fear, living for today, and disrespecting authority.

      A. Cultural deviance   C. Choice

      B. Social disorganization   D. Differential association

17. Shaw and McKay are most closely associated with _____ theory.

      A. trait   C. strain

      B. choice   D. social disorganization

18. According to the labeling theory, what is an important consideration in the study of delinquency?

      A. the motivation of the delinquent act

      B. the age of the delinquent

      C. the economic status of the victim

      D. the societal response to the delinquent act

19. Which of the following would best fit the restorative justice ideal?

      A. boot camp

      B. curfews

      C. meetings between offenders and victims

      D. victim testimony at sentencing

20. From a labeling theory perspective, what would be the primary criticism of juvenile diversion and restitution programs?

      A. They are inefficiently operated programs.

      B. They often result in a monetary penalty for lower economic class clients.

      C. They widen the net of social control.

      D. They create recidivists by forcing poor delinquents to steal to make the restitution payments.

21. Which of the following descriptions best describes the theoretical orientation of conflict theory?

      A. They view delinquents as rebels who cannot conform to proper social norms.

      B. They try to devise innovative ways of controlling youthful misbehavior.

      C. They evaluate how the criminal law is used as a mechanism of social control by the elite.

      D. They explain crime as a function of individual choice.

22. A young person is repeatedly called a juvenile delinquent and then begins to act like a serious delinquent by hanging out with the tough crowd, dressing different, and even acting different. Labeling theorists would say this is an example of what?

      A. self-fulfilling prophecy   C. stigma transformation

      B. escalating deviance   D. delinquent branding

23. Which theory refers to attachment, commitment, involvement and belief?
    - A. techniques of neutralization
    - B. differential association
    - C. containment theory
    - D. social control theory

24. _____ refers to being labelled by agents of social control, like school officials and the police.
    - A. Stigmatized
    - B. Socially branded
    - C. Degraded
    - D. Capitulated

25. Which of the following statements is true of the Hirschi's social control theory?
    - A. Delinquents are a product of blocked means to conventional goals.
    - B. Delinquents are influenced by diet and potential toxins in the environment.
    - C. Delinquents are children who learned the attitudes and techniques of crime from deviant peers.
    - D. People are born selfish, or "bad", and are socialized by others to control themselves.

26. Which of Agnew's sources of strain is similar to what Merton spoke of in his theory of anomie?
    - A. strain caused by the failure to achieve positively valued goals
    - B. strain as the transference of negatively valued goals
    - C. strain as the removal of positively valued stimuli from the individual
    - D. strain as the presentation of negative stimuli

27. Which theory argues that crime and delinquency are the result of the frustration and anger that people experience when the means to achieve social and financial success are blocked to them?
    - A. social ecology
    - B. social disorganization
    - C. frustration-aggression amplification
    - D. strain

28. What causes normlessness according to Merton?
    - **A.** when personal goals cannot be achieved using available means.
    - B. divorce and family violence and the negative affective states they create
    - C. racial discrimination
    - D. all of the above

29. What is the major premise of social disorganization theory?
    - A. Crime is a function of individual decision making and choice.
    - B. Crime is a product of the individual traits of individuals living in urban areas.
    - C. Crime is a function of community level social forces operating in an urban environment.
    - D. Crime is a consequence of inadequate educational opportunities.

30. According to Shaw and McKay, what produced delinquency?
    A. delinquents chose criminal actions over noncriminal actions
    B. blocked conventional opportunities to achieve success
    C. transitional neighborhoods exhibiting culture conflict and ineffective
        community controls
    D. cultural isolation

TRUE/FALSE

1. Restorative justice attempts to address the issues that produced conflict between people, rather than treating one as a victim deserving sympathy and the other as a delinquent deserving punishment.
    A. True
    B. False

2. Learning theories assume that children are born good and learn to be bad.
    A. True
    B. False

3. Learning theories assume that children are born bad and learn to be good.
    A. True
    B. False

4. The author notes that political unrest and mistrust, economic stress, and family disintegration are social changes that have been found to precede sharp increases in crime rates, when traditional social institutions and values predominate, crime rate declines.
    A. True
    B. False

5. According to social disorganization theory, rates of delinquency are highest in the central city and decline as one moves outward from the center.
    A. True
    B. False

6. There is little empirical evidence to suggest that Hirschi's social control theory is valid.
    A. True
    B. False

7. Labeling theory is primarily concerned with identifying why an individual committed the initial act of delinquency.
    A. True
    B. False

8. Sociological theories of crime contend that explanations of delinquency as individual level phenomenon fail to account for the consistent social patterns in found in delinquency.
    A. True
    B. False

9. According to strain theory, if juveniles' social bonds are weakened, they are able to engage in antisocial but personally desirable behaviors.
    A. True
    B. False

10. Communities with low collective efficacy generally experience low violence rates and low levels of physical and social disorder; in contrast, neighborhoods with high collective efficacy suffer high rates of violence and significant disorder.
    A. True
    B. False

11. Communities with high collective efficacy generally experience low violence rates and low levels of physical and social disorder; in contrast, neighborhoods with low collective efficacy suffer high rates of violence and significant disorder.
    A. True
    B. False

12. According to social reaction theory, people enter into law-violating careers when they are labeled for their acts and organize their personalities around the labels.
    A. True
    B. False

13. According to conflict theory, obedience to the norms of their lower-class culture puts people in conflict with the norms of the dominant culture.
    A. True
    B. False

14. According to strain theory, people who adopt the goals of society but lack the means to attain them seek alternatives, such as crime.
    A. True
    B. False

15. The social structure view is that position in the socioeconomic structure influences the chances of becoming a delinquent.
    A. True
    B. False

16. Strain occurs when kids experience anger over their inability to achieve legitimate social and economic success.
    A. True
    B. False

17. Siegel and Welsh note that the best-known strain theory is Robert Merton's theory of anomie, which describes what happens when people have inadequate means to satisfy their goals.
	A. True
	B. False

18. Strain according to Agnew as the presentation of negative stimuli is illustrated with the loss of a girlfriend or boyfriend, the death of a loved one, moving to a new neighborhood, or the divorce or separation of parents
	A. True
	B. False

19. Hirschi contends that if the social bond is weakened, youths are free to deviate.
	A. True
	B. False

20. Hirschi contends that delinquents are "lone wolves," detached from family and friends, while some critics believe that delinquents do maintain close peer group ties.
	A. True
	B. False

21. According to labeling theory, most youths may violate the law at some point for a variety of reasons, including poor family relationships, peer pressure, psychological abnormality, and prodelinquent learning experiences.
	A. True
	B. False

22. According to differential association theory, all people have the potential to become delinquents, but their bonds to conventional society prevent them from violating the law.
	A. True
	B. False

23. In *The Child Savers,* Anthony Platt documented the creation of the delinquency concept and the role played by wealthy child savers in forming the philosophy of the juvenile court; he believed that the child-saving movement's real goal was to maintain order and control while preserving the existing class system.
	A. True
	B. False

24. Siegel and Welsh note that there is no documented evidence linking family poverty with children's health, achievement, and behavior.
	A. True
	B. False

25. Lewis contends that mistrust of authority prevents the impoverished inner city residents from taking advantage of the few conventional opportunities available to them; the result is a permanent underclass whose members have little chance of upward mobility.
    A. True
    B. False

FILL IN

1. _____ theory holds that delinquency is a result of youths' desire to conform to lower-class neighborhood cultural values that conflict with those of the greater society; lower-class values include being tough, never showing fear, living for today, and disrespecting authority.

2. _____ justice attempts to address the issues that produced conflict between people rather than treating one as a victim deserving sympathy and the other as a delinquent deserving punishment.

3. According to the concept of _____, most neighborhood residents share the common goal of living in a crime-free area.

4. Diversion and deinstitutionalization may actually bring more youths into the system who previously would have avoided any type of formal action because of the availability of the program; this is referred to as _____.

5. _____ is a pervasive, strain-producing sense of injustice which develops in communities in which the poor and wealthy live in close proximity to one another.

6. According to Sutherland's _____ theory, if the pro-delinquency definitions youths have learned outweigh the anti-delinquency definitions, they will be vulnerable to choosing criminal behaviors over conventional ones.

7. _____ theorists view delinquent behavior as a function of the capitalist system's inherent inequity; youths who are judged inferior as potential job prospects become known as losers and punks and wind up in delinquent roles.

8. _____ is the process by which a person who has been negatively labeled accepts the label as a personal role or identity.

9. According to labeling theory, deviant behavior that is a response to an earlier labeling experience is called a _____; youths act out these social roles even if they were falsely bestowed.

10. _____ theory is the view that intergroup conflict, born out of the unequal distribution of wealth and power, is the root cause of delinquency.

11. _____ is removing juveniles from adult jails and placing them in community-based programs to avoid the stigma attached to these facilities.

12. _____ is the process of transforming a lower-class area into a middle-class enclave through property rehabilitation.

13. _____ is a process in which mutual trust and a willingness to intervene in the supervision of children and help maintain public order creates a sense of well being in a neighborhood and helps control anti-social activities.

14. _____ is a condition caused by the failure to achieve one's social goals.

15. Shaw and McKay are most closely associated with _____ theory.

ESSAY

1. Discuss Shaw and McKay's social disorganization theory. What are some of the policies or programs to reduce delinquency based on this perspective?

2. Discuss Hirschi's social control theory. What are some of the policies or programs to reduce delinquency based on this perspective?

3. Discuss Agnew's general strain theory. What are some of the policies or programs to reduce delinquency based on this perspective?

4. Discuss labeling theory. What are some of the policies or programs to reduce delinquency based on this perspective?

5. Discuss conflict theory. What are some of the policies or programs to reduce delinquency based on this perspective?

ANSWER KEY

MULTIPLE CHOICE

1. A	11. C	21. C
2. B	12. A	22. A
3. A	13. D	23. D
4. A	14. A	24. A
5. D	15. A	25. D
6. D	16. A	26. A
7. C	17. D	27. D
8. A	18. D	28. A
9. A	19. C	29. C
10. C	20. C	30. C

TRUE FALSE

1. T	11. T	21. T
2. T	12. T	22. F
3. F	13. F	23. T
4. T	14. T	24. F
5. T	15. T	25. T
6. F	16. T	
7. F	17. T	
8. T	18. F	
9. T	19. F	
10. F	20. T	

FILL IN

1. cultural deviance
2. restorative
3. collective efficacy
4. widening the net
5. relative deprivation
6. differential association
7. conflict
8. self-labeling
9. self-fulfilling prophecy
10. social conflict
11. deinstitutionalization
12. gentrified
13. collective efficacy
14. strain
15. social disorganization

1. Social disorganization theory discusses in reference to delinquency
    A. ecological relationships between socio-economic disorder and crime and delinquency
    B. lack of the family bond
    C. lack of religion
    D. alienation of the working class from the social structure and government.

2. Relative deprivation
    A. is based upon the average income of the society
    B. would exist in a socialist society as well as a capitalist society due to non-economic social stratification
    C. is unrelated to crime.
    D. relates to perceptions that poor people may adopt when they live close to affluent people.

3. The lack of access to legitimate means to universally accepted material goods is central to which theory
    A. Merton's Anomie/Strain theory
    B. Hirschi's social control theory
    C. Akers' social learning theory
    D Sutherland's differential association theory

4. Agnew
    A. considers Merton's anomie theory erroneous because there was a great deal of strain in the Soviet Union despite economic equality.
    B. removed economic factors from Merton's theory
    C. considers sociological strain without economic factors since the sociological perspective considers social institutions such as the family, school, and religion to be primary determinants of behaviour not economic structures.
    D. adds a variety of strains in addition to strain that occurs from disjuncture between the aspirations and expectations of individuals based upon their relationship with the opportunity structures.

5. According to the *Code of the Streets*
    A. a violent subculture has replaced pro-social culture in many inner-city communities
    B. a violent subculture competes with a pro-social culture in many inner-city communities.
    C. a violent inner city subculture is primarily interested in increasing profits from drug sales.
    D. a violent inner city subculture based on materialistic values prevents youth from doing well in school.

6. According to social process theory, although social position is important, what is a key determinant of behaviour?
    A. socialization
    B. school curricula
    C. parental income
    D. housing arrangements

7. Parental efficacy
    A. means consistent and stern punishment for delinquents
    B. relates to parents having the money to pay for good schools for their children
    C. relates to parents who can be supportive and effectively control their children in a non-coercive fashion.
    D. is directly related to income levels.

8. Unsupervised summer employment in which youth work together unsupervised
    A. reduces crime
    B. has no effect on crime
    C. is a perfect environment for positive peer culture
    D. may increase crime

9. Labelling theory considers
    A. the examination of whatever pushed or pulled a youth to a commit a delinquent act as the primary concern of the justice system
    B. harsher punishments would deter crime
    C. heavy handed approaches as counter productive
    D. boot camps as good investment of public money

10. According to Hirschi,
    A. delinquent peers are responsible for steering good boys to commit crime
    B. lack of attachment, commitment, involvement, and belief would almost inevitably lead to deviance
    C. jobs programs would prevent delinquency by providing legitimate means to obtain socially recognized goals.
    D youth should not be sent to juvenile court so they are not labelled.

True False:

1. The Balanced Approach stresses punishment in sentencing, with community service, restitution, and incapacitation as secondary. T F

2. Theories that attribute delinquency to individual traits, personality, or choice have been criticized for not being able to explain why such individual characteristics are often concentrated in certain geographic areas of a city or country. T F

3. Racial disparity refers to statistical differences in how people of color are found in the criminal justice system T F

4. According to the text, community fear is characterized by deficits in many quality of life aspects of the environment   T F

5 Critical theories are primarily interested in reforming our criminal justice system so that it can function more efficiently T F

Multiple Choice
1. D
2. D
3. A
4 D
5. B
6. A
7. C
8. D
9. C
10. B

True False
1. F
2. T
3. T
4. T
5 F

CHAPTER FIVE
DEVELOPMENTAL THEORIES

LEARNING OBJECTIVES

- Be familiar with the concept of developmental theory.
- Know the factors that influence the life course.
- Recognize that there are different pathways to delinquency.
- Be able to discuss the social development model.
- Describe what is meant by interactional theory.
- Be familiar with the turning points in delinquency.
- Be able to discuss the influence of social capital on delinquency.
- Know what is meant by a latent trait.
- Be able to discuss Gottfredson and Hirschi's general theory of crime.
- Be familiar with the concepts of impulsivity and self-control.

CHAPTER OUTLINE

I.   Introduction
    A.   1. Kia moves comes to US from Vietnam at age 11.
       2. He has problems at school and is referred to Family Court Crisis Intervention.
       3. During counseling meant to prevent him from being seriously delinquent his parents reveal to him the reasons why they had left for the US years earlier when he was in the care of his grandmother.
       4. In an emotional session, Kia understood that he was not abandoned, that his parents had worked to bring him as soon as possible, and his school problems disappeared.
    B.   Developmental theory
       1.   view that looks at the specific aspects of the delinquent career
          a.   onset
          b.   continuity
          c.   termination of delinquency
    C.   Life course theory
       1.   people have multiple traits: social, psychological, economic
       2.   people change over the life course
       3.   family, job, and peers influence behavior
    D.   Latent trait theory
       1.   people have a master trait: personality, intelligence, genetic makeup
       2.   people do not change
       3.   criminal opportunities change; maturity brings fewer opportunities

4. early social control and proper parenting can reduce criminal propensity
5. criminal careers are a passage
6. personal and structural factors influence crime
7. change affects crime
8. unchanging personal factors are more important determinants of behavior

II. The Life Course View
   A. Perspective
      1. conform to social rules and function effectively in society
      2. transitions expected to take place in an orderly fashion
         a. beginning with finishing school
         b. entering the workforce
         c. getting married
         d. having children
      3. some kids are incapable of maturing in a reasonable and timely fashion
      4. in some cases transitions can occur too early
      5. sometimes disruption of one trajectory can harm another
      6. negative life experiences can become cumulative
      7. disruptions in life's major transitions can be destructive
      8. disruptions in life's major transitions can be ultimately promote criminality
      9. it is a developmental process
      10. delinquent careers are interactional
      11. as people mature the factors that influence their behavior change
   B. Glueck research
      1. renewed interest in the research efforts of Sheldon and Eleanor Glueck
      2. they followed the careers of known delinquents
      3. made extensive use of interviews and records
      4. comparisons of delinquents and nondelinquents
      5. focused on early onset of delinquency as a harbinger of a delinquent career
      6. identified a number of personal and social factors related to persistent offending
      7. most important of these factors was family relations
      8. quality of discipline and emotional ties with parents
      9. did not restrict their analysis to social variables

III. Life Course Concepts
   A. Age of onset
      1. seeds of a delinquent career are planted early in life
      2. early onset strongly predicts more frequent, varied, and sustained criminality

3. early starters begin offending before age 14
   a. poor parenting to
   b. deviant behaviors to
   c. involvement with delinquent groups
4. late starters, who begin offending after age fourteen
   a. poor parenting leads to
   b. identification with delinquent groups
   c. deviant behaviors

B. Adolescent-limiteds versus life course persisters
   1. concepts identified by Moffitt
   2. adolescent-limited offenders get involved with antisocial activities early in life
      a. begin to phase out of delinquent behaviors as they mature
      b. considered typical teenagers
   3. life course persisters remain high-rate offenders into young adulthood

C. Problem behavior syndrome
   1. delinquency is but one of many social problems faced by at-risk youth
   2. behaviors include:
      a. family dysfunction
      b. substance abuse
      c. smoking
      d. precocious sexuality and early pregnancy
      e. educational underachievement
      f. suicide attempts
      g. sensation seeking
      h. unemployment

D. Multiple pathways
   1. delinquents may travel more than a single road in their delinquent career
   2. Loeber and his associates have identified three distinct paths to a delinquent
   3. authority conflict pathway begins at an early age with stubborn behavior
   4. covert pathway begins with minor, underhanded behavior
      a. leads to property damage
   5. overt pathway escalates to aggressive acts beginning with aggression

E. Continuity of crime and delinquency
   1. best predictor of future criminality is past criminality
   2. early delinquent activity is likely to be sustained
   3. offenders seem to lack the social survival skills
      a. necessary to find work or to develop the interpersonal relations

IV.   Life Course Theories
    A.   Social development model
        1.   focus on factors affecting child's social development over the life course
        2.   all children face the risk of delinquent behavior
            a.   especially those forced to live in the poorest neighborhoods
            b.   and attend substandard schools
        3.   child must develop and maintain prosocial bonds
            a.   developed in the context of family life
            b.   parents routinely praise children
            c.   give them consistent, positive feedback
        4.   parental attachment affects a child's behavior for life
        5.   children who cannot form prosocial bonds in their family are at risk
        6.   adolescents who perceive opportunities and rewards for antisocial behavior
            a.   will form deep attachments to deviant peers
            b.   become committed to a delinquent way of life
        7.   commitment and attachment to conventional institutions, activities, and beliefs
            a.   insulate youths from the delinquency-producing influences
    B.   Interactional theory
        1.   onset of delinquent behavior can be traced to a deterioration of the social bond
            a.   marked by weakened attachment to parents
            b.   weakened commitment to school
            c.   weakened belief in conventional values
        2.   delinquency is a dynamic developmental process that takes on different meanings and forms as a person matures
        3.   delinquency is bidirectional
        4.   delinquency-promoting factors tend to reinforce one another
        5.   early and persistent involvement in antisocial behavior generates consequences that are hard to shake
        6.   delinquency does not terminate in a single generation
    C.   Age-graded theory
        1.   Sampson and Laub identified turning points in a delinquent career
        2.   reanalyzed the original Glueck data
        3.   stability of delinquent behavior can be affected by events that occur later in life
        4.   two critical turning points are career and marriage
        5.   at risk adolescents can live conventional lives if they can find good jobs or achieve successful careers
        6.   adolescents are able to desist from delinquency if, as adults,
            a.   they become attached to a spouse who supports and sustains them
        7.   spending time in marital and family activities reduces exposure to deviant peers

103

8. people build social capital

9. positive relations with individuals and institutions that are life sustaining

10. a successful marriage creates social capital when it improves a person's stature creates feelings of self-worth, and encourages others to trust the person

D. Testing age-graded theory

1. children raised in two-parent families are more likely to grow up to have happier marriages than children whose parents were divorced or never married

2. delinquent youth who enter the military, serve overseas, and receive veterans' benefits enhance their occupational status

E Tracking down five hundred delinquent boys in the new millennium

1. Sampson and Laub have located the survivors of the delinquent sample

2. oldest being 70 and the youngest 62

3. they are reinterviewing this cohort

4. delinquency is strongly related to adult delinquency and drug and alcohol abuse

5. most antisocial children do not remain antisocial as adults

6. of men in the study cohort who survived to age fifty
   a. 24% had no arrests for acts of violence and property after age 17
   b. 48% had no arrests for predatory delinquency after age 25
   c. 60% had no arrests for predatory delinquency after age 31
   d. 79% had no arrests for predatory delinquency after age 40

7. they conclude that desistance from delinquency is the norm

8. building social capital through marriage and jobs were key components

9. one important element for "going straight" is the "knifing off" of individuals

10. former delinquents who "went straight" were able to put structure into their lives

11. former delinquents faced the risk of an untimely death

12. four significant life-changing events
    a. marriage
    b. joining the military
    c. getting a job
    d. changing one's environment or neighborhood

F. Policy Implications

1. Youth problems such as delinquency, substance abuse, violence, dropping out, and teenage pregnancy often share common root.

2. Intervention strategies must address a broad array of antisocial, criminal, and deviant behaviors not limited to one subgroup of delinquents

3.   Prevention strategies would provide both supervision and monitoring as well as new opportunities of social support and growth; and new situations that provide the opportunity for transforming identity.

V.   The Latent Trait View
     A.   Crime and Human Nature
          1.   Wilson and Herrnstein contend that personal traits influence people
               a.   choose delinquency over noncrime
          2.   people have a personal attribute that controls their propensity to commit crime
          3.   latent trait is either present at birth or established early in life
               a.   remains stable over time
               b.   defective intelligence
               c.   impulsive personality
               d.   genetic abnormalities
          4.   the propensity or inclination to commit delinquency is stable
          5.   the opportunity to commit delinquency fluctuates over time
          6.   adult responsibilities provide them with fewer opportunities to do so

     B.   General theory of crime
          1.   Gottfredson and Hirschi's general theory of crime (GTC)
          2.   modifies and redefines some of the principles from social control
                a.   integrates concepts of control with other theories
          3.   the act and the offender – consider the delinquent offender and the delinquent act as separate concepts
          4.   people engage in delinquent acts when they perceive them to be advantageous
          5.   delinquency provides easy, short-term gratification
          6.   delinquency is rational and predictable
          7.   delinquent offenders are predisposed to commit crimes
          8.   stable differences in people's propensity to commit delinquent acts
          9.   may be inherited or may develop through incompetent or absent parenting
    C. What makes people delinquency-prone?
          1.   Gottfredson and Hirschi attribute delinquency to a person's level of self-control
          2.   low self-control develops early in life and remains stable into and through adulthood
          3.   elements of impulsivity
                i.   insensitive
               ii.   physical (rather than mental)
               iii.   risk taker
               iv.   shortsighted
               v.   non-verbal
               vi.   here-and-now orientation

              vii.   refuses to work for distant goals
             viii.   lacks diligence
             ix.   lacks tenacity
             x.   lacks persistence
             xi.   adventuresome
             xii.   active
             xiii.   self-centered
             xiv.   have unstable marriages
             xv.   have unstable jobs
             xvi.   have unstable friendships
             xvii.   less likely to feel shame if engaging in deviant acts
             xviii. finds deviant behaviors pleasureable
             ixx.   more likely to engage in dangerous behaviors

        4.   Gottfredson and Hirschi trace the root cause of poor self-control to inadequate child-rearing practices
            a.   parents who are unwilling or unable to monitor a child's behavior
            b.   fail to recognize deviant behavior when it occurs
            c.   fails to punish that behavior

D.   Self-control and delinquency
     1.   theory can explain all varieties of delinquent behavior and all the social and behavioral correlates of delinquency

E.   Supporting evidence for the GTC
     1.   dozens of research efforts have tested the validity of Gottfredson and Hirschi's views

F.   Analyzing the GTC
     1.   integrating concepts of socialization and criminality helps Gottfredson and Hirschi explain why some who lack self-control can escape criminality and vice versa

G.   Empirical evidence supporting the general theory of crime
     1.   offenders lacking in self-control commit a garden variety of delinquent acts
     2.   drunk drivers are impulsive individuals with low self-control
     3.   kids who take drugs and commit delinquency enjoy engaging in risky behaviors
     4.   gender differences in self-control explain delinquency rate differences
     5.   victims have lower self-control than nonvictims

H.   Questions and criticisms
     1.   circular reasoning
     2.   personality disorder
     3.   ecological-individual differences
     4.   racial and gender differences
     5.   people change
     6.   modest relationship
     7.   cross-cultural differences

VI.   Evaluating the Developmental View
      A.   Developmental view
          1.   understood as a passage along which people travel
          2.   events and life circumstances influence the journey
          3.   emphasize the influence of changing interpersonal and structural factors
      B.   Latent trait theories
          1.   assume that an individual's behavior is linked changes in the surrounding world
          2.   evidence supporting both latent trait and life course theories
          3.   maintaining positive social bonds helps reduce
     C. Developmental Theory and Delinquency Prevention
       1. reduce risk factors in children's school, family, and personal environment.
       1. multisystemic treatment
       2 targeting youth as early as preschool through elementary school
       3. strengthening social-emotional competencies and positive coping skills while at the same time suppressing antisocial aggressive behavior.
       4. improving youth's developing skills to succeed in school, after school, and with the help of the parents, at home.

CHAPTER SUMMARY

Life course theories argue that events that take place over the life course influence delinquent choices. The cause of delinquency constantly changes as people mature. At first, the nuclear family influences behavior; during adolescence, the peer group dominates; in adulthood, marriage and career are critical. There are a variety of pathways to delinquency: some kids are sneaky, others hostile, and still others defiant. According to the concept of problem behavior syndrome, delinquency may be just one of a variety of social problems, including health, physical, and interpersonal troubles.

The social development model theory finds that living in a disorganized neighborhood helps weaken social bonds and sets people off on a delinquent path. According to interactional theory, delinquency influences social relations, which in turn influence delinquency; the relationship is interactive. The sources of delinquency evolve over time. Sampson and Laub's age-graded theory holds that the social sources of behavior change over the life course. People who develop social capital are best able to avoid antisocial entanglements. Important life events, or turning points, enable adult offenders to desist from delinquency. Among the most important are getting married and serving in the military.

Latent trait theories hold that some underlying condition present from birth or soon after controls behavior. Suspect traits include low IQ, impulsivity, and personality structure. This underlying trait explains the continuity of offending because, once present, it remains with a person throughout the lifetime. The General Theory of Crime, developed by Gottfredson and Hirschi, integrates rational choice theory concepts. Gottfredson and Hirschi trace the root cause of poor self-control to inadequate child-rearing practices. Parents who are unwilling or unable to monitor a child's behavior, to recognize deviant behavior when it occurs, and to punish that behavior, will produce children who lack self-control. Children who are not attached to their parents, who are poorly supervised, and whose parents are delinquent, are the most likely to develop poor self-control and to become delinquent or deviant themselves. In a sense, lack of self-control occurs naturally when steps are not taken to stop its development. Whereas the propensity for delinquency is stable throughout life, the opportunity for delinquency, that is, the presence of suitable targets and capable guardians, mediates choice.

KEY TERMS

adolescent-limited: Offender who follows the most common delinquent trajectory, in which antisocial behavior peaks in adolescence and then diminishes.

authority conflict pathway: Pathway to delinquent deviance that begins at an early age with stubborn behavior and leads to defiance and then to authority avoidance.

covert pathway: Pathway to a delinquent career that begins with minor underhanded behavior, leads to property damage, and eventually escalates to more serious forms of theft and fraud.

overt pathway: Pathway to a delinquent career that begins with minor aggression, leads to physical fighting, and eventually escalates to violent delinquency.

developmental theory: The view that criminality is a dynamic process, influenced by social experiences as well as individual characteristics.

early onset: Most early onset delinquents begin their careers with disruptive behavior, truancy, cruelty to animals, lying, and theft. Early onset strongly predicts more frequent, varied, and sustained criminality later in life.

general theory of crime (GTC): A developmental theory that modifies social control theory by integrating concepts from biosocial, psychological, routine activities, and rational choice theories.

impulsive: Lacking in thought or deliberation in decision making. An impulsive person lacks close attention to details, has organizational problems, is distracted and forgetful.

interactional theory: A developmental theory that attributes delinquent trajectories to mutual reinforcement between delinquents and significant others over the life course—family in early adolescence, school and friends in midadolescence, and social peers and one's own nuclear family in adulthood.

life course theory: A developmental theory that focuses on changes in behavior as people travel along the path of life and how these changes affect crime and delinquency.

latent trait: A stable feature, characteristic, property, or condition, such as defective intelligence or impulsive personality, that makes some people delinquency-prone over the life course.

latent trait theory: The view that delinquent behavior is controlled by a "master trait," present at birth or soon after, that remains stable and unchanging throughout a person's lifetime.

life course persister: One of the small group of offenders whose delinquent career continues well into adulthood.

problem behavior syndrome (PBS): A cluster of antisocial behaviors that may include family dysfunction, substance abuse, smoking, precocious sexuality and early pregnancy, educational underachievement, suicide attempts, sensation seeking, and unemployment, as well as delinquency.

pro-social bonds: Socialized attachment to conventional institutions, activities, and beliefs.

pseudomaturity: Characteristic of life course persisters, who tend to engage is early sexuality and drug use.

self-control: Refers to a person's ability to exercise restraint and control over his or her feelings, emotions, reactions, and behaviors.

social capital: Positive relations with individuals and institutions, as in a successful marriage or a successful career, that support conventional behavior and inhibit deviant behavior.

social development model (SDM): A developmental theory that attributes delinquent behavior patterns to childhood socialization and pro- or antisocial attachments over the life course.

turning points: Critical life events, such as career and marriage, that may enable adult offenders to desist from delinquency.

SELF TEST QUESTIONS

MULTIPLE CHOICE

1. Which of the following best describes developmental theory?
    A. A delinquent career is a dynamic process, influenced by internal and external factors, with pauses, escalations, and changes of direction along the way.
    B. Human development is controlled by a stable and unchanging personality trait.
    C. Behavior is influenced by goals, aspirations, and bonds to conventional society.
    D. Juveniles choose to commit delinquent acts because benefits outweigh costs.

2. According to _____, delinquent behavior is a dynamic process influenced by individual characteristics as well as social experiences, and the factors that cause antisocial behaviors change dramatically over a person's life span.
    A. developmental theory   C. latent trait theory
    B. life course theory   D. social disorganization

3. According to _____, human development is controlled by a master trait that remains stable and unchanging throughout a person's lifetime; these theorists believe that people don't change, opportunities do.
    A. developmental theory   C. latent trait theory
    B. life course theory   D. social disorganization

4. Current developmental research was inspired by the early efforts of Sheldon and Eleanor _____; they followed the careers of known delinquents to determine the factors that predicted persistent offending.
    A. Glueck   C. Rigby
    B. Jones   D. Smith

5. Based on a _____ view, disruptions in life's major transitions can be destructive and ultimately may promote criminality; a positive life experience may help some delinquents desist from crime for a while, whereas a negative one may cause them to resume their activities.
    A. latent trait   C. subcultural
    B. developmental   D. social disorganization

6. Referred to as _____, developmental theorists realize that crime occurs when a group of antisocial behaviors cluster together and typically involve family dysfunction, substance abuse, smoking, precocious sexuality, educational underachievement, suicide, and unemployment.
    A. intractable requisite   C. problem behavior syndrome
    B. stubborn child condition   D. infantile malady

110

7. Which of the following would a person with low self-control be likely to do?
   - A. study for exams
   - B. exercise regularly
   - C. read books instead of watching tv
   - D. sit in a bar, smoke cigarettes, and gamble

8. Which of the following would a person with high self-control be likely to do?
   - A. smoke cigarettes
   - B. use drugs
   - C. gamble
   - D. be a designated driver

9. Siegel and Welsh note that the best predictor of future criminality is _____.
   - A. grades in high school
   - B. body type and personality
   - D. parenting style
   - D. past criminality

10. Which of the following pathways identified by Leober et. al's research describes a situation where a school bully grows up to rob old ladies and intimidate neighbors?
   - A. authority-conflict pathway
   - B. covert pathway
   - C. overt pathway
   - D. sadistical pathway

11 Which of the following pathways identified by Leober's research describes a situation where a delinquent career begins with lying and shoplifting, leading to property damage and eventually escalating to more serious forms of delinquency, such as larceny and the use of stolen credit cards?
   - A. authority-conflict pathway
   - B. covert pathway
   - C. overt pathway
   - D. menacing pathway

12. Which of the following pathways identified by Leober's research describes a situation where a delinquent career begins with defiance of parents, which leads to truancy, running away, and staying out late?
   - A. authority-conflict pathway
   - B. covert pathway
   - C. overt pathway
   - D. transforming pathway

13. Which of the following statements is best associated with the earlier onset of criminality?
   - A. the sooner they stop committing delinquent acts
   - B. the worse their grades will be
   - C. the more frequent, varied, and sustained the criminal career
   - D. the more likely they are to go on to college

14. According to Moffitt, _____ combine family dysfunction with severe neurological problems that predispose them to antisocial behavior patterns; they may have low verbal ability, which inhibits reasoning skills, learning ability, and school achievement.
   - A. adolescent-limiteds
   - B. life-course persisters
   - C. pseudomature people
   - D. teenage marauders

15. _____ delinquents reduce the frequency of their offending as they mature to around age eighteen; these kids may be considered typical teenagers who get into minor trouble.
    A. Adolescent-limited
    B. Life-course persister
    C. Pseudomature
    D. Teenage marauder

16. Developmental criminology
    A. is inconsistent with developmental psychology
    B. was developed in the Chicago School
    C. is part and parcel of the social disorganization school of criminology
    D. features theories viewed through the prism of life trajectory

17. Moffitt notes that life-course persisters seem to mature faster and engage in early sexuality and drug use, referred to as _____.
    A. semi-adolescence
    B. pseudomaturity
    C. pseudo-ritualism
    D. anti-establishment

18. Drawing from Sampson and Laub's follow up, what was one technique used by former delinquents for going straight?
    A. looking to make a big score to give them money to leave crime
    B. knifing off of individuals from their immediate environment
    C. getting a girlfriend who supported their criminal habits and lifestyle
    D. maintaining strong bonds with delinquent friends as they grow old together

19. Siegel and Welsh note that people build _____; that is, positive relations with individuals and institutions that are life-sustaining.
    A. social capital
    B. financial capital
    C. restricting nets
    D. moral calculations

20. Implications from Gottfredson and Hirschi's General Theory of Crime would be to
    A. examine twin studies to understand delinquency better
    B. divert most youth from the juvenile court system
    C. avoid labeling by tracking in the schools
    D. encourage parenting classes and fund quality day care.

21. According to Loeber et. al, the authority conflict pathway
    A. begins in early adulthood
    B. is exacerbated by drug abuse
    C. begins at an early age with stubborn behavior
    D. first becomes evident when neurotransmitters double and triple in adolescence

22. Which of the following is considered most critical in delinquency prevention according to the social development model?
    A. reducing the rewards of crime
    B. children must develop pro-social bonds with the family and school
    C. the genetic trait causing crime must be located and treated with medication
    D. delinquency is but one of a cluster of related social problems

23. Which developmental criminology theory discussed in this chapter could make one reconsider the implications of Wolfgang's and Moffit's research (discussed in chapters two and three) that found that chronic recidivists or life course persisters rarely age out of crime?
    A. Age-Graded Theory
    B. General Theory of Crime
    C. Interactional Theory
    D. Latent-trait theory

24. The authors present studies around the world which found that delinquent kids score higher on scales measuring impulsivity than non-delinquent youth as supporting which theory. This is called:
    A. Age-Graded Theory
    B. General Theory of Crime
    C. Interactional Theory
    D. Latent-trait theory

25. Which of the following statements best describes the relationship between delinquent bonds and delinquency according to interactional theory?
    A. Delinquency causes strong bonds to delinquent friends.
    B. Delinquency causes weak bonds to delinquent friends.
    C. Delinquency and bonds to delinquents are bi-directional.
    D. Interactional theory does not talk about delinquency and attachment to
        delinquent peers.

26. Which of the following was identified by Sampson and Laub as the two critical turning points in life?
    A. graduation and marriage
    B. marriage and divorce
    C. birth and death
    D. marriage and a career

27. In Sampson and Laub's _____, they identify the life events that enable young offenders to desist from crime as they mature.
    A. interactional theory
    B. age-graded theory
    C. social control theory
    D. transitional theory

28. According to Sampson and Laub, which of the following is a social process variable?
    A. residential mobility
    B. difficult temperament
    C. family disruption
    D. parental supervision

29. Which theory states that casual influences are bi-directional such that weak bonds lead kids to develop friendships with deviant peers, which leads to delinquency (and frequent delinquency further weakens social bonds)?
    A. master trait
    B. General Theory of Crime
    C. Interactional Theory
    D. Social Development Model

30. According to Gottfredson and Hirschi, individuals who are impulsive, insensitive, physical, risk takers, short sighted, and nonverbal are said to have _____.
    A. low self control
    B. sociopathic personality
    C. hedonistic psychopathy
    D. an unusual medulla oblongata

TRUE/FALSE

1. The social development model holds that commitment and attachment to conventional institutions, activities, and beliefs insulate youths from the criminogenic influences of their environment; the pro-social path inhibits delinquency by strengthening bonds to pro-social others and activities.
    A. True
    B. False

2. Age-graded theory relies heavily on biological determinism
    A. True
    B. False

3. General Theory of Crime with the breakdown of the nuclear family considers school attachment of greater concern than familial attachments.
    A. True
    B. False

4. Delayed or late transitions in the life course only insulate a youth from delinquency and cannot lead to delinquent acts.
    A. True
    B. False

5. Siegel and Welsh note that delinquents who start their delinquent careers early are the ones most likely to stop offending before age eighteen.
    A. True
    B. False

6. The general theory of crime holds that crime is learned in adolescence and unlearned in adulthood.
    A. True
    B. False

7. Juvenile delinquents are fairly homogenous in terms of age of onset, frequency, duration, and type of offending.
    A. True
    B. False

8. Moffitt contends that life course persisters may have lower verbal ability, inhibited reasoning skills, lower learning ability, and poor school achievement; they seem to mature faster and engage in early sexuality and drug use, referred to as pseudomaturity.
    A. True
    B. False

9. Research indicates that children who are more likely to go on to become adult offenders begin their delinquent careers at a very early age, and that the earlier the onset of criminality, the more frequent, varied, and sustained the criminal career.
    A. True
    B. False

10. Loeber et. al contend that youths can enter two or three delinquent pathways simultaneously.
    A. True
    B. False

11. Siegel and Welsh contend that late starters to delinquency, who begin offending after age fourteen, may follow a path beginning with poor parenting which leads to identification with delinquent groups, and then to delinquent behaviors.
    A. True
    B. False

12. Siegel and Welsh note that early starters, who begin offending before age fourteen, follow a path that travels from poor parenting to deviant behaviors to involvement with delinquent groups.
    A. True
    B. False

13. According to Loeber et. al's research, youths can enter a delinquent career only through one specific pathway.
    A. True
    B. False

14. Siegel and Welsh note that youths who drink in the late elementary school years, who are aggressive, and who have attention problems are more likely to be offenders during adolescence.
    A. True
    B. False

15. Youths who are less attached to their parents and school and have antisocial friends are more likely to be offenders.
    A. True
    B. False

16. Loeber notes that not all youth travel down a single path; those who travel more than one path are the most likely to become persistent offenders as they mature.
    A. True
    B. False

17. Delinquency may be contagious: kids at risk for delinquency may be located in families and neighborhoods in which they are constantly exposed to deviant behavior, or they may have brothers, fathers, neighbors, and friends who engage in and support their activities and thus reinforce their deviance
    A. True
    B. False

18. Latent trait theories hold that some underlying condition present from birth or soon after controls behavior; suspect traits include low IQ, impulsivity, and personality structure.
    A. True
    B. False

19. Interactional theory assumes a physical or psychological trait makes some people delinquency-prone.
    A. True
    B. False

20. The social development model assumes that the opportunity to commit delinquency varies; an individual has a latent criminal trait that remains stable.
    A. True
    B. False

21. Research that finds that low self-control is significantly related to antisocial behavior and that the association can be seen regardless of culture or national settings supports general theory of crime.
    A. True
    B. False

22. Siegel and Welsh note that the general theory of crime sufficiently addresses ecological variations in crime.
    A. True
    B. False

23. Latent trait theories assume a physical or psychological trait makes some people delinquency-prone.
    A. True
    B. False

24. There is a great deal of cross cultural research evidence to suggest that low self-control is a universal characteristic of offenders.
    A. True
    B. False

25. Some research results support the proposition that self-control is a causal factor in delinquent and other forms of deviant behavior, but that the association is quite modest; low self-control alone cannot predict the onset of a delinquent or deviant career.
    A. True
    B. False

FILL IN

1. The key latent trait in Gottfredson and Hirschi's general theory of crime is

_____.

2. The authors note that people build _____; that is, positive relations with individuals and institutions that are life-sustaining.

3. According to general theory of crime, people who commit white-collar crimes and workplace delinquency have lower levels of _____ than nonoffenders.

4. Rather than focusing on human change and development, _____ view regards the opportunities people have to commit crime at various stages of their life as critical; they believe that people don't change, opportunities do.

5. According to Moffitt, _____ combine family dysfunction with severe neurological problems that predispose them to antisocial behavior patterns; they may have low verbal ability, which inhibits reasoning skills, learning ability, and school achievement.

6. Moffitt contends that life course persisters may have lower verbal ability, which inhibits reasoning skills, learning ability, and school achievement; they seem to mature faster and engage in early sexuality and drug use, referred to as _____.

7. _____ delinquents reduce the frequency of their offending as they mature to around age eighteen; these kids may be considered typical teenagers who get into minor trouble.

8. According to Sampson and Laub, the best way to transition out of delinquency is through four significant life-changing events: marriage, _____, getting a job, and changing one's environment or neighborhood.

9. According to _____, predispositions to aggress on others are activated by environmental and situational variables.

10. According to Gottfredson and Hirschi, people with limited self-control tend to be _____; they are insensitive to other people's feelings, physical (rather than mental), risk-takers, short-sighted, and nonverbal.

117

11. According to _____, the adolescent raised in a large, single-parent family of limited economic means and educational achievement was the most vulnerable to delinquency.

12. The _____ pathway begins with minor, underhanded behavior (lying, shoplifting) that leads to property damage; this behavior eventually escalates to more serious forms of criminality.

13. In Sampson and Laub's _____ theory, they identify the life events that enable young offenders to desist from crime as they mature.

14. Laub and Sampson's most important contribution is identifying the life events that enable young offenders to desist from crime as they mature; two critical turning points are _____ and career.

15. Referred to as _____ syndrome, developmental theorists realize that crime occurs among a group of antisocial behaviors that cluster together and typically involve family dysfunction, substance abuse, smoking, precocious sexuality, early pregnancy, educational underachievement, and unemployment.

ESSAY

1. Discuss Gottfredson and Hirschi's general theory of crime. What are the policy implications of this theory?

2. Discuss Sampson and Laub's age-graded theory of crime.

3. Identify and define the three pathways for delinquency developed by Loeber et al.

4. Discuss the differences between developmental theories and latent trait theories.

5. Identify and discuss the significance of the Gluecks' research.

ANSWER KEY

MULTIPLE CHOICE

1. A	11. B	21. C
2. B	12. A	22. B
3. C	13. C	23. A
4. A	14. B	24. B
5. B	15. A	25. C
6. C	16. D	26. D
7. D	17. B	27. B
8. D	18. B	28. D
9. D	19. A	29. C
10. C	20. D	30. A

TRUE FALSE

1. T	11. T	21. T
2. F	12. T	22. F
3. F	13. F	23. T
4. F	14. T	24. T
5. F	15. T	25. T
6. F	16. T	
7. T	17. T	
8. T	18. T	
9. T	19. F	
10. T	20. F	

FILL IN

1. self control
2. social capital
3. self-control
4. latent trait
5. life course persisters
6. pseudomaturity
7. adolescent-limiteds
8. joining the military
9. latent trait theory
10. impulsive
11. Sheldon and Eleanor Glueck
12. covert
13. age graded
14. marriage
15. problem behavior

Multiple Choice:

1. Gottfredson and Hirschi mention which of the following variables as significant factors leading to low self-control and delinquency
   A. inconsistent parenting, lack of supervision, monitoring and punishment
   B. low IQ, mesomorph body shape, and extra Y chromosome
   C. drug dependent parents, homelessness, and child abuse
   D. poverty, racial discrimination, and unresponsive schools.

2. The life course view
   A. considers biological determinants of crime as robust variables
   B. believes that Freud was right concerning the first two years of life and personality development
   C. assumes that delinquency, school, and crime problems often follow similar life trajectories
   D. was first proposed by Travis Hirschi in *Causes of Delinquency* in 1969.

3. Developmental views of delinquency
   A. consider labeling by social institutions as determinant of delinquency trajectories as youths struggle with stigma
   B. consider economic factors as determining which adaptation to strain youth adopt.
   C. do not distinguish between the life paths of girls and boys.
   D. recognize that the social environment and significant others can have great influence on a person's life trajectory.

4. According to Terry Moffitt's research, early onset is usually associated with
   A. adolescent limiteds
   B. life-course persisters
   C. psychopaths
   D. sex offenders

5. Youth suffering from problem behavior syndrome
   A. must be treated differently from most offenders
   B. are usually drug addicts
   C. are good candidates for psychotherapy
   D. need multidimensional treatment approaches

6. Sampson and Laub following up on Glueck and Glueck's research found that
   A. Only adolescent limiteds knife out of crime
   B. Life course persisters as well as adolescent limiteds can knife out of crime
   C. Chronic recidivists, those arrested more than five times, almost never knife out of crime
   D. Biological defects usually prevent knifing out of crime.

7. Life-course theories
   A. Concentrate on early childhood experiences
   B. Recognize that multiple pathways and trajectories of crime and delinquency must be examined
   C. Consider the adolescent limited versus life-course persister dichotomy as presumptively correct
   D. Usually use cross-sectional data

8. According to the research of Sampson and Laub, which of the following would not lead to knifing out of crime:
   A. marrying a women who is a criminal
   B. marrying a prosocial woman
   C. joining the army
   D. obtaining steady employment

9. Latent trait theory
   A. assumes that many people are pretty much born criminal
   B. asserts that propensity to commit crimes can become a reality if opportunity presents itself
   C. asserts that low IQ causes crime
   D. denies any significant influence of the environment since one cannot change his character very easily

10. Which theorist(s) stated that some offenders enjoy "money without work, sex without courtship, revenge without court delays"
   A. Sampson and Laub
   B. Thornberry and Nagin
   C. Loeber and Loeber
   D. Gottfredson and Hirschi

True False:
 1. Latent trait theories focus upon knifing out of crime possibilities T F

 2. General Theory of Crime examines propensities, rational choice, and opportunities. T F

 3. Life course theories adopt multidisciplinary approaches to delinquency T F

 4.   Problem behavior syndrome focuses primarily on substance abuse and child abuse. T F

 5. Lack of inner controls has been related to parenting style T F

Multiple Choice
1. A
2. C
3. D
4. B
5. D
6. B
7. B
8. A
9. B
10. D

True False
1. F
2 T
3 T
4 F
5 T

CHAPTER SIX
GENDER AND DELINQUENCY

LEARNING OBJECTIVES

- Be familiar with the changes in the female delinquency rate.
- Understand the cognitive differences between males and females.
- Be able to discuss the differences in socialization between boys and girls and how this may affect their behavior.
- Understand the psychological differences between the sexes.
- Be able to discuss the early work on gender, delinquency, and human traits.
- Know the elements contemporary trait theorists view as the key to understanding gender differences, such as psychological makeup and hormonal differences.
- Know how socialization is thought to affect delinquency rates.
- Discuss the views of contemporary socialization theorists.
- Know the basic tenets of liberal feminism.
- Discuss how critical feminists view female delinquency and describe Hagan's power-control theory
- Be familiar with how the treatment girls receive by the juvenile justice system differs from the treatment of boys.

CHAPTER OUTLINE

I.   Introduction
     A.   Laticia
          1. Laticia, a fifteen-year-old female of African descent, was referred to the teen center for her involvement in a gang-related physical assault
          2. Her mother worked three low-income jobs; her father was not in the picture
          3. She was referred to juvenile court she had not attended school for several months.
          4. She is nearly six feet tall, and almost 300 pounds
          5. Laticia has threatened a number of teachers and was often suspended from school for unruly behavior until she finally dropped out. She has had numerous sexual encounters, but no relationships.
          8. Laticia was generally responsible for taking care of her siblings, which she resented.
          5. One counselor at the drop-in center made it his mission to help Laticia
          6. The counselor helped her focus on her positive attributes and to respect herself.
          7. The counselor suspected the mother of being physically abusive

9. Laticia at the program at the drop-in center participated in anger management issues in groups, community service, and continued to see her counselor. She returned to school and then graduated and was able to continue her education in a community college.

B. Early experts
1. female offender was an aberration
2. their crimes usually had a sexual connotation
3. criminologists often ignored female offenders
4. few "true" female delinquents were considered anomalies
5. explained by masculinity hypothesis

C. Contemporary interest
1. female delinquency is growing at a faster pace than male Delinquency in US and around the world.
2. Criminologists no longer portray female delinquents as "fallen women", exploited by men and involved in illicit sexual activities.
3. feminist approach to understanding crime is now firmly established

II. Gender Differences in Development
A. Gender differences
1. may exist as early as infancy
2. infant girls show greater control over their emotions

B. Socialization differences
1. males learn to value independence
2. females' self-worth depends on their ability to sustain relationships
3. boys may experience a chronic sense of alienation
4. girls are socialized to be less aggressive than boys
5. girls are supervised more closely
6. males are more likely to display physical aggression
7. whereas females display relational aggression
8. females are more likely to be targets of sexual and physical abuse

C. Cognitive differences
1. girls learn to speak earlier and faster, and with better pronunciation
2. boys do much better on standardized math tests
3. cognitive differences are small and narrowing
4. differences usually attributed to cultural expectations

D. Personality differences
1. girls are often stereotyped as talkative
2. boys spend more time talking than girls do
3. gender differences may have an impact on self-esteem and self-concept
4. girls are regularly confronted with unrealistically high standards of slimness
   a. may make them extremely unhappy with their own bodies

E. What causes gender differences?
1. some experts suggest that gender differences may have a biological origin

2. they have somewhat different brain organizations
3. they have been exposed to different styles of socialization
4. Bem's gender-schema theory
   a. our culture polarizes males and females
   b. forcing them to obey mutually exclusive gender roles or scripts
5. self-esteem tied to how closely their behavior conforms to stereotype

II. Gender Differences and Delinquency
   A. Gender differences
      1. may partly explain the significant gender differences in delinquency rate
      2. males seem more aggressive and less likely to form attachments to others
      3. boys are also more likely than girls to socialize with deviant peers
      4. girls are shielded by their moral sense
      5. females display more self-control than males
      6. females are more verbally proficient
   B. Gender patterns in delinquency
      1. females have increased their participation in delinquent behaviors
      2. today females make up about 24 percent of all arrests and 18 percent of all arrests for serious violent crimes
   C. Monitoring the Future
      1. patterns of male and female criminality appear to be converging
      2. illegal acts most common for boys are also frequently committed by girls
   D. Violent behavior
      1. gender differences in the delinquency rate may be narrowing
         a. males continue to be overrepresented in arrests for violent crimes
      2. in 2005, of the approximately 900 juveniles arrested for murder, only 90 were female
      3. males and females display differences in the victims they target and the weapons
         a. typical male juvenile kills a friend or acquaintance
         b. males kill with a handgun during an argument
         c. female is as likely to kill a family member
         d. female is more likely to use a knife
         e. both males and females tend to kill males

III. Are Female Delinquents Born That Way?
   A. Early biological explanations
      1. tradition of tracing gender differences to traits that are uniquely male or female
      2. publication in 1895 of The Female Offender by Lombroso

3. maintained that women were lower on the evolutionary scale than men
4. women who committed crimes could be distinguished from "normal" women
   a. distinct physical characteristics
5. delinquent females appeared closer to men than to other women
6. in 1925 Cyril Burt linked female delinquency to menstruation

B. Chivalry hypothesis
1. female delinquency goes unrecorded because the female is the instigator
2. females first use their sexual charms to instigate crime
   a. beguile males in the justice system to obtain deferential treatment
3. female criminality is overlooked by male agents of the justice system

C. Early psychological explanations
1. Freud and penis envy
   a. inferiority complex in girls
   b. boys learn to fear women
   c. girls identify with their mothers and accept a maternal role
2. psychodynamic theorists suggested that girls are socialized to be passive
3. females susceptible to being manipulated by men
4. male delinquency reflects aggressive traits
5. female delinquency is a function of:
   a. repressed sexuality
   b. gender conflict
   c. abnormal socialization

D. Contemporary trait views
1. early theorists linked female delinquency to early or precocious sexuality
2. evidence suggests that girls who reach puberty at an early age
   a. at the highest risk for delinquency
   b. early bloomers may be more attractive to older adolescent boys
   c. and increased contact with this high-risk group
   d. socialized into party deviance
3. hormonal imbalance may influence aggressive behavior
4. excessive amounts of male androgens are related to delinquency
   a. testosterone
5. some females are overexposed to male hormones in utero
6. conflicting evidence on the relationship between PMS and female delinquency
7. Fishbein notes the evidence does show a link between PMS and delinquency
8. males are inherently more likely to be aggressive

127

9.   males seem to be more aggressive in all societies for which data are available

10. gender differences in aggression can even be found in nonhuman primates

E.   Biosocial theorists

    1.   males wish to possess as many sex partners as possible

        a.   increase their chances of producing offspring

    2.   females concentrate on acquiring things that will help them rear their offspring

F.   Contemporary psychological views

    1.   female delinquents suffer from some mental abnormality

    2.   running away and truancy suggest underlying psychological distress

    3.   female offenders have more acute mental health symptoms

    4.   serious female delinquents linked to callous-unemotional (CU) traits

        a.   an affective disorder described by a lack of remorse or shame

        b.   poor judgment

        c.   failure to learn by experience

        d.   chronic lying

IV.   Socialization Views

A.   Socialization views

    1.   child's social development the key to understanding delinquent behavior

    2.   W. I. Thomas published The Unadjusted Girl in 1928

    3.   some females can become impulsive thrill seekers

    4.   poor girls from demoralized families use sex as a means to gain:

        a.   amusement

        b.   pretty clothes

        c.   other luxuries

B.   Lifestyle

    1.   girls may be supervised more closely than boys

    2.   closer supervision restricts the opportunity for crime and time available

    3.   three assumptions about gender differences in socialization:

        a.   families exert a more powerful influence on girls than on boys

        b.   girls do not form close same-sex

        c.   females get into affairs with older men who exploit them and involve then in sexual deviance

D.   Contemporary socialization views

    1.   female delinquents have more dysfunctional home lives than male offenders

    2.   girls seem to be more deeply affected than boys by child abuse

3.   girls may be forced into a life of sexual promiscuity
4.   institutionalization does not help matters. Those sent away are much more likely to develop criminal records as adults than similarly troubled girls who manage to stay with families throughout their childhood
5.   runaways are regularly victimized and practice survival sex.
6.   Chesney-Lind states: "Young women on the run from homes characterized by sexual abuse and parental neglect are forced, by the very statutes designed to protect them, into the life of an escaped convict." Many of these girls may find themselves pregnant at a very young age. Physical and sexual abuse takes its toll on young girls.

E.   Abusive homes
1.   linking abusive home lives to gang participation and crime
2.   Moore's gang girls in East LA came from troubled homes
   a.   68% were afraid of their fathers
   b.   55% reported fear of their mothers
   c.   30% reported that family members had made sexual advances
   d.   many had overly strict parents
3.   poor home life is likely to have a more damaging effect on females

F.   Human Trafficking and the Sexual Exploitation of Children
1.   human trafficking includes all forms of transportation of women and girls (as well as young boys) through the use of force, abduction, fraud, coercion for the purpose of sexual and/or commercial exploitation this includes sexual slavery, prostitution, pornography, being used as human containers for drug smuggling, labor servitude, or organ donation.
2.   facilitated by global economy and the relaxation of corporate borders
3.   debts may be passed on to other family members or even entire villages from generation to generation.
4.   Sex tourism is a booming industry.
5.   poverty, sexual abuse, and family obligations are main reasons given by children for entering into prostitution
6.   the United States passed the Trafficking Victims Protection Act of 2003 and strengthened it in 2005.

V.   Liberal Feminist Views
A.   Liberal feminism
1.   female social roles provide fewer opportunities to commit crime
2.   as roles of women become more similar to those of men so will their crime
3.   female criminality is motivated by the same influences as male criminality
4.   female delinquency would be affected by the changing role of women

B. Support for liberal feminism
    1. as women were empowered economically and socially
        a. they would be less likely to feel dependent and oppressed
    2. their new role as breadwinner might encourage traditional male crimes
    3. correlation between the women's rights movement and the female crime rate
    4. gender differences in delinquency are fading
    5. girls may be committing crimes to gain economic advancement

VI. Critical Feminist Views
  A. Marxist feminists
    1. inequality stems from unequal power of men and women in a capitalist society
    2. exploitation of females by fathers and husbands
    3. under capitalism women are a commodity like land or money
    4. female delinquency originates with the onset of male
    5. critical feminists focus on the social forces that shape girls' lives
    6. young males learn to be exploitive of women
    7. women are inherently powerless in such a society
    8. male exploitation acts as a trigger for female delinquent behavior
    9. female attempts at survival are then labeled delinquent
  B. Crime and patriarchy
    1. capitalist society is characterized by both patriarchy and class conflict
    2. capitalists control workers
    3. men control women both economically and biologically
    4. females denied access to male-dominated street crimes
  C. Power-control theory
    1. gender differences in delinquency are a function of class differences
    2. Hagan calls his view power-control theory
    3. class influences delinquency by controlling the quality of family life
    4. fathers assume the role of breadwinners
    5. mothers have menial jobs or remain at home
    6. mothers are expected to control the behavior of their daughters
    7. parent-daughter relationship viewed as a prep for the cult of domesticity
  D. Egalitarian families
    1. husband and wife share similar positions of power at home and work
    2. daughters gain a kind of freedom that reflects reduced parental control
    3. produce daughters whose law-violating behaviors mirror those of their brothers

4. middle-class girls are most likely to violate the law
   a. because they are less closely controlled than lower-class girls
5. relationship between social class and delinquency has been challenged
6. addresses gender differences, class position, and family structure
7. stresses the significance of changing feminine roles
8. daughters of successful and powerful mothers are more at risk for delinquency
   a. encouraged to take prosocial risks
   b. engaging in athletic competition
   c. breaking into traditional male-dominated

VII. Gender and the Juvenile Justice System
   A. Justice system
      1. police are more likely to arrest female adolescents for sexual activity
         a. ignore the same behavior among male delinquents
      2. girls were also more likely to be sent to a detention facility before trial
      3. girls are far more likely than to be picked up by police for status offenses
      4. juvenile justice system still categorizes female offenders into 2 distinct groups:
         a. girls who momentarily strayed from the "good girl" path
         b. dangerously wayward girls who have serious problems
      5. institutionalized girls report that they are given fewer privileges
         a. less space
         b. less equipment
         c. fewer programs
      6. girls subject to harsh punishments if they are considered dangerously immoral
      7. association between male standards of "beauty" and sexual behavior
      8. respond to attractive girls who engage in sexual behavior more harshly
      9. officials still show a lack of concern about girls

CHAPTER SUMMARY

The relationship between gender and delinquency has become a topic of considerable interest to criminologists. At one time, attention was directed solely at male offenders and the rare female delinquent was considered an oddity. The nature and extent of female delinquent activities have changed, and girls are now engaging in more frequent and serious illegal activity. Sociologists and psychologists recognize that there

131

are differences in attitudes, values, and behavior between boys and girls. There are cognitive differences. Females process information differently than males do and have different cognitive and physical strengths. These differences may, in part, explain gender differences in delinquency. Girls are socialized differently, which causes them to internalize rather than externalize anger and aggression. There are also psychological differences between the sexes. Girls may actually be at risk for a greater level of mental anguish than boys.

There are a number of different views of female delinquency. Trait views are concerned with biological and psychological differences between the sexes. Early efforts by Cesare Lombroso and his followers placed the blame for delinquency on physical differences between males and females. Girls who were delinquent had inherent masculine characteristics. Contemporary trait theorists view girls' psychological makeup and hormonal and physical characteristics as key to their delinquent behavior. Socialization has also been identified as a cause of delinquency. Males are socialized to be tough and aggressive, females to be passive and obedient. Early socialization views portrayed the adolescent female offender as a troubled girl who lacked love at home and supportive peer relations. These theories treated female delinquents as sexual offenders whose criminal activities were linked to destructive relationships with men.

Contemporary socialization views continue to depict female delinquents as being raised in hellish homes where they are victims of sexual and physical abuse. More recent views of gender and delinquency incorporate the changes brought about by the women's movement. Liberal feminists argue that, as the roles of women change, so will their crime patterns. Critical feminists view female delinquency as a function of patriarchy and the mistreatment and exploitation of females in a male-dominated society. Hagan's power-control theory helps us understand why these differences exist and whether change may be coming. The treatment girls receive by the juvenile justice system has also been the subject of debate. Originally, it was thought that police protected girls from the stigma of a delinquency label. Contemporary criminologists charge, however, that girls are discriminated against by agents of the justice system.

KEY TERMS

masculinity hypothesis: View that women who commit crimes have biological and psychological traits similar to those of men.

gender-schema theory: A theory of development that holds that children internalize gender scripts that reflect the gender-related social practices of the culture. Once internalized, these gender scripts predispose the kids to construct a self-identity that is consistent with them.

chivalry hypothesis (also known as paternalism hypothesis): The view that low female crime and delinquency rates are a reflection of the leniency with which police treat female offenders.

precocious sexuality: Sexual experimentation in early adolescence.

liberal feminism: Asserts that females are less delinquent than males because their social roles provide them with fewer opportunities to commit crimes; as the roles of girls and women become more similar to those of boys and men, so too will their crime patterns.

critical feminists: Hold that gender inequality stems from the unequal power of men and women and the subsequent exploitation of women by men; the cause of female delinquency originates with the onset of male supremacy and the efforts of males to control females' sexuality.

power-control theory: Holds that gender differences in the delinquency rate are a function of class differences and economic conditions that influence the structure of family life.

egalitarian families: Husband and wife share power at home; daughters gain a kind of freedom similar to that of sons and their law-violating behaviors mirror those of their brothers.

SELF TEST QUESTIONS

MULTIPLE CHOICE

1. With the publication in 1895 of _____, Lombroso (with William Ferrero) extended his work on criminality to females; Lombroso maintained that women were lower on the evolutionary scale than men, more childlike and less intelligent.
   A. *The Female Offender*
   B. *Girls in the Gang*
   C. *The Femme Criminale*
   D. *The Sex, Drugs, and Crime Chronicles*

2. According to Lombroso, in physical appearance, delinquent females appeared closer both to criminal and noncriminal men than to other women; the _____ hypothesis suggested that delinquent girls have excessive male characteristics.
   A. power control theory   C. psychodynamic theory
   B. masculinity hypothesis   D. gender schema theory

3. In 2005, of the approximately _____ juveniles arrested for murder, 90 were female.
   A. 500   C. 900
   B. 600   D. 1,300

4. The text mentions that boys who "aren't tough" are labeled sissies and girls are expected to form closer bonds with their friends and to share feelings as explaining
   A. cognitive and personalty differneces   C. mating practices
   B. sexual development   D. criminal propensities

5. The authors note that the patterns of male and female criminality appear to be _____.
   A. converging   C. equal
   B. diverging   D. becoming less similar

6. Healy and Bronner's research suggested that males physical superiority enhanced their criminality; their research showed that about seventy percent of the delinquent girls they studied had abnormal, masculine weight and size characteristics, a finding which supported the _____.
   A. gender schema theory   C. psychodynamic theory
   B. masculinity hypothesis   D. power control theory

7. Early biotheorists suspected that premenstrual syndrome (PMS) was a direct cause of the relatively rare instances of female violence: "For several days prior to and during menstruation, the stereotype has been that 'raging hormones' doom women to irritability and _____, two facets of premenstrual syndrome."
   A. poor judgment   C. unexplained convulsions
   B. explosive rage   D. temporary insanity

8. According to the text, the main reasons girls gave for entering into prostitution were
    A. they were abducted and drugged by organized gangs
    B. they had penis envy and were masochistic
    C. poverty, sexual abuse, and family obligations
    D. all of the above

9. James Messerschmidt argues that
    A. males commit much more crime than females because of high levels of testosterone
    B. misguided concepts of "masculinity" flow from the inequities built into "patriarchal capitalism."
    C. women are underrepresented in the criminal justice system because of chivalry: society does not want to incarcerate females, especially if they have young children.
    D. The women's liberation movement has lead to women's freedom to commit crimes.

10. What stereotype of female delinquency is no longer taken seriously?
    A. that the female delinquent comes from a paternalistic family
    B. that the female delinquent is a sexual deviant
    C. that the female delinquent suffers from physical and sexual abuse
    D. that the female delinquent is a product of the feminist movement

11. What is the left side of the brain believed to control?
    A. gross motor function   C. visual-spatial orientation
    B. language   D. maps and directions

12. According to Siegel and Welsh, _____ display relational aggression; for example, by excluding disliked peers from play groups.
    A. females   C. both genders
    B. males   D. adults

13. According to Siegel and Welsh, _____ are socialized to sustain relationships, be less aggressive, blame themselves, have lower self-esteem, and have superior verbal ability.
    A. females   C. both genders
    B. males   D. adults

14. According to Siegel and Welsh, _____ are socialized to be independent, be aggressive, externalize anger, have high self-esteem, and have a low attention span.
    A. females   C. both genders
    B. males   D. adults

15. According to Siegel and Welsh, what was seen as a key factor in how harsh the juvenile court's punishment is for female status offenders was?
    A. race   C. demeanor
    B. attractiveness   D. intelligence

16. Which of the following perspectives views female delinquency as a consequence of the unequal power between males and females in a capitalist society?
   A. liberal feminists
   B. radical feminists
   C. trait theorists
   D. gender schema theory

17. In the patriarchal family type, fathers are the breadwinners of the family, and mothers stay home; mothers are expected to control the behavior of their daughters while _____.
   A. granting freedoms to their sons
   B. giving the same treatment to their sons
   C. closely monitoring the activities of their sons
   D. leaving the supervision and discipline of sons to her husband

18. According to _____ theory, gender differences in the delinquency rate can be traced to differences in psychological orientation; male delinquency reflects aggressive personality traits, while female delinquency is a product of young girl's psychosexual development, repressed sexuality, gender conflict, and abnormal socialization.
   A. liberal feminism
   B. psychoanalytic
   C. power control
   D. radical feminism

19. Some biosocial theorists link antisocial behavior to hormonal influences; the argument is that the male sex hormone _____ accounts for their more aggressive behavior, and that gender related hormonal differences can also explain the gender gap in delinquency.
   A. testosterone
   B. carcinogens
   C. ammonium nitrates
   D. estrogen

20. According to _____, some impoverished girls who have not been socialized under middle class family controls can become impulsive thrill seekers; female delinquency is linked to the wish for luxury and excitement.
   A. Freud
   B. Lombroso
   C. Fishbein
   D. W.I. Thomas

21. Whereas boys usually use _____ when they kill, girls usually use _____
   A. knives, guns
   B. guns, knives
   C. poison, guns
   D. guns, poison

22. Data indicates that, while women make up twenty percent of all arrestees, they account for less than five percent of all inmates; this statistics could be used to support the _____.
   A. masculinity hypothesis
   B. gender identification process
   C. chivalry hypothesis
   D. feminine tolerance factor

23. The Monitoring the Future self-report study shows that patterns of male and female criminality appear to be converging. Self-report data indicate that the rank-ordering of male and female deviant behaviors is _____.
   A. still extremely different
   B. similar
   C. not measured
   D. somewhat different

24. According to power control theory, gender differences in delinquency rates are a function of _____ and economic conditions that influence the structure of family life.
        A. class differences   C. differences in academic abilities
        B. cognitive differences   D. media socialization

25. Liberal feminists see increasing female offending patterns caused by _____.
        A. cognitive differences in development
        B. experiences of abuse and unreasonable parental control
        C. structured opportunities in work, politics, and school
        D. exploitation of females by fathers and husbands

26. According to Hagan, in _____ families—those in which the husband and the wife share similar positions of power at home and in the workplace—daughters gain a kind of freedom that reflects reduced parental control.
        A. patriarchal   C. matriarchal
        B. egalitarian   D. dysfunctional

27. What two factors make up the double marginality Messerschmidt identifies?
        A. low math score and verbal ability
        B. patriarcy and capitalism
        C. gender and race
        D. less aggressive and more emotional

28. Until contemporary feminist movements,
        A. Female crime was not serious investigated
        B. Most criminologists like Lombroso examined female and male offenders
        C. Female delinquent behavior was tied to their sexuality
        D. Female criminologists wrote a variety of theories about female deviance.

29. According to the text, liberal feminists are most likely to agree with
        A. Marxist feminists
        B. Socialist feminists
        C. Radical feminists
        D. None of the above

30. Freud and Lombroso had a(n)
        A. sociological perspective of sexual development
        B. economic explanation of gender and crime
        C. cultural explanation of gender and crime
        D. biological component in their view of gender and crime

TRUE FALSE

1. According to liberal feminists, the women's liberation movement would produce even less female crime because women would no longer be exploited sexually by males.
    A. True
    B. False

2. According to radical feminism, the cause of female delinquency originates with the onset of male supremacy, or patriarchy, the subsequent subordination of women, male aggression, and the efforts of men to control females sexually.
    A. True
    B. False

3. Performance on the mathematics portion of the Scholastic Aptitude Test (SAT) still favors males: twice as many boys as girls attain scores over 500, and thirteen times as many boys as girls attain scores over 700.
    A. True
    B. False

4. Girls are often stereotyped as talkative, but research shows that in many situations boys spend more time talking than girls do; males are more likely to introduce new topics and to interrupt conversations.
    A. True
    B. False

5. According to radical feminism, our culture polarizes males and females by forcing them to obey mutually exclusive gender roles; girls are expected to be "feminine," exhibiting traits such as being sympathetic and gentle, and boys are expected to be "masculine," exhibiting assertiveness and dominance.
    A. True
    B. False

6. Over the past decades, females have increased their participation in delinquent behaviors at a faster rate than males.
    A. True
    B. False

7. There is a connection between the hormone cortisol and conduct disorders in girls
    A. True
    B. False

8. According to the text, Dr. Sigmund Freud has had a great influence on theoretical criminology, penology, and correctional intervention programs.
    A. True
    B. False

9. According to the text, the primary reason for the great disparity in lethal violence of males and females is that girls learn to play with dolls and boys with trucks.

     A True

     B False

10. Males account for 76 percent of the total number of arrests and 82 percent of all serious violent crime arrests.

     A. True

     B. False

11. Siegel and Welsh note that the typical male juvenile kills a friend or acquaintance with a handgun during an argument.

     A. True

     B. False

12. Siegel and Welsh note that the typical female juvenile kills a friend, rival gang member, or acquaintance with a handgun during an argument.

     A. True

     B. False

13. William Healy and Augusta Bronner suggested that males' physical superiority enhanced their criminality; their research showed that about seventy percent of the delinquent girls they studied had abnormal weight and size, a finding that supported the masculinity hypothesis.

     A. True

     B. False

14. Siegel and Welsh note that empirical evidence suggests that girls who reach puberty at an early age are at the highest risk for delinquency. One reason is that early bloomers are more attractive to older adolescent boys, and increased contact with this high-risk group places the girls in jeopardy for antisocial behavior.

     A. True

     B. False

15. Females who test higher for testosterone are more likely to engage in stereotypical male behaviors.

     A. True

     B. False

16. Diana Fishbein has reviewed the literature in this area and finds that, after holding constant a variety of factors (including IQ, age, and environment), females exposed to male hormones *in utero* are more likely to engage in aggressive behavior later in life.

     A. True

     B. False

17. Adler argued that female delinquency would be affected by the changing role of women: as females entered new occupations and participated in sports, politics, and other traditionally male endeavors, they would also become involved in crimes that had heretofore been male-oriented; delinquency rates would then converge.
    A. True
    B. False

18. Females involved in violent crime more often than not have some connection to a male partner who influences their behavior. One study of women who kill in the course of their involvement in the drug trade found that they kill on behalf of a man or out of fear of a man.
    A. True
    B. False

19. In egalitarian families, in which the husband and wife share similar positions of power at home and in the workplace, daughters gain a kind of freedom that reflects reduced parental control. These families produce daughters whose law-violating behaviors mirror those of their brothers.
    A. True
    B. False

20. Over the past decades, males have increased their participation in delinquent behaviors at a faster rate than females.
    A. True
    B. False

21. According to psychologist Sandra Bem's gender-schema theory, our culture polarizes males and females by forcing them to obey mutually exclusive gender roles; girls are expected to be "feminine," exhibiting traits such as being sympathetic and gentle and boys are expected to be "masculine," exhibiting assertiveness and dominance.
    A. True
    B. False

22. Males and females have somewhat different brain organizations; females are more left-brain oriented and males more right-brain oriented.
    A. True
    B. False

23. Siegel and Welsh note that young girls are regularly confronted with unrealistically high standards of slimness that make them extremely unhappy with their own bodies; the incidence of eating disorders such as anorexia and bulimia have increased markedly in recent years.
    A. True
    B. False

24. Boys are often stereotyped as talkative, but research shows that in many situations girls spend more time talking than girls do; girls are more likely to introduce new topics and to interrupt conversations.
    A. True
    B. False

25. According to liberal feminists, the women's liberation movement would produce more female crime because women would have greater opportunities to commit crimes.
    A. True
    B. False

FILL IN

1. _____ asserts that females are less delinquent than males because their social roles provide them with fewer opportunities to commit crimes; as the roles of girls and women become more similar to those of boys and men, so too will their crime patterns.

2. _____ theory holds that children internalize gender scripts that reflect the gender-related social practices of the culture; once internalized, these gender scripts predispose the kids to construct a self-identity that is consistent with them.

3. Precocious sexuality is _____ experimentation in early adolescence.

4. _____ contends that low female crime and delinquency rates are a reflection of the leniency with which police treat female offenders.

5. _____ theory contends that gender differences in the delinquency rate are a function of class differences and economic conditions that influence the structure of family life.

6. The _____ hypothesis view is that women who commit crimes have biological and psychological traits similar to those of men.

7. _____ families are best illustrated when the husband and wife share power at home; daughters gain a kind of freedom similar to that of sons, and their law-violating behaviors mirror those of their brothers.

8. _____ hold that gender inequality stems from the unequal power of men and women and the subsequent exploitation of women by men; the cause of female delinquency originates with the onset of male supremacy and the efforts of males to control females' sexuality.

141

9. In a(n) _____ family, fathers are the bread winners of the family and mothers stay home; mothers are expected to control the behavior of their daughters while granting freedoms to their sons.

10. In _____ families—those in which the husband and the wife share similar positions of power at home and in the workplace—daughters gain a kind of freedom that reflects reduced parental control.

11. According to power control, gender differences in delinquency rates are a function of _____ and economic conditions that influence the structure of family life.

12. With the publication in 1895 of *The Female Offender*, _____ (with William Ferrero) extended his work on criminality to females; he maintained that women were lower on the evolutionary scale than men, more childlike and less intelligent.

13. According to Siegel and Welsh, _____ are socialized to sustain relationships, be less aggressive, blame themselves, have lower self-esteem, and have superior verbal ability.

14. According to Siegel and Welsh, _____ are socialized to be independent, be aggressive, externalize anger, have high self-esteem, and have a low attention span.

15. Infant _____ show greater control over their emotions

ESSAY

1. Discuss the idea that males are more aggressive than females. Is this caused by biological, psychological, or social factors?

2. Why has society responded more severely to sexual transgressions by females?

3. Are lower and working class females more strictly supervised than upper and middle class females? Explain.

4. Compare and contrast the views of liberal feminism to radical feminism.

5. What are some of the explanations offered to explain the divergent trends in delinquency by males and females?

143

ANSWER KEY

MULTIPLE CHOICE

1. A	11. B	21. B
2. B	12. A	22. C
3. C	13. A	23. B
4. A	14. B	24. A
5. A	15. B	25. C
6. B	16. B	26. B
7. A	17. A	27. B
8. C	18. B	28 C
9. B	19. A	29 D
10. B	20. D	30 D

TRUE FALSE

1. F	11. T	21. T
2. T	12. F	22. T
3. T	13. T	23. T
4. T	14. T	24. F
5. F	15. T	25. T
6. T	16. T	
7. T	17. T	
8. F	18. T	
9. F	19. T	
10. T	20. F	

FILL IN

1. liberal feminism
2. gender-schema
3. sexual
4. chivalry hypothesis
5. power-control
6. masculinity
7. egalitarian
8. radical feminists
9. patriarchal
10. egalitarian
11. class
12. Lombroso
13. females
14. males
15 girls

Multiple Choice

1. According to the text, the increase in female delinquency
   A. is found in many countries around the world
   B. is found primarily in the United States
   C. is primarily found in countries with high unemployment
   D. is directly caused by increased sexual abuse.

2. Which feminist condemned society's reaction to runaways as being part of the problem, not the solution
   A. Adler
   B. Chesney-Lind
   C. Thomas
   D. Fishbein

3. Female adolescents
   A. are less interested in relationships with boys than boys are with girls
   B. with problems at home may seek affection elsewhere leading to exploitation by older males
   C. usually act out rather than internalize their problems
   D. need more Freudian psychoanalysis to find out the root cause of the problem so they can come to grips with it.

4. Research conducted in our country and abroad found that the factors that generate male delinquency
   A. are quite different than those that direct female delinquency
   B. are quite similar as those that direct female delinquency
   C. are not consistent in cross-cultural research
   D. are unrelated to aggression, cognitive scripts, or socialization

5. According to the text, in comparison to typical male murderers, female murderers
   A. kill strangers
   B. kill their children
   C. kill an acquaintance or a friend during an argument
   D. kill a family member or an acquaintance

6. Lombroso who was a medical doctor
   A. used random samples of males and females to come up with his theories about the female offender
   B. believed that post partum depression leads women to kill
   C. believed that female offenders' etiology could be explained the same as male criminal etiology.
   D. stated that female offenders had excessive body hair, wrinkles and an abnormal cranium

7. The chivalry hypothesis
   A. explains why women who kill their abusers get hard time and male batterers get light if any punishment
   B. requires equalization of justice for men and women
   C. cannot explain treatment of most female offenders according to critical feminists
   D. explains the increase in female crime rates and needs to be examined closer.

8. Clinical interviews indicate that, in comparison to male delinquents, female delinquents
   A. are more likely to be diagnosed as having Anti Social Personality Disorder
   B. are more likely to be diagnosed as ADHD
   C. are significantly more likely to suffer from mood disorders
   D. suffer from less schizophrenia, but more neurosis

9. Institutionalization of wayward girls
   A. does not help girls in trouble
   B. is required to prevent them from being victimized
   C. is effective if run by private or religious organizations
   D. is less expensive than community treatment

10. Human trafficking
    A. is aggressively attacked by INTERPOL
    B. is pretty much restricted to the third world
    C. is a global epidemic
    D. has lead to significant action by the UN

True False:

1. According to Bem, gender-schema theory may or may not be related to the concept of gender scripts. T F

2. According to the text, early physical development and precocious sex with older boys almost always leads to a life of crime. T F

3. According to the text, reduced supervision of girls may explain their increased crime rates T F

4. Liberal feminists, as opposed to radical feminists, promote a feminist agenda demanding structural changes in child rearing, financial resources, and representation in government and industry T F

5. Liberal feminists point out that increases in female delinquency occur at the same time that girls and women have greater opportunity to commit crimes.
T F

Answer Key

<u>Multiple Choice</u>
1. A
2 B
3 B
4 A
5 D
6 D
7 C
8 C
9 A
10 C

<u>True False</u>
1. F
2. F
3. T
4. F
5. T

CHAPTER SEVEN
THE FAMILY AND DELINQUENCY

LEARNING OBJECTIVES

- Be familiar with the link between family relationships and juvenile delinquency.
- Understand the complex association between family breakup and delinquent behavior.
- Understand why families in conflict produce more delinquents than those that function harmoniously.
- Know the association between inconsistent discipline and supervision and juvenile crime.
- Be able to discuss how parental and sibling misconduct influences delinquent behaviors.
- Define the concept of child abuse.
- Know the nature and extent of abuse.
- Be able to list the factors that are seen as causing child abuse.
- Be familiar with the complex system of state intervention in abuse cases.
- Discuss the association between child abuse and delinquent behavior.

CHAPTER OUTLINE

I.   Changing American Family
        A. Joey's Story:
                1. Joey and his sister and brother were neglected and sexually abused before being placed in foster homes.
                2. Joey did not adjust well to foster care and was charged with sexual assault at age 12.
                3. Joey spends years in residential treatment centers and mental health hospitals
                4, As Joey approaches age 17 attempts are made to return him home where his siblings already have been reunited with the mother.
                5. Joey and his family participate in therapy which is strength based and provides wrap around services.
                6. Joey shows marked improvement, obtains his GED, and is employed full time
        A.   Family dysfunction
                1. family dysfunction is key to understanding deviance and delinquency.
                2. good families protect youths from risk factors
                3. without relief from extended family members, nuclear families can be "dangerous hothouses of emotions"
                4. television and daycare raise many children today.
        B.   So-called traditional family
                1.   extended families more uncommon; in their place is the nuclear family

148

          2.   male breadwinner, female who cares for the home is thing of the past

          3.   no longer can this family structure be considered the norm

          4.   women play a much greater role in the economic process

          5.   created a more egalitarian family structure

          6.   three-quarters of all mothers of school-age children are employed

          7.   fathers are now spending more time with their children

    C.   Family makeup

          1.   After decades-long decline, two-thirds of underage minors now live in two-parent families.

          2.   will experience parental separation or divorce before they reach age sixteen

              a.   40% of White children

              b.   75% of African-American children

          3.   Through there has been a sharp decline in teen pregnancies over the last decade, more than 1.3 million children are still born to unmarried women annually.

    D.   Child care

          1.   family daycare homes are of special concern

          2.   90% or more of the facilities operate underground

          3.   working poor families are most likely to suffer from inadequate child care

          4.   about 3.5 million children under age thirteen are latch key kids

    E.   Economic stress

          1.   family is also undergoing economic stress

          2.   about 20 percent of all children live in poverty

          3.   about 8 percent live in extreme poverty

          4.   About 33 percent of all children live in families where no parent has full time, year-round employment

II.   The Family's Influence on Delinquency

    A.   Socialization

          1.   disturbed home environment has significant impact on delinquency

          2.   family is the primary unit of socialization

    B.   Four categories of family dysfunction

          1.   families disrupted by spousal conflict or breakup

          2.   families involved in interpersonal conflict

          3.   negligent parents

          4.   families with deviant parents

    C.   Family breakup

          1.   one of the most enduring controversies in the study of delinquency

          2.   strong determinant of a child's law-violating behavior

          3.   connection seems self-evident since family is primary socialization

          4.   if present trends continue, less than half of all children will live continuously with mother and father throughout childhood

          5.   children who have experienced family breakup demonstrate behavior problems and hyperactivity

6. family breakup is often associated with conflict, hostility, and aggression
7. since blended families are less stable than families consisting of two biological parents, an increasing number of children will experience family breakup two or there times during childhood
8. family breakup associated with conflict, hostility and aggression. children of divorce suspected of having lax supervision, weakened attachment, and greater susceptibility to peer pressure
9. more transitions associated with delinquent activity

D. Effects of divorce
1. relationship between broken homes and delinquency has been controversial
2. children growing up in broken homes were more likely to be delinquent
3. question the link between broken homes and delinquency
4. research may be tainted by sampling bias
5. system may treat children from disrupted households more severely
6. *parens patriae* philosophy calls for official intervention where parental supervision is considered inadequate
7. self-report data does not corroborate official data of relationship of broken homes and delinquency

E. Divorce reconsidered
1. family breakup is traumatic
2. McLanahan research on children who grow up apart from biological fathers
   a. less likely to finish high school and attend college
   b. less likely to find and keep a steady job
   c. more likely to become teen mothers
3. fairly good evidence that father absence is responsible for some social problems
4. effects of divorce seem gender-specific:
   a. boys seem to be more affected by the postdivorce absence of the father
   b. fathers seem less likely to be around to solve problems
   c. girls are more affected by quality of the mother's parenting
   d. girls also affected by postdivorce parental conflict
5. Parents who are in post-divorce turmoil may influence their children to misbehave.
6. Jaffee research indicates quality of marriage more important than makeup

F. Family conflict
1. not all unhappy marriages end in divorce
2. intrafamily conflict is a common experience in many American families
3. parents' marital happiness was a significant predictor of delinquency

      4.   damaged parent-child relationships are associated with delinquency

      5.   little difference between the behavior of children who witness intra family violence and those who are victims.

      6.   conflict-prone youth may destabilize households; parents may give in to difficult children and teach that aggression pays off.

      7.   conflict or divorce question

           a.   children in both broken homes and high-conflict intact homes

           b.   worse off than children in low-conflict, intact families

      8.   family incompetence: children raised by parents who lack proper parents skills are at risk

      9.   delinquency will be reduced if parents provide the type of structure that integrates children into families, while giving them the ability to assert their individuality and regulate their own behavior.

G.   Focus on Delinquency

The Chicken or the Egg: Which comes first, bad kids or bad parents?

1. Huh's survey of 500 adolescent girls and found that children's misbehavior undermines parenting effectiveness, not that poor parenting was a direct cause of children's misbehavior.

2. Harris asserts that genetics and environment primarily determine how a child turns out.

H.   Family neglect

      1.   Parental efficacy key to delinquency prevention

      2.   Poor child-parent communications have been related to dysfunctional activities

      3.   strong attachment to parents helps youth resist delinquency.

      4.   family influence remains considerable throughout life

I.   Inconsistent discipline

      1.   parents of delinquent youths tend to be inconsistent disciplinarians

      2.   most Americans still support the use of corporal punishment

      3.   physical punishment weakens the bond between parents and children

      4.   lowers the children's self-esteem

      5.   undermines their faith in justice

      6.   abused children have a higher risk of neurological dysfunction

J.   Supervision

      1.   inconsistent supervision can promote delinquency

      2.   effective supervision can reduce children's involvement in delinquency

K.   Resource dilution

      1.   resources in large families may be spread too thin

      2.   relationship may be indirect

      3.   resource dilution may force some mothers into the workforce

      4.   working mothers are unable to adequately supervise their children

L. Family deviance
  1. parental deviance has a powerful influence on delinquent behavior
  2. the children of deviant parents produce delinquent children themselves
  3. Cambridge Youth Survey
     a. a significant number of delinquent youths have criminal fathers
     b. 8% of the sons of noncriminal fathers became chronic offenders
     c. 37% of youths with criminal fathers became delinquent
  4. genetic, environmental, psychological, and child-rearing are factors.
  5. substance abuse: children of drug abusing parents are more likely to get involved in drug abuse and delinquency
  6. parenting
     a deviant parents are the least likely to have close relationships with their offspring and are more likely to be overly harsh and inconsistent.
  6. sibling delinquency related to delinquency

III. Child Abuse And Neglect
  A. Historical foundation
     1. parental abuse and neglect is not a modern phenomenon
     2. child named Mary Ellen Wilson landmark case
     3. battered child syndrome nonaccidental injury of children by their parents
  B. Defining abuse and neglect
     1. Kempe's work expanded in a more generic expression of child abuse
     2. includes neglect and physical abuse
        a. any physical or emotional trauma to a child for which no reasonable explanation can be found
        c. generally seen as a pattern of behavior rather than a single act
     3. neglect refers to deprivations children suffer at the hands of their caregivers
     4. abuse is a more overt form of aggression against the child
     5. emotional abuse is manifested by constant criticism and rejection of the child
     6. abandonment when parents leave their children
        a. the intention of severing the parent-child relationship
     7. sexual abuse refers to the sexual exploitation of children
  C. Sexual abuse
     1. sexual abuse can vary in content and style
     2. abused children suffer disrupted ego and personality development
     3. correlation between the severity of abuse and its long-term effects

D. Extent of child abuse
  1. it is almost impossible to estimate the extent of child abuse
  2. many victims are so young that they have not learned to communicate
  3. groundbreaking 1980 survey by Gelles and Straus
     a. between 1.4 and 1.9 million children were subject to physical abuse
     b. average number of assaults per year was 10.5
  4. surveys conducted in 1985 and 1992
     a. incidence of severe violence toward children had declined
     b. parental approval of corporal punishment also decreased
E. Monitoring abuse
  1. DHHS conducts an annual survey of CPS agencies
  2. determine the number of reported child abuse victims
     a. three and a half million referrals
     b. 870,000 children were found to be victims of abuse or neglect
F. Who are the victims of abuse?
  1. younger children are the most likely to be abused and neglected
  2. 1,500 children die each year from abuse
G. Sexual abuse
  1. one in ten boys and one in three girls were victims of sexual exploitation
  2. 325,000 children are subjected to some form of sexual exploitation
  3. number of reported cases has been in significant decline
H. Causes of child abuse and neglect
  1. parents who themselves suffered abuse tend to abuse their own children
  2. the presence of an unrelated adult increases the risk of abuse
  3. isolated and alienated families tend to become abusive
  4. cyclical pattern of violence seems to be
  5. particularly acute in homes where there has been divorce or separation
  6. abusive punishment in single-parent homes double that of two -parent families
  7. parents who are unable to cope with stressful events are most at risk
I. Substance abuse
  1. strong association between child abuse and parental alcoholism
  2. significant relationship between cocaine and heroin abuse and neglect/abuse
J. Stepparents and abuse
  1. stepchildren share a greater risk for abuse than do biological offspring
  2. stepparents may have less emotional attachment to the children of another

3.   stepchildren are over-represented in cases of familicide

K.   Social class and abuse
1.   high rate of reported abuse and neglect among people in lower economic classes
2.   subject to greater environmental stress and have fewer resources
3.   stress on low-income parents is especially severe when children are handicapped

L.   Child protection system: philosophy And practice
1.   Parental rights
2.   courts assumed parents have the right to bring up their children as they see fit
3.   *Troxel v. Granville* (2000)
      a.   due process clause of the constitution
      b.   protects against government interference with certain rights
      c.   including parents' right to make decisions about their children
4.   rights of both parents and children are constitutionally protected
5.   USSC cases for abuse and neglect
      a.   *Lassiter v. Department of Social Services*
      b.   *Santosky v. Kramer*
      c.   child's right to be free from parental abuse
      d.   set down guidelines for a termination-of-custody hearing
      e.   right to legal representation
      f.   states provide a *guardian ad litem*
6.   In 1974 Congress passed the Child Abuse Prevention and Treatment Act (CAPTA)
      a.   provides funds for services for maltreated children and parents
7.   abusive parents are subject to prosecution

N.   Investigating and reporting abuse
1.   many states require selected occupations to report suspected cases
2.   many have made failure to report child abuse a criminal offense
3.   case is screened by an intake worker
4.   turned over to an investigative caseworker
5.   case may be referred to a law enforcement agency
6.   if child is in imminent danger of severe harm
      a.   caseworker may immediately remove the child from the home
      b.   court hearing must be held shortly after to approve custody
7.   most common reasons for screening out cases
      a.   the reporting party is involved in a child custody case
8.   an advisement hearing is held
      a.   court will review the facts of the case
      b.   determine whether permanent removal of the child is justified
      c.   notify the parents of the charges against them

<table>
<tr><td></td><td></td><td>d.</td><td colspan="2">parents have the right to counsel in all cases of abuse and neglect</td></tr>
</table>

                      d.   parents have the right to counsel in all cases of abuse and neglect

                      e.   many states require the court to appoint an attorney for the child

              9.   if the parents admit the allegations

                      a.   court enters a consent decree

                      b.   case is continued for disposition

                      c.   one-half of all cases are settled by admission at the advisement hearing

            10.   if the parents deny the petition

                      a.   an attorney is appointed for the child

                      b.   case is continued for a pretrial conference

            11.   at the pretrial conference

                      a.   attorney for the social service agency presents an overview

                      b.   admissibility of photos and written reports are settled

                      c.   attorneys can negotiate a settlement of the case

            12.   types of services that the child and the child's family will receive

                      a.   parenting classes

                      b.   mental health counseling

                      c.   substance abuse treatment

                      d.   family counseling

                      e.   reunification goals

O.   Process of state intervention in cases of abuse and neglect

            1.   most crucial part of an abuse or neglect proceeding is the disposition hearing

            2.   agreements are reached between parents and state

            3.   half to two-thirds of all convicted parents will serve time in incarceration

            4.   about one half of all cases are settled by admission at the advisement hearing

            5.   courts are guided by three interests

                      a.   role of the parents

                      b.   protection for the child

                      c.   responsibility of the state

                      d.   balancing-of-the-interests approach used to guide decisions

P.   Abused child in court

            1.   traumatic experience–children get confused and frightened and may change their testimony

            2.   controversy over the accuracy of children's reports

                      a.   McMartin Day Care case in California

            3.   procedures to minimize the trauma to the child

                      a.   allowing videotaped statements

             4.   states that allow videotaped testimony usually put some restrictions

                      a.   some prohibit the government from calling the child to testify at trial

                      b.   some require a finding that the child is medically

unavailable
5. states now allow a child's testimony to be given on CCTV
6. some states require a compelling need for CCTV testimony
7. some allow anatomically correct dolls to demonstrate happenings
   a. allowed when testifying in federal courts
8. physicians and mental health professionals testify about statements
   a. made to them by children
   b. children are incapable of testifying
Q. *White v. Illinois*
1. state's attorney is required neither to:
   a. produce young victims at trial
   b. nor to demonstrate the reason why they were unavailable to serve
2. White removed the requirement that prosecutors produce child victims in court
   a. testimony would prove too disturbing or where the victim is too young
R. *Coy v. Iowa*
1. victims of sexual or physical abuse often make poor witnesses
2. USSC placed limitations on efforts to protect child witnesses in court
3. Sixth Amendment grants defendants "face-to-face" confrontation with accusers
S. *Maryland v. Craig*
1. one-way CCTV testimony was used during the trial
2. Maryland statute that allows CCTV testimony is sufficient
   a. requires a determination that the child will suffer distress
   b. if forced to testify
   c. serve as the equivalent of in-court testimony
   d. would not interfere with the defendant's right to confront witnesses
T. Disposition of abuse and neglect cases
1. social service agents avoid removing children from the home whenever
2. placement of children in foster care is intended to be temporary
3. power to terminate the rights of parents over their children
U. Abuse, neglect, and delinquency
1. effects of child abuse are long-term
2. abused kids will experience mental and social problems across their life span
3. area of concern is the child's own personal involvement with violence
4. link between maltreatment and delinquency is focus of criminological theories
   a. social control theory and disrupting normal relationships
   b. social learning theory and teaching children aggressive

behavior

        c.   general strain theory and negative affective states

V.   Clinical histories

    1.   between 70 and 80% of juvenile offenders have abusive backgrounds

    2.   possible that angry parents attack their delinquent and drug-abusing children

        a.   child abuse is a result of delinquency, not its cause

W.   Cohort studies

    1.   children treated for abuse were disproportionately involved in violent offenses

    2.   Widom's research comparing abused and nonabused children

        a.   26% of the abused sample had juvenile arrests

        b.   17% of the comparison group had juvenile arrests

        c.   29% of those who were abused had adult criminal records

        d.   21% of the control group had adult criminal records

        e.   abused children were the most likely to get arrested for violent crimes

        f.   their violent crime arrest rate was double that of the control group

X.   Child victims and persistent offending

    1.   consequences of childhood victimization continue throughout life

    2.   abused children had a higher frequency of adult offending than the nonabused

    3.   sexually abused youths are more likely to suffer an arrest

Y.   Abuse-delinquency link

    1.   many delinquent youths come from what appear to be model homes

    2.   majority of both groups did not become delinquent

    3.   Ireland's research

        a.   link may be a function of when the abuse occurred

CHAPTER SUMMARY

Poor family relationships have been linked to juvenile delinquency. Early theories viewed the broken home as a cause of youthful misconduct, but subsequent research found that divorce and separation play a smaller role than was previously believed. However, contemporary studies now show that parental absence may have a significant influence on delinquency because it is more difficult for one parent to provide the same degree of discipline and support as two. The quality of family life also has a great influence on a child's behavior. Families in conflict produce more delinquents than those that function harmoniously. Families who neglect their children are at risk for delinquency. Inconsistent discipline and supervision have also been linked to juvenile crime. Parental and sibling misconduct is another factor that predicts delinquent behaviors.

Concern over the relationship between family life and delinquency has been heightened by reports of widespread child abuse. Cases of abuse and neglect have been found in every social class and racial group. It has been estimated that there are three and one half million reported cases of child abuse each year, of which almost one million are confirmed by child welfare investigators. Two factors are seen as causing child abuse. First, parents who themselves suffered abuse as children tend to abuse their own children. Second, isolated and alienated families tend to become abusive. Local, state, and federal governments have attempted to alleviate the problem of child abuse. All fifty states have statutes requiring that suspected cases of abuse be reported. There is a complex system of state intervention once allegations of child abuse are made. Thousands of youths are removed from their homes every year.

A number of studies have linked abuse to delinquency. They show that a disproportionate number of court-adjudicated youths had been abused or neglected. Although the evidence is not conclusive, the data suggest that a strong relationship exists between child abuse and delinquent behavior. To make it easier to prosecute abusers, the Supreme Court has legalized the use of closed-circuit TV in some cases. Most states allow children to use anatomically correct dolls when testifying in court.

KEY TERMS

nuclear family: A family unit composed of parents and their children; this smaller family structure is subject to great stress due to the intense, close contact between parents and children.

broken home: Home in which one or both parents is absent due to divorce or separation; children in such an environment may be prone to antisocial behavior.

blended families: Nuclear families that are the product of divorce and remarriage, blending one parent from each of two families and their combined children into one family unit.

intrafamily violence: An environment of discord and conflict within the family; children who grow up in dysfunctional homes often exhibit delinquent behaviors, having learned at a young age that aggression pays off.

resource dilution: A condition that occurs when parents have such large families that their resources, such as time and money, are spread too thin, causing lack of familial support and control.

battered child syndrome: Nonaccidental physical injury of children by parents or guardians.
child abuse: Any physical, emotional, or sexual trauma to a child, including neglecting to give proper care and attention, for which no reasonable explanation can be found.

neglect: Passive neglect by a parent or guardian, depriving children of food, shelter, health care, and love.

abandonment: Parents physically leave their children with the intention of completely severing the parent-child relationship.

familicide: Mass murders in which a spouse and one or more children are slain.

advisement hearing: A preliminary protective or temporary custody hearing in which the court will review the facts and determine whether removal of the child is justified and notify parents of the charges against them.

pretrial conference: The attorney for the social services agency presents an overview of the case, and a plea bargain or negotiated settlement can be agreed to in a consent decree.

parental efficacy: parents providing the type of structure that integrates children into families, while giving them the ability to assert their individuality and regulate their own behavior

disposition hearing: The social service agency presents its case plan and recommendations for care of the child and treatment of the parents, including incarceration and counseling or other treatment.

balancing-of-the-interests approach: Efforts of the courts to balance the parents' natural right to raise a child with the child's right to grow into adulthood free from physical abuse or emotional harm.

review hearings: Periodic meetings to determine whether the conditions of the case plan for an abused child are being met by the parents or guardians of the child.

hearsay: Out-of-court statements made by one person and recounted in court by another; such statements are generally not allowed as evidence except in child abuse cases wherein a child's statements to social workers, teachers, or police may be admissible.

SELF TEST QUESTIONS

MULTIPLE CHOICE

1. A nuclear families that is the product of divorce and remarriage is called a(n) _____ family.
    A. blended   C. extended
    B. dysfunctional   D. patriarchal

2. _____ is manifested by constant criticism and rejection of the child.
    A. physical abuse   C. emotional abuse
    B. physical neglect   D. abandonment

3. About _____ percent of African American children will experience parental separation or divorce before they reach age sixteen.
    A. 10   C. 40
    B. 25   D. 75

4. About _____ of mothers of school aged children are employed outside the home.
    A. one-quarter   C. three-quarters
    B. one-half   D. two-thirds

5. Siegel and Welsh note that fathers are spending _____ with their children on workdays than they did 20 years ago.
    A. less time   C. about the same time
    B. more time   D. almost no time

6. As many as _____ percent of European American children and ___ percent of African American children will experience parental separation or divorce before they reach age sixteen, and many of these children will experience multiple family disruptions over time.
    A. 40 and 77   B. 30 and 50
    B. 40 and 60   C. 45 and 65

7. Which of the following best describes the findings of F. Ivan Nye concerning parental supervision and delinquency?
    A. There is no association between parental supervision and delinquency.
    B. Greater the level of supervision the more likely parents are to uncover delinquency.
    C. The less parental supervision the youth receives the better socially adjusted they are.
    D. Mothers who threatened discipline but failed to carry it out produced delinquent kids.

8. Data from the Cambridge Youth Survey indicates that about 8 percent of the sons of noncriminal fathers became chronic offenders, compared to _____ percent of youths with criminal fathers.
>A. 6   C. 37
>B. 13   D. 63

9. Siegel and Welsh note that _____ % of low-income households with children which do not have a fully employed parent year round.
>A. 24   C. 45
>B. 33   D. 59

10. Which of the following was identified by Farrington as one type of parental deviance that appears to be inter-generational?
>A. stealing cars   C. bullying
>B. robbing banks   D. vandalism

11. According to the legend, who arranged for the removal of Mary Ellen Wilson from her abusive parents?
>A. Society for the Prevention of Cruelty to Children
>B. Society for the Prevention of Cruelty to Animals
>C. New York City's Child Protection Services
>D. a man known simply as Charley

12. According to Estes and Weiner, each year in the United States _____ children are subjected to some form of sexual exploitation, which includes sexual abuse, prostitution, use in pornography and molestation by adults.
>A. 4,500   C. 35,400
>B. 19,300   D. 325,000

13. _____ refers to any physical or emotional trauma to a child for which no reasonable explanation, such as an accident, can be found.
>A. child abuse   C. battered child syndrome
>B. child trauma   D. parental discipline

14. By disrupting normal relationships and impeding socialization, maltreatment reduces the social bond and frees individuals to become involved in deviance. This statement is best associated with _____.
>A. social control theory   C. general strain theory
>B. social learning theory   D. social disorganization theory

15. Maltreatment leads to delinquency because it teaches children that aggression and violence are justifiable forms of behavior. This statement is best associated with _____.
>A. social control theory   C. general strain theory
>B. social learning theory   D. social disorganization theory

16. Maltreatment creates the "negative affective states" that are related to strain, anger, and aggression. This statement is best associated with _____.
    A. social control theory
    B. social learning theory
    C. general strain theory
    D. social disorganization theory

17. Based on a 1980 survey, Gelles and Straus estimated that between _____ children in the United States were subject to physical abuse from their parents.
    A. 200,000 to 350,000
    B. 600,000 to 690,000
    C. 1.4 to 1.9 million
    D. 3.4 to 3.9 million

18. In _____, the Court ruled that CCTV could serve as the equivalent of in court testimony and would not interfere with the defendant's right to confront witnesses.
    A. *Jones v. Kentucky*
    B. *White v. Illinois*
    C. *Maryland v. Craig*
    D. *Kramer v. PA*

19. Attempts to determine the extent of sexual abuse indicate that perhaps 1 in 10 boys and 1 in _____ girls have been the victims of some form of sexual exploitation.
    A. 3
    B. 5
    C. 7
    D. 12

20. In reference to broken homes, the relationship to delinquency
    A. Is clear and consistent
    B. Depends on the nature of the family dynamics before and after the divorce
    C. Is spurious
    D. Has not yet been explored through valid studies.

21. In the 2000 case _____, the United States Supreme Court ruled that the due process clause of the Constitution protects against government interference with certain fundamental rights and liberty interests, including parents' fundamental right to make decisions concerning the care, custody, and control of their children.
    A. *Jones v. Kentucky*
    B. *White v. Illinois*
    C. *Courtright v. Pennsylvania*
    D. *Troxel v. Granville*

22. What did the cases of *Lassiter v. Department of Social Services* and *Santosky v. Kramer* involve?
    A. recognition of a child's right to be free from parental abuse
    B. the unrestrained authority of the state to intervene in families
    C. evidentiary standards of hearsay in child protection cases
    D. the legal nature of CCTV testimony

23. Some states have relaxed their laws of evidence to all out of court statements by the child to a social worker, teacher, or police officer to be used as evidence, such statements would otherwise be considered _____.
    A. tainted
    B. hearsay
    C. word of mouth
    D. perjured

24. _____ includes throwing, shooting, stabbing, burning, drowning, suffocating, biting, or deliberately disfiguring a child; the greatest number of injuries result from beatings.

      A. physical abuse   C. emotional abuse

      B. physical neglect   D. abandonment

25. _____ results from parents' failure to provide adequate food, shelter, or medical care for their children, as well as failure to protect them from physical danger.

      A. physical abuse   C. emotional abuse

      B. physical neglect   D. abandonment

26. Which of the following statements is false concerning divorce and delinquency?

      A. remarriage does not lessen the effects of divorce on youth

      B. postdivorce conflict between parents is related to child maladjustment

      C. continued contact with the noncustodial parent is strongly associated with less delinquency

      D. children living with a stepparent exhibit as many problems as youths in divorce

27. In explaining heightened rates of child abuse among stepchildren, Siegel and Welsh assert that

      A. step parents usually try to obtain finances set aside for the children

      B. step parents are usually innocent of any charges of abuse

      C. step parents have less emotional attachment to the step children

      D. there is no difference between abuse of natural and step children

28. In explaining higher levels of child abuse among low-income families, Siegel and Welsh point out that

      A. Child abuse statistics are generated by agencies that focus upon the poor, and therefore their statistics lack validity

      B. Heightened levels of abuse may result from heightened levels of stress caused by poverty

      C. We should not judge the use of violence among the lower classes, since it is unethical to judge other cultures.

      D. Sometimes children need to be physically disciplined, and the definition of abuse by Child Protective Services incorrectly identifies effective parenting as abuse.

29. According to Siegel and Welsh,

      A. Most states now allow a child's testimony to be given on closed circuit television

      B. All states now allow a child's testimony to be given on closed circuit television

      C. Federal law mandates that states allow a child's testimony to be given on closed circuit television

      D. CCTV prevents the accused from seeing the child.

30. In considering the potential effects of abuse, those who subscribe to Trait Theory
    A. consider how disruption of social bonds frees individuals to deviate from social norms
    B. examine how the victims of abuse model the behavior of the abusers
    C. focus upon the negative affective states such as anger and aggression that will result
    D. consider psychological abnormality as leading to antisocial behaviors.

TRUE FALSE

1. According to social control theory, maltreatment reduces the social bond and frees individuals to become involved in deviance by disrupting normal relationships and impeding socialization.
    A. True
    B. False

2. According to social learning theory, maltreatment creates the negative affective states that are related to strain, anger, and aggression.
    A. True
    B. False

3. According to general strain theory, maltreatment leads to delinquency because it teaches children that aggression and violence are justifiable forms of behavior.
    A. True
    B. False

4. According to Siegel and Welsh, studies of juvenile offenders have confirmed that between 70 and 80 percent may have had abusive backgrounds; many of these juveniles report serious injury, including bruises, lacerations, fractures, and being knocked unconscious by a parent or guardian.
    A. True
    B. False

5. According to Siegel and Welsh, larger families are more likely to produce delinquents than smaller ones, and middle children are more likely to engage in delinquent acts than first- or last-born children.
    A. True
    B. False

6. Farrington found that one type of parental deviance, bullying, may be both inter- and intragenerational; bullies have children who bully others, and these second-generation bullies grow up to become the fathers of children who are also bullies
    A. True
    B. False

7. According to Widom's research, 4 percent of older Black males who had suffered abuse went on to become adult criminals while only 67 percent of young, White, nonabused females became adult offenders.
    A. True
    B. False

8. According to Widom's research, 67 percent of older Black males who had suffered abuse went on to become adult criminals while only 4 percent of young, White, nonabused females became adult offenders.
    A. True
    B. False

9. Early theories viewed the broken home as a cause of youthful misconduct, but subsequent research found that divorce and separation play a smaller role than was previously believed.
    A. True
    B. False

10. According to social learning theory, maltreatment leads to delinquency by disrupting normal relationships and impeding socialization, maltreatment reduces the social bond and frees individuals to become involved in crime.
    A. True
    B. False

11. Attempts to determine the extent of sexual abuse indicate that perhaps 1 in 10 boys and 1 in 3 girls have been the victims of some form of sexual exploitation.
    A. True
    B. False

12. Research conducted in ten European countries shows that the degree to which parents and teachers approve of corporal punishment is related to the homicide rate.
    A. True
    B. False

13. The Victims of Child Abuse Act of 1990 allows children to use anatomically correct dolls to demonstrate happenings when testifying in federal court.
    A. True
    B. False

14. In the 1992 case Craig v Maryland the Court ruled that the state's attorney is not required to produce young victims at trial
    A. True
    B. False

15. As recent studies of more than four thousand youths in Denver, Pittsburgh, and Rochester found, the more often children are forced to go through family transitions the more likely they are to engage in delinquent activity.
    A. True
    B. False

16. About 20 percent of all children live in poverty and about 8 percent live in extreme poverty which is at least 50 percent below the poverty line.
    A. True
    B. False

17. Children growing up in families disrupted by parental death are better adjusted than children of divorce; parental absence is not a per se cause of antisocial behavior.
    A. True
    B. False

18. Remarriage lessens the effect of divorce on delinquency.
    A. True
    B. False

19. Research indicates that children growing up in homes with high levels of conflict were less socially adjusted than children growing up in broken homes.
    A. True
    B. False

20. Research indicates that children growing up in broken homes were less adjusted than children growing up homes with high levels of conflict.
    A. True
    B. False

21. It is clear that single-parent homes cause delinquency.
    A. True
    B. False

22. Isolated and alienated families have higher incidents of child abuse.
    A. True
    B. False

23. The McMartin Day Care case revealed that much of sexual abuse is repressed.
    A. True
    B. False

24. According to the text, in making decisions about dispositions in child abuse proceedings, cost is often a determinant factor
    A. True
    B. False

166

25. Fathers are now spending more time with children on workdays than they did 20 years ago and women are spending somewhat less time than they did 20 years ago.
　　　A. True
　　　B. False

FILL IN

1. _____ neglect includes inadequate nurturing, inattention to a child's emotional development, and lack of concern about maladaptive behavior.

2. Siegel and Welsh note that, according to legend, Mary Ellen's removal from her parents had to be arranged through the _____ on the ground that she was a member of the animal kingdom.

3. Parents may find it hard to control their children because they have such large families that their resources, such as time, are spread too thin; this concept is called

_____.

4. About _____ percent of all children live in poverty.

5. Strong _____ to a parent can prevent delinquency in any family structure.

6. As a recent study of more than four thousand youths in Denver, Pittsburgh, and Rochester found, the more often children are forced to go through family _____ the more likely they are to engage in delinquent activity.

7. Research conducted in ten European countries shows that the degree to which parents and teachers approve of _____ is related to the homicide rate.

8. The Victims of _____ Act of 1990 allows children to use anatomically correct dolls to demonstrate happenings when testifying in federal court

9. According to _____ theory, maltreatment reduces the social bond and frees individuals to become involved in deviance by disrupting normal relationships and impeding socialization.

10. According to _____ theory, maltreatment leads to delinquency because it teaches children that aggression and violence are justifiable forms of behavior.

11. According to _____ theory, maltreatment creates negative affective states that are related to anger and aggression.

12. The _____ philosophy of the juvenile court calls for official intervention when parental supervision is considered inadequate.

13. A _____ home is one in which one or both parents are absent due to divorce or separation.

14. A _____ family is a nuclear family that is the product or divorce and remarriage.

15. States have relaxed laws of evidence to allow out of court statements by a child, otherwise considered _____, to be used as evidence.

ESSAY

1. Describe parenting styles that can insulate a youth from delinquency while also producing a well-socialized adolescent.

2. Discuss the association between family size and delinquency. What are some reasons you would expect large families to have more delinquency? What are some reasons you would expect small families to have less delinquency?

3. How does General Strain Theory view the link between child abuse and delinquency?

4. What are some possible reasons to explain why juveniles are more likely to be delinquents if a sibling is delinquent?

5. What is the US Supreme Court's ruling on the use of CCTV in child abuse cases?

ANSWER KEY

MULTIPLE CHOICE ITEMS

1. A	11. B	21. D
2. C	12. D	22. A
3. D	13. A	23. B
4. C	14. A	24. A
5. B	15. B	25. B
6. A	16. C	26. C
7. D	17. C	27. C
8. C	18. C	28. B
9. B	19. A	29. A
10. C	20. B	30. D

TRUE FALSE ITEMS

1. T	11. T	21. F
2. F	12. T	22. T
3. F	13. T	23. F
4. T	14. T	24. F
5. T	15. T	25. T
6. T	16. T	
7. F	17. T	
8. T	18. F	
9. T	19. T	
10. F	20. F	

FILL IN ITEMS

1. emotional	11. general strain
2. SPCA	12. *parens patriae*
3. resource dilution	13. broken
4. 20	14. blended
5. attachment	15. hearsay
6. transitions	
7. corporal punishment	
8. Child Abuse	
9. social control	
10. social learning	

Multiple Choice

1. The authors connect the massive increase in employed mothers to
   A. immorality.
   B. drug use.
   C. changing economic structure of our society.
   D. radical feminists and their social agenda.

2. According to the text, about what percentage of day care providers are not regulated:
   A. 20
   B. 40
   C. 60
   D. 90

3. Mary Ellen
   A. was removed from the home on the ground that she was part of the animal kingdom.
   B. died two years after being removed from her biological parents.
   C. was placed in an orphanage.
   D. became a school teacher.

4. Sara Jaffee found that
   A. divorce doubles child abuse.
   B. latch-key kids are three times as likely to become delinquents.
   C. drugs and child abuse have reciprocal effects.
   D. whether children are better off if their parents divorce depends on the level of parental deviance.

5. Research on intra-family violence found that
   A. witnessing violence has similar effects as direct child abuse on youth.
   B. females are less likely to suffer from depression than males when abused.
   C. females are more likely to harm animals if abused than males who are abused.
   D. all of the above

6. According to the text, parental efficacy
   A. translates into effective frameworks and structures.
   B. is more of an art than a science and cannot be evaluated.
   C. is caused by class differences.
   D. has predominantly indirect effects on delinquency.

7. Huh found that
   A. children's behaviors are determined in the first year of life.
   B. difficult children influence parents' ability to parent.
   C. almost all of personality is determined by nurture, not nature.
   D. parents cannot significantly mitigate difficult child's behavior and trajectories in life.

171

8. According to the text, psychologists suggest that maltreatment encourages children
   A. to seek out deviant subcultures for comfort.
   B. to empathize with others.
   C. to use violence to solve their problems.
   D. to join religious cults in search of answers.

9. Parental use of physical punishment
   A. has been criminalized in most states in America in the last 20 years.
   B. has been rejected by organized religion.
   C. teaches self-reliance.
   D. can weaken the parent-child bond and model and justify violence.

10. According to the test, separation caused by parental imprisonment predicted antisocial behavior up to age
   A. 12.
   B. 17.
   C. 21.
   D. 32.

True/False

1. Most experts agree that parental influence on adolescents may be less than for younger children and may take a different form, but it remains robust. T F

2. In the 1992 White v Illinois case the Supreme Court ruled that the state's attorney is not required to produce young victims at trial T   F

3. Justice O'Connor dissented in the Maryland v Craig decision, stating that defendants had a right to physically confront their child accuser T F

4. Social control theories assert that the reason why youth in abusive homes have a greater chance of themselves becoming offenders is that they bond with their father or other abuser and learn their behavior   T   F

5. According to the text, pretrial conferences in child abuse can negotiate a settlement with a detailed treatment plan T F

Multiple Choice:

1. C
2. D
3. D
4. D
5. A
6. A
7. B
8. C
9. D
10. D

True False

1. T
2. T
3. F
4. F
5. T

CHAPTER EIGHT
PEERS AND DELINQUENCY: JUVENILE GANGS AND GROUPS

LEARNING OBJECTIVES

- Be familiar with the development of peer relations.
- Know the various views of peer group cohesiveness.
- Be able to define the concept of the gang.
- Be familiar with the history of gangs.
- Know the nature and extent of gang activity.
- Recognize the various types of gangs.
- Understand how gangs are structured.
- Be familiar with the racial and ethnic makeup of gangs.
- Discuss the various theories of gang development.
- Know how police departments are undertaking gang prevention and suppression

CHAPTER OUTLINE

Luis's Story
   1. Luis is a 16 -year old Latino male who identified himself as involved in a gang.
   2. Luis is charged with substantial battery and resisting arrest.
   3. He has a history of truancy and nonviolent offenses.
   4. Luis lives with his mother and three younger siblings
   5. Luis is referred to a correctional facility, but the order is stayed pending his entering treatment. In treatment Luis attends programs to maintain sobriety, learn anger management, prevent gang involvement, and address criminal thinking concerns.
   6. Luis successfully completed the program, the order to send him to a correctional facility was not invoked, and he was not arrested again as a juvenile.

I.   Adolescent Peer Relations
   A.   Adolescent peer relations
      1.   parents are primary source of influence in children's early years
      2.   between ages 8 and 14 children seek out a stable peer group
      3.   friends begin to have a greater influence over decision making than parents
      4.   children form cliques
         a.   small groups of friends who share activities and confidences
      5.   they belong to crowds
         a.   loosely organized groups of children who share interests and activities

6. acceptance by peers has a major impact on socialization
7. some juveniles are controversial status youth
 a. aggressive kids
 b. either highly liked or intensely disliked by their peers
8. peer relations are a significant aspect of maturation

B. Peer relations and delinquency
 1. peer group relationships are closely tied to delinquent behaviors
  a. delinquent acts tend to be committed in small groups rather than alone
  b. process referred to as co-offending
  c. inadequate peer relations associated with delinquency
  d. delinquent friends also linked to antisocial behavior and drug abuse
 2. boys who go through puberty at an early age
  a. more likely to later engage in violence, property crimes, and drugs
  b. more likely to engage in precocious sexual behavior
  c. most likely to develop strong attachments to delinquent friends

C. Impact of peer relations
 1. birds of a feather flock together
  a. control theory approach
  b. delinquents are detached from their peers
  c. detached from other elements of society
  d. antisocial youths seek out like-minded peers for criminal associations
 2. delinquent friends cause law-abiding youth to get in trouble
  a. youths fall in with a bad crowd
 3. antisocial youths join up with like-minded friends
  a. deviant peers sustain and amplify delinquent careers
 4. troubled kids choose delinquent peers out of necessity rather than desire
 5. loyalty to delinquent friends is associated with delinquency
 6. delinquents report caring and trust in their peer relations

II. Youth Gangs
A. What are gangs?
 1. gangs are groups of youths who engage in delinquent behaviors
 2. gang delinquency differs from group delinquency
 3. gangs involve long-lived institutions
  a. distinct structure and organization
  b. identifiable leadership, division of labor, rules, rituals, and possessions
 4. gangs are seen as an interstitial group
  a. one falling within the cracks and crevices of society
  b. maintains standard group processes

5.   Klein argues that two factors stand out in all definitions
       a.   members have self-recognition of their gang status
       b.   there is a commitment to criminal activity

B.   How did gangs develop?
   1.   gangs have been reported in several other nations
   2.   gangs are not a recent phenomenon
   3.   in 1920s, Thrasher initiated the study of the modern gang
       a.   analysis of more than thirteen hundred youth groups in Chicago
       b.   gangs linked to an interstitial area
       c.   groups become more solidified through conflict with authorities
       d.   gang is not a haven for disturbed youths
       e.   viewed as an alternative lifestyle for normal boys
   4.   National Youth Gang Center defined gangs
       a.   self-formed association of peers having the following characteristics:
       b.   three or more members, generally ages twelve to twenty-four
       c.   a gang name and some sense of identity
       d.   generally indicated by symbols
       e.   some degree of permanence and organization
       f.   elevated level of involvement in delinquent or criminal activity

C.   Gangs in the 1950s and 1960s
   1.   threat of gangs and violence swept the public consciousness
   2.   movies and Broadway musicals romanticized violent gangs
   3.   by the mid-1960s, the gang menace seemed to have disappeared
       a.   police gang-control units infiltrated gangs
       b.   increase in political awareness that developed during the 1960s
       c.   many gang members were drafted
       d.   gang members became active users of heroin and other drugs

D.   Gangs reemerge
   1.   interest in gang activity began anew in the early 1970s
   2.   275 police-verified gangs with 11,000 members in 1975
   3.   involvement in the sale of illegal drugs
   4.   natural consequence of the economic and social
   5.   media fell in love with gang images

E.   Why did gangs reemerge?
   1.   involvement in sale of drugs
   2.   natural consequence of economic and social disorganization
   3.   media fell in love with gang images

III.   Contemporary Gangs
    A.   Extent
        1.   youth gangs are active in over 2,900 jurisdictions
        2.   over 90% of large cities reported gang
        3.   estimated 24,000 gangs containing about 760,000 gang members
        4.   significant number of youths are now or have been gang members
    B.   Location
        1.   15,000 gangs with 300,000 members located in small cities and suburbs
        2.   gangs have operated in transitional neighborhoods
        3.   areas eventually evolve into permanently disorganized neighborhoods
        4.   growth of gangs in suburbs attributed to a restructuring of the population
        5.   massive movement of people out of the central city
        6.   downtown areas have undergone extensive renewal
            a.   there are few residential areas and thus few adolescent recruits
            b.   there is intensive police patrol
    C.   Migration
        1.   gangs in some areas have relocated or migrated
        2.   most recent NYGS found many jurisdictions have experienced gang migration, and in a few areas more than half of all gang members had come from other areas.
        3.   20% of gang members were migrants from another jurisdiction
        4.   700 U.S. cities have experienced some form of gang migration in the last ten years
        5.   most common reason for migrating is personal and social
            a.   family relocation causes gang boys to move or stay with relatives
        6.   most migrators are African-American or Hispanic males
            a.   maintain close ties with members of their original gangs
            b.   some migrants join local gangs, shedding old friends
        7.   most gangs actually are homegrown
    D.   Types
        1.   Fagan found that most gangs fall into one of these four categories
            a.   social gang
            b.   party gang
            c.   serious delinquent gang
            d.   organized gang
    E.   Cohesion
        1.   definition of a gang implies that it is a cohesive group
        2.   some experts refer to gangs as near-groups
            a.   limited cohesion
            b.   impermanence
            c.   minimal consensus of norms

                    d.   shifting membership
                    e.   disturbed leadership
                    f.   limited definitions of membership expectations
            3.   Vigil identified different types of Latino barrio gang members
                    a.   regular members
                    b.   peripheral
                    c.   temporary
                    d.   situational
    F. Age
            1.   ages of gang members range widely
            2.   time line
                    a.   youths first hear about gangs at around nine years of age
                    b.   get involved in violence at ten or eleven
                    c.   join their first gang at twelve
            3.   gang members are getting older
                    a.   loss of relatively high-paid, low-skilled factory jobs
                    b.   inability of inner-city males to obtain adequate jobs
                    c.   cannot afford to marry and raise families
                    d.   criminal records lock these youths out of the job market
            4.   Hagedorn identified four types of adult gang members:
                    a.   legits
                    b.   dope fiends
                    c.   new jacks
                    d.   homeboys
    G. Gender
            1.   gangs were considered a male-dominated enterprise
            2.   number of female gang members and female gangs is rapidly
                    increasing
            3.   less than 10% of the gang members are female
            4.   liberation view
                    a.   sense of sisterhood
                    b.   independence
                    c.   solidarity
                    d.   chance to earn profit through illegal activities
            5.   social injury view
                    a.   female members are still sexually exploited by male gang
                            boys
                    b.   males also play a divisive role in the girls relationships
            6.   most girls join gangs in an effort to cope with their turbulent
                    personal lives
            7.   female gang membership did have some benefits
                    a.   protected females from sexual assault by nongang men
    H. Formation
            1.   gang formation involves a sense of territoriality
            2.   most gang members live in close proximity to one another

3.   Moore's research on klikas
      a.   remain together as unique groups with separate identities
      b.   have more intimate relationships among themselves
      c.   can expand by including members' kin

I.   Leadership
1.   gangs tend to be small and transitory
2.   group roles can vary
3.   Klein observed that many gang leaders deny leadership

J.   Communications
1.   gangs seek recognition, both from their rivals and from the community
2.   major source of communication is graffiti
3.   gangs also communicate by means of a secret vocabulary
4.   representing
      a.   flashing gang signs in the presence of rivals
      b.   often escalates into a verbal or physical confrontation
      c.   in some areas, gang members were jackets with their gang name or certain articles of clothing

K.   Ethnic and racial composition
1.   nearly half of all gang members are Hispanic/Latino
2.   about one-third are African American/Black
3.   10% are Caucasian/White
4.   6% are Asian and other races
5.   most intergang conflict is among groups of the same ethnicity
6.   African-American Gangs
      a.   Boozies formed in 1920s
      b.   Crips gang was formed in the 1970s in Los Angeles
      c.   Crips and Bloods membership exceeds 25,000 youths
      d.   Chicago's Blackstone Rangers from 1960s to early 1990s
      e.   Black Gangster Disciples are now the dominant gang in Chicago
7.   Hispanic gangs
      a.   gang culture is relatively popular
      b.   gangs frequently use initiation
      c.   hispanic gangs have a fixed leadership hierarchy
      d.   hispanic gang members are known for their dress codes
      e.   members mark off territory with graffiti
      f.   hispanic gangs have a strong sense of turf
8.   Asian gangs
      a.   reliance on making money through extortion
      b.   Asian gangs tend to victimize members of their own ethnic group
      c.   recruit new members from disaffected youths with problems in school
      d.   distrust of outside authorities

9. Anglo Gangs
    a. many are derivatives of English punk and skinhead movement of 1970s
    b. white gang members are often alienated middle-class youths
    c. get involved in devil worship, tattoo themselves with occult symbols, and gauge their bodies to draw blood for rituals

L. Criminality and violence
  1. gang members typically commit more crimes than any other group of youths
  2. gang criminality has numerous patterns
  3. the gang–crime association theory.
Thornberry et al.'s data:
    a. only 30% of the youths report being gang members
    b. accounted for 65% of all reported delinquent acts

M. Gang violence
  1. gang members are heavily armed and dangerous
  2. gang members were about ten times more likely to carry
  3. gang violence is impulsive and therefore comes in spurts
  4. violence is a core fact of gang formation and life

N. Revenge, honor, courage, and prestige
  1. gang members are sensitive to any rivals who question their honor
  2. violence is used to maintain the gang's internal discipline
  3. turf tax or extortion is common gang crime

IV. Why Do Youths Join Gangs?
A. Anthropological view
  1. gangs appeal to adolescents' longing for the tribal process
  2. gang processes do seem similar to the puberty rites of some tribal cultures
  3. active gang members whose parents are also active members
  5. rituals of initiation show that the boy is ready to leave his matricentric home

B. Social disorganization/sociocultural view
  1. destructive sociocultural forces in poor inner-city areas
  2. dysfunctional and destitute families and lacked adequate role models
  3. gang members pushed into membership because of poverty and minority status
  4. gangs are a natural response to lower-class life
  5. gangs provide a status-generating medium for boys
  6. youths are encouraged to join gangs during periods of anomie
    a. can include immigration or emigration
    b. rapidly expanding or contracting populations
    c. incursion of different racial/ethnic groups

C. Psychological view
1. gangs serve as an outlet for disturbed youths who
   a. suffer a multitude of personal problems and deficits
2. many suffer from a variety of personal deficits including
   a. low self-concept
   b. social deficits
   c. poor impulse control
   d. limited life skills
D. Rational choice view
1. some youths may make a rational choice to join a gang
2. turn to gangs as a method of obtaining desired goods and services
3. gang membership is not a necessary precondition for delinquency
4. substance abuse and delinquency no higher than those of nongang members
5. crime and drug abuse rates increase while youths are in gangs
6. gangs facilitate criminality rather than provide a haven for disturbed youths
E. Personal safety view
1. rational calculation to achieve safety
2. fear being harassed or attacked if they remain unaffiliated
3. gang members are more likely to be attacked than nonmembers
F. Fun and support view
1. some youths join gangs simply to have fun
2. some youths join gangs in an effort to obtain a family-like atmosphere

V. Controlling Gang Activity
A. Law enforcement efforts
1. youth services programs
   a. traditional police personnel from the youth unit
   b. given responsibility for gang control
2. gang details
   a. one or more police officers, usually from youth or detective units
   b. assigned exclusively to gang-control work
3. gang units
   a. established solely to deal with gang problems
   b. one or more officers are assigned exclusively to gang -control work
B. National assessment
4. one in four law enforcement agencies with a gang problem now operate a gang unit, including more than half of larger cities.
5. Chicago Police Department's gang crime section
   a. maintains intelligence on gang problems
   b. trains its more than 400 officers to deal with gang problems
6. some police departments engage in "gang-breaking" activities

C.   Community control efforts
    1.   social workers of the YMCA worked with youths in Chicago gangs
    2.   during the 1950s, the detached street worker program was developed
        a.   social workers went into the community to work with gangs on their own turf
        b.   participated in gang activities and tried to get to know their members
        c.   purpose was to
            i.   act as advocates for the youths
            ii.   provide them with positive role models
            iii.   treat individual problems
    3.   today's programs employ recreation areas open in the evening hours
        a.   provide supervised activities
    4.   coordinating groups help orient gang-control efforts
    5.   some community efforts are partnerships with juvenile justice agencies
    6.   involve schools in gang-control programs
D.   Elements of Spergel's Community Gang Control Program
    1.   community mobilization
    2.   provision of academic, economic, and social opportunities
    3.   social intervention
    4.   gang suppression
    5.   organizational change and development

F.   Why gang control is difficult
    1.   heavy-handed approaches can lead to abuse.
        Los Angeles's Community Resources Against Street Hoodlums (CRASH) anti-gang unit reduced gang activity but used excessive Force, was corrupt, and violated civil rights.
    2.   hundreds of thousands of high-paying jobs are needed
    3.   the more embedded youths become in criminal enterprise
        a.   the less likely they are to find meaningful adult work
        b.   unlikely they can suddenly be transformed into effective workers
    4.   social causes demand social solutions

CHAPTER SUMMARY

Peer relations are a critical element of maturation. Many experts believe that maintaining delinquent friends is a significant cause of antisocial behaviors. Some experts believe that criminal kids seek each other out. Gangs are law-violating youth groups that use special vocabulary, clothing, signs, colors, graffiti, and names, and whose members are committed to antisocial behavior. Gangs are a serious problem in many cities.

Gangs have been around since the eighteenth century. The gang problem died down for a while in the 1960s, then reemerged in the 1970s. There are now thousands of gangs containing an estimated 760,000 members. Most gang members are male and live in urban areas. Whereas most gang members used to be 14-21 years of age, gang members are getting older and the majority of them are now legal adults. Gangs can be classified by their structure, behavior, or status. Some are believed to be social groups, others are criminally oriented, and still others are violent. Hundreds of thousands of crimes are believed to be committed annually by gangs. Although some gangs specialize in drug dealing, gang kids engage in a wide variety of criminal offenses. Violence is an important part of being a gang member.

Although most gang members are male, the number of females in gangs is growing at a faster pace. African-American and Hispanic gangs predominate, but Anglo and Asian gangs are also quite common. We are still not sure what causes gangs. One view is that they serve as a bridge between adolescence and adulthood when adult control is lacking. Another view suggests that gangs serve as an alternative means of advancement for disadvantaged youths. Still another view is that some gangs are havens for disturbed youths.

KEY TERMS

cliques: Small groups of friends who share intimate knowledge and confidences.

crowds: Loosely organized groups who share interests and activities.

controversial status youth: Aggressive kids who are either highly liked or intensely disliked by their peers and who are the ones most likely to become engaged in antisocial behavior.

gang: Group of youths who collectively engage in delinquent behaviors.

interstitial group: Delinquent group that fills a crack in the social fabric and maintains standard group practices.

disorganized neighborhood: Inner-city areas of extreme poverty where the critical social control mechanisms have broken down.

near-groups: Clusters of youth who, outwardly, seem unified but actually have limited cohesion, impermanence, minimal consensus of norms, shifting membership, disturbed leadership, and limited definitions of membership expectations.

barrio: A Latino word meaning neighborhood.

klikas: Subgroups of same-aged youths in Hispanic gangs that remain together and have separate names and a unique identity in the gang.

graffiti: Inscriptions or drawings made on a wall or structure and used by delinquents for gang messages and turf definition.

representing: Tossing or flashing gang signs in the presence of rivals, often escalating into a verbal or physical confrontation.

skinhead: Member of White supremacist gang, identified by a shaved skull and Nazi or Ku Klux Klan markings.

prestige crimes: Stealing or assaulting someone to gain prestige in the neighborhood; often part of gang initiation rites.

detached street workers: Social workers who go out into the community and establish close relationships with juvenile gangs with the goal of modifying gang behavior to conform to conventional behaviors and help gang members get jobs and educational opportunities.

MULTIPLE CHOICE

1. According to _____ theorists, delinquents are as detached from their peers as they are from other elements of society; while delinquent youths may acknowledge that they have friends, their actual personal relationships are cold and exploitive.
    A. control   C. learning
    B. strain   D. conflict

2. An interstitial group_____.
    A. falls within the cracks and crevices of society
    B. lacks cohesive bonds
    C. by definition is an organized gang
    D. has no true bourndaries

3. _____ involves long-lived, complex institutions that have a distinct structure and organization, including identifiable leadership, division of labor, rules, rituals, and possessions.
    A. Gang delinquency   C. Cohort delinquency
    B. Group delinquency   D. Pluralistic offending

4. _____ consists of a short-lived alliance created to commit a particular crime or engage in a random violent act.
    A. Gang delinquency   C. Cohort delinquency
    B. Group delinquency   D. Pluralistic offending

5. According to _____, a gang is any denotable adolescent group of youngsters who are generally perceived as a distinct aggregation by others in their neighborhood; and recognize themselves as a denotable group
    A. Thrasher   C. Klein
    B. Short   D. Miller

6. What view of gang members does Lewis Yablonsky ascribe to?
    A. gangs are a result of blocked opportunities
    B. gangs are a rite of passage
    C. gangs are a means for the poor to integrate into the economic structure
    D. gangs are outlets for youth with a multitude of personal problems and deficits

7. Strength or power is frequently asserted through the use of the term _____, which means to rule, and *controllo*, indicating that the gang controls the area.
    A. *rifa*   C. *loco*
    B. *wiffa*   D. *por vida*

8. Fagan described this type of gang as being involved in few delinquent activities and little drug use other than alcohol and marijuana; membership is more interested in the social aspects of group behavior.

A. social   C. serious

B. party   D. organized

9. Fagan described this type of gang as concentrating on drug use and sales, while forgoing most delinquent behavior except vandalism; drug sales are designed to finance members' personal drug use.

A. social   C. serious

B. party   D. organized

10. What does it mean when gang graffiti is crossed out?

A. The writer made a mistake.

B. The police are trying to get kids mad.

C. The youth is no longer in the gang.

D. The territory is disputed by gangs.

11. A _____ are subgroups of same-aged youths in Hispanic gangs that remain together and have separate names and unique identity within the gang.

A. klikas   C. banditos

B. cholo   D. barrio

12. Siegel and Welsh note that movies such as *The Wild Ones* and *Blackboard Jungle* were made about gangs, and the Broadway musical (and later movie) _____ romanticized violent gangs.

A. *West Side Story*   C. *American Me*

B. *Colors*   D. *A Bronx Tale*

13. Fagan described the _____ as one heavily involved in criminality and drug use and sales; drug use and sales reflect a systemic relationship with other criminal acts.

A. social   C. serious

B. party   D. organized

14. The text mentions the alienation thesis of gang affiliation in reference to

A. Hispanic gangs

B. contemporary gangs in Germany

C. Asian gangs

D. African American gangs

15. In their early work, Richard Cloward and Lloyd Ohlin recognized that some gangs specialized in violent behavior, others were _____ whose members actively engaged in substance abuse, and a third type were criminal.

A. retreatists   C. rebels

B. anarchists   D. innovators

16. Los Angeles' CRASH unit
    A. did not reduce gang activity
    B. violated citizens' civil rights
    C. followed departmental standard operating procedures
    D. is still in existence, although under greater monitoring by Chief Bratton's office

17. William Julius Wilson contends that older members are still active to some degree in gangs because _____.
    A. young adults choose gang life over conventional roles
    B. older gang members are forced to remain through fear and intimidation
    C. they occupy lucrative leadership roles in the gang
    D. inability of inner-city males to obtain adequate employment

18. What gang prevention approach would be most effective according to the Social Disorganization view of gang formation?
    A. psychological counseling
    B. drug counseling
    C. pre-natal screening
    D. community economic development

19. Block and Niederhoffer contend that marks, uniforms, tattoos, and hazing as an initiation ritual support the _____ view of gang membership.
    A. psychological   C. anthropological
    B. rational choice   D. social disorganization

20. The _____ perspective assumes that gangs are a natural and normal response to the privations of lower-class life and that gangs are a status-generating medium for boys whose aspirations cannot be realized by legitimate means.
    A. psychological   C. anthropological
    B. rational choice   D. social disorganization

21. The Rochester Youth Development Study found that gang members account for what percentage of serious delinquent acts?
    A. 46 percent
    B. 56 percent
    C. 76 percent
    D. 86 percent

22. In Los Angeles and Chicago, the most gang-populated cities in the USA, gangs account for how many homicides?
    A. one quarter
    B. one third
    C. over half
    D. three quarters

23. The most dangerous spots in the Rochester study were found to be
    A. near bus terminals.
    B. along disputed borders where a drug spot intersects with a turf hot spot.
    C. where marauders travel to enemy territory in search of victims.
    D. in parks and underpasses.

24. The 2001 the National Youth Gang Survey found that the race/ethnicity composition of gangs is as follows: about half of all gang members are _____.
    A. Hispanic/Latino   C. Asian
    B. African American   D. white, non Hispanic

25. Admission to a Hispanic gang usually involves an initiation ritual in which boys are required to prove their _____; the most common test requires novices to fight several established members or to commit some crime, such as a robbery.
    A. machismo   C. verbal reasoning
    B. bravado   D. pain tolerance

26. The _____ are now the dominant gang(s) in Chicago; its members are actively involved in politics and have extensive ownership of legitimate private businesses.
    A. Siegel's Marauders   C. Dead Rabbits
    B. Gangster Disciples and Latin Kings D. Crips and Bloods

27. In Los Angeles, the first black youth gang formed in the 1920s was the _____.
    A. Boozies   C. Stantons
    B. Wilsons   D. Williamsons

28. When gang members toss or flash signs to proclaim their gang membership, this is called _____.
    A. fronting   C. badging
    B. passing   D. representing

29. _____ occur when a gang youth steals or assaults someone, even a police officer, to gain prestige in the gang and neighborhood; these crimes may be part of an initiation right or an effort to establish a special reputation or to respond to a challenge.
    A. Double dog dare syndromes   C. Prestige crime
    B. Gang hazing   D. Status booster offenses

30. The selection hypothesis explaining the association of gang membership and delinquency holds that
    A. kids with a history of crime and violence join gangs and maintain their delinquency.
    B. gang membership facilitates deviant behavior because it provides the structure and group support for antisocial behaviors.
    C. selection and facilitation work interactively increasing criminality.
    D. none of the above

TRUE/FALSE

1. According to social control theorists, delinquents are as detached from their peers as they are from other elements of society.
 A. True
 B. False

2. According to social learning theorists, delinquents are as detached from their peers as they are from other elements of society.
 A. True
 B. False

3. Learning theorists view the delinquency experience as one marked by close peer group support; they link delinquency to the rewards gained by associating with like-minded youth and being influenced by peer pressure.
 A. True
 B. False

4. Social control theorists view the delinquency experience as one marked by close peer group support; they link delinquency to the rewards gained by associating with like-minded youth and being influenced by peer pressure.
 A. True
 B. False

5. Siegel and Welsh note that today, American White gang members are often alienated middle-class youths, rather than poor lower-class youths.
 A. True
 B. False

6. In the United States, gangs first appeared in the 1960s in Los Angeles.
 A. True
 B. False

7. Most gangs are racially and ethnically heterogeneous.
 A. True
 B. False

8. Most gangs are racially and ethnically homogeneous.
 A. True
 B. False

9. One aspect of Spergel's Community Gang Control Program includes community mobilization, including citizens, youth, community groups, and agencies.
 A. True
 B. False

10. One aspect of Spergel's Community Gang Control Program is the provision of academic, economic, and social opportunities.
   A. True
   B. False

11. Two types of areas are identified as gang-prone: the transitional neighborhood and the middle class suburb.
   A. True
   B. False

12. Regardless of their type, gang members typically commit more crimes than any other youths in the social environment; gang membership enhances any pre-existing propensity to commit crime.
   A. True
   B. False

13. According to the anthropological view, gang processes and functions seem similar to the puberty rites of some tribal cultures; gangs help the child bridge the gap between childhood and adulthood.
   A. True
   B. False

14. Although many youths join gangs for personal protection, gang members are more likely to be victimized than non-gang members.
   A. True
   B. False

15. According to the text gang affiliation has increased in the last 5 years.
   A. True
   B. False

16. The number one reason cited for females leaving gangs is getting married.
   A. True
   B. False

17. The number of migrants is relatively small in proportion to the overall gang population, supporting the contention that most gangs are actually homegrown.
   A. True
   B. False

18. The number of migrant gang members is relatively large in proportion to the overall gang population, supporting the contention that most gangs are branch offices or satellites of larger established gangs.
   A. True
   B. False

19. Recent data indicates that about ninety percent of all gang members are male.
   A. True
   B. False

20. The detached street worker program was developed in major centers of gang activity; social workers went into the community to work with gangs on their own turf, and they participated in gang activities and tried to get to know their members.
   A. True
   B. False

21. Malcolm Klein argues that two factors stand out in all definitions of "gang": there is an official rulebook for all members to follow and a set schedule of face-to-face meetings.
   A. True
   B. False

22. Siegel and Welsh note that, by the mid 1960s, the gang menace seemed to have disappeared.
   A. True
   B. False

23. Recent data reveal that an estimated 24,000 gangs containing about 760,000 gang members were active in the United States.
   A. True
   B. False

24. The standard definition of a gang implies that it is a near-group.
   A True
   B. False

25. By age thirteen, most gang members have (a) fired a pistol, (b) seen someone killed or seriously injured, (c) gotten a gang tattoo, and (d) been arrested.
   A. True
   B. False

FILL IN

1. Reviews of the research show that delinquent acts tend to be committed in small groups, rather than alone; a process called _____.

2. According to _____ theorists, delinquents are as detached from their peers as they are from other elements of society.

3. _____ theorists view the delinquency experience as one marked by close peer group support; they link delinquency to the rewards gained by associating with like-minded youth and being influenced by peer pressure.

4. In the 1600's the city of _____ was terrorized by organized gangs, who called themselves Hectors, Bugles, and Dead Boys.

5. _____ are subgroups of same-aged youths in Hispanic gangs that remain together and have separate names and a unique identity in the gang.

6. According to _____, a gang is any denotable adolescent group of youngsters who are generally perceived as a distinct aggregation by others in their neighborhood; recognize themselves as a denotable group; and have been involved in a number of delinquent incidents.

7. The text points out that many _____ gang members are not from the lower class, but are alienated or anomic middle class youth

8. Thrasher called a group that develops in the cracks and crevices of society an_____ group.

9. _____ refers to inscriptions or drawings made on a wall or structure and used by delinquents for gang messages and turf definition.
10. Fagan described the _____ gang as one concentrating on drug use and sales, while forgoing most delinquent behavior except vandalism; drug sales are designed to finance members' personal drug use.

11. Fagan described the _____ gang as one heavily involved in criminality and drug use and sales; drug use and sales reflect a systemic relationship with other criminal acts.

12. The _____ program was developed in major centers of gang activity; social workers went into the community to work with gangs on their own turf, and they participated in gang activities and tried to get to know their members.

13. A _____ is a member of White supremacist gang, identified by a shaved skull and/or Nazi or Ku Klux Klan markings.

14. According to the _____ view, gangs appeal to adolescents' longing for the tribal process that sustained their ancestors; gang rituals help the child bridge the gap between childhood and adulthood.

15. Most gangs are racially and ethnically _____.

ESSAY

1. What explanations are provided by the authors to account for the reemergence of gangs after their decline in the 1960's? Which sound most plausible?

2. Describe Fagin's gang taxonomy.

3. Summarize the social disorganizational/sociocultural view of why youths join gangs.

4. Summarize the psychological view of why youths join gangs.

5. How does Spergel's Community Gang Control paradigm incorporate law enforcement and community control efforts to reduce gangs?

ANSWER KEY

MULTIPLE CHOICE

1. A	11. A	21. D
2. B	12. A	22. C
3. A	13. D	23. B
4. B	14. B	24. A
5. C	15. A	25. A
6. A	16. B	26. B
7. A	17. D	27. A
8. A	18. D	28. D
9. B	19. C	29. C
10. D	20. D	30 A

TRUE FALSE

1. T	11. F	21. F
2. F	12. T	22. T
3. T	13. T	23. T
4. F	14. T	24. F
5. T	15. F	25. T
6. F	16. T	
7. F	17. T	
8. T	18. F	
9. T	19. F	
10. T	20. T	

FILL IN

1. co-offending	11. organized
2. social control	12. detached street worker
3. learning	13. skinhead
4. London	14. anthropological
5. klikas	15. homogenous
6. Klein	
7. Anglo	
8. interstitial	
9. graffiti	
10. party	

Multiple Choice:

1. According to the text, boys who mature early
   A. become loners.
   B. are more likely to develop strong attachments to delinquent friends.
   C. are more likely to join school activities and excel in athletics.
   D. none of the above

2. Which theorist described delinquent peer relations as only appearing to be close, but in fact explained by the phrase "birds of a feather flock together?"
   A. Richard Cloward
   B. Lloyd Ohlin
   C. Albert Cohen
   D. Travis Hirschi

3. Approximately how many gang members live in small cities, suburban, and rural areas?
   A. 300,000
   B. 400,000
   C. 500,000
   D. 600,000

4. Which gang which has its origins in Latin America and has been classified by some experts as the nation's most dangerous gang?
   A. Mexican Mafia
   B. Columbian Mafia
   C. MS-13
   D. 18th street gang

5. A gang which lacks cohesion, permanence, with minimal consensus of norms, shifting membership, disturbed leadership, and limited definitions of membership expectations could be described as a(n)
   A. neighborhood association.
   B. near group.
   C. guild.
   D. interstitial group.

6. Why are gang members getting older?
   A. greater spending on social spending by the federal government
   B. drug use prevents them from going to college and getting jobs
   C. the loss of manufacturing and other low-skilled jobs.
   D. increased child abuse has destroyed their autonomy

7. _____ noted that music has had a strong influence on gangs in the US and abroad.
   A. Hagedorn

B. Klein
C. Spergel
D. Thrasher

8. Gangs usually migrate
    A. to sell drugs to new customers.
    B. to avoid law enforcement.
    C. to maintain contacts with others.
    D. to support terrorism.

9. MS-13 original members originated in
    A. El Salvador.
    B. Mexico.
    C. The former Soviet Union.
    D. Columbia.

10. Which of the following is not true about gangs?
    A. Violence and crime is an important component of gang life.
    B. Although some gangs specialize in drug dealing, gang members engage in a
    variety of criminal offenses.
    C. most researchers agree that gangs are havens for disturbed youth.
    D. most research on gangs has concentrated on poor communities.

True False:

1. Law enforcement gang details include one or more police officers assigned exclusively
    to gang-control work.
        A. True
        B. False

2. Rational choice theory considers gang membership a sign of lack of rationality.
        A. True
        B. False

3. Detached social workers try to provide intelligence to anti-gang units.
        A. True
        B. False

4. Experts are not hopeful that promising economic opportunities will be provided to help give
    gang members stakes in conformity so they do not commit crimes.
        A. True
        B. False

5. Most of the research supports Hirschi's theory that delinquents lack of social skills
    prevents them from forming close relationships.

A. True
B. False

<u>Answer Key</u>

<u>Multiple Choice:</u>
1. B
2. D
3. A
4. C
5. B
6. C
7. A
8. C
9. A
10. C

<u>True/False</u>
1. T
2. F
3. F
4. T
5. F

CHAPTER NINE
SCHOOLS AND DELINQUENCY

LEARNING OBJECTIVES

- Understand the crisis that is facing the education system.
- Be aware of the association between school failure and delinquency.
- Be familiar with the factors that cause school failure.
- Know what is meant by the term tracking.
- Recognize the problem of truancy and what is being done to limit its occurrence.
- Be familiar with the reasons why kids drop out of school.
- Understand the nature of school crime and school shootings.
- Know what school administrators are now doing to prevent delinquency on campus.
- Be familiar with the various school-based delinquency prevention efforts.
- Know the legal rights of students.

CHAPTER OUTLINE

Ciara,
  1. age 11, lives in Harlem with mother and 3 siblings.
  2. has problems in school behaviorally and academically
  3. she challenges her teachers and seeks refuge among group of older troubled teens and is great risk of dropout
  4. Ciara is required to attend after school Drug Power, a youth leadership program
  5. Ciara loves the music and connects with the youth counselors
  6. Ciara learns self control and importance of rational productive decision-making
  7. Ciara graduates high school and hopes to attend college

I. The School in Modern American Society
   A. Role in shaping the values of children
      1. today more than 90% of school-age children attend school
      2. only 7% of school-age children attended school in 1890
      3. today's young people spend most of their time in school
      4. adolescence is prolonged because young people spend a longer time in school
      5. they are not considered adults because they have not entered the work world
   B. Socialization and status
      1. children spend their school hours with their peers
      2. school has become a primary determinant of economic and social status
      3. educational achievement has become of equal determinant of economic success
      4. many youths do not meet acceptable standards of school

199

achievement

      5. school failure continues to be a major problem for U.S. society

C. Education in crisis

      1. U.S. trails in critical academic areas

      2. U.S. 8th-graders lag behind students in some less affluent nations

      3. U.S. devotes less of its resources to education than do many other Nations

      4. about 18 percent of children are not familiar with basic rules of print or writing

D. Dropping out

      1.   74 percent of freshman graduate high school

      2.   dropouts are much more likely to be unemployed

      3.   kids drop out because they do not like school or need to get a job. Other reasons are low academic achievement, poor problem-solving ability, low self esteem, difficulty getting along with teachers, and substance abuse. Almost half of all female dropouts did so because they were pregnant. Poverty and family dysfunction are correlated with dropout.

      4.   each dropout costs society about 243,000 to 388,000 dollars in his or her lifetime, and if she or he turns to crime, each future criminal costs 1.3-1.5 million.

II. Academic Performance and Delinquency

    A. Poor academic performance

      1. directly linked to delinquent behavior

      2. school failure is a stronger predictor of delinquency

      3. delinquents are often academically deficient

      4. self-report delinquent acts correlated with school attachment and achievement

      5. academic failure and delinquency is commonly among chronic offenders

      6.   only 9 percent of the chronic offenders in Wolfgang's cohort graduated from high school, compared to 74 percent of non-offenders.

      7. 40% of incarcerated felons had twelve or more years of education

    B. School failure and delinquency

      1. school experience is a direct cause of delinquent behavior

      2. children who fail at school soon feel frustrated and rejected

      3. school failure leads to psychological dysfunction causing antisocial behavior

      4. academic failure reduces self-esteem

      5. view is that school failure and delinquency share a common cause

          a. delinquents may have lower IQs than non-delinquents

          b. delinquent behavior has been associated with a turbulent family life

          c. delinquency has been associated with low self-control and

impulsivity
        d. drug use, depression, abuse, and disease symptoms of troubled lifestyle

C. Causes of school failure
1. social class and school failure
    a. delinquency was a phenomenon of working-class students
    b. failure to live up to middle-class measuring rods
    c. school disadvantages of lower-class caused by social structure
    d. economic problems require them to take part-time jobs
    e. boys who do poorly in school are more likely to be delinquent
        i. regardless of their socioeconomic background
    f. middle-class delinquents are more likely to experience school failure
2. tracking is dividing students into groups according to ability level
    a. contributor to student delinquency
    b. participate less in extracurricular activities
    c. some school officials begin tracking students in the lowest grade levels
    d. effects of school labels accumulate over time
alienation
    e. has been identified as a link between school failure and delinquency
    f. attachment to teachers helps insulate high-risk adolescents from delinquency
    g. some students to feel that the school experience is a waste of time
    h. hundreds of thousands of youth are absent from school

III. Delinquency in The School
A. Violent Schools—Safe Schools (1977)
1. 40% of robberies and 36% of physical attacks involving teenagers occur in school
2. students from pre-kindergarten through grade 12 were victims of about 1.9 million total crimes
3. amount and rate of school crime has actually been in decline
B. Focus on Delinquency: Bullying in School
1.   bullying is repeated, negative acts toward a child
2.   may be physical or verbal
3.   30-50 percent of gay, lesbian, and bisexual young people are harassed in an educational setting
4.   both bully and victim(s) suffer short- and long-term consequences tend to not grow out of victim role
5.   chronic victims of bullying may suffer depression, poor self-esteem, and other mental problems as adults
6.   aggression at age eight powerful predictor of criminality and violence well into adulthood (up to age 30)

7. Olweus prevention plan
   a. school wide interventions
   b. classroom-level interventions
   c. individual-level interventions
7. Olweus program receives positive evaluation and is used in US and a number of countries around the world

C. School shootings
   1. 10% of students report bringing weapons to school on a regular basis
   2. Secret Service has developed a profile of school shootings and shooters
      a. more than half had considered the attack for at least two weeks and had a plan for at least two days
      b. attackers' mental anguish was well known
      c. threats were communicated in more than three-fourths of the cases
      d. no accurate or useful profile of at-risk kids developed
      e. drugs and alcohol had little involvement in school violence
      f. shooters had a history of feeling extremely depressed or desperate
      g. most frequent motivation was revenge
   3. factors linked to children who engage in serious school violence
      a. social withdrawal
      b. excessive feelings of isolation and being alone
      c. excessive feelings of rejection
      d. being a victim of violence
      e. feelings of being picked on and persecuted
      f. low school interest and poor academic performance
      g. expression of violence in writings and drawings
      h. uncontrolled anger
      i. history of discipline problems
      j. history of violent and aggressive behavior
      k. membership in hate groups
      l. drug use and alcohol use
      m. inappropriate access to, possession of, and use of firearms
      n. serious threats of violence

D. Who commits school crime?
   1. most likely to be found in socially disorganized neighborhoods
   2. high proportion of students behind grade level in reading
   3. school crime is a function of the community in which the school is located
   4. school-based crimes have survival value
   5. high population density and transient populations have problem-prone schools

202

E. Reducing school crime
    1. crime-free, weapon-free, or safe-school zone statutes
    2. defined zones to include school transportation and school
    -sponsored functions
    3. schools have instituted strict controls over student activity
    4. zero tolerance policy mandates predetermined punishments for
    specific offenses
    5. schools restrict entry of dangerous persons by having visitors sign
    in before entry
    6. most close the campus for lunch
    7. mechanical security devices such as surveillance cameras
    8. 4% of schools use random metal detectors
    9. infiltrate undercover detectives on school grounds
    10. improving the school climate and increasing educational standards

IV. Role of the School in Delinquency Prevention
    A. Reform efforts
        1. make the educational system more responsive to the needs of
        students
        2. children undergo enormous pressures while in school
        3. U.S. is facing an educational crisis
        4. alternative schools
            a. positive learning environment
            b. low student-teacher ratios
            c. individualized learning
    B. School-based prevention programs
        1. cognitive
        2. affective
        3. behavioral
        4. environmental
        5. therapeutic
        6. personalized student-teacher relationships have been recommended
        7. integrate job training and experience with classroom instruction
        8. growing need for after-school programs
        9. Twenty-First Century Community Learning Centers
        10. teens who attend after-school activities achieve higher grades

V. Legal Rights in the School
    A. Right to personal privacy
        1. right of school officials to search students and possessions on
        school grounds
        2. in 1984, *New Jersey v. T.L.O.*
        3. students are constitutionally protected from illegal searches
        4. school officials are not bound by the same restrictions as police
        5. school officials legally search students based on reasonable
        suspicion

B. Drug testing

     1. in 1995, *Vernonia School District 47J v. Acton*

     2. legalized a random drug-testing policy for student athletes

C. Academic privacy

     1. right to expect that their records will be kept private

     2. 1974 federal Family Educational Rights and Privacy Act (FERPA)

     3. restricts disclosure of student's education records without parental consent

D. Free speech

     1. freedom of speech is guaranteed in the First Amendment

     2. passive speech is a form of expression not associated with speaking words

          a. in 1969, *Tinker v. Des Moines Independent Community School District*

          b. conduct will interfere with the discipline required to operate the school

     3. right to discipline a student who uses obscene or profane language and gestures

     4. ruled that the principal could censor articles in a student publication

     5. suspended students for posting defamatory messages on Web sites

E. School prayer

     1. many view it as a violation of the principle of separation of church and state

     2. in 2000, *Santa Fe Independent School District, Petitioner v. Jane Doe*

     3. student council chaplain delivered a prayer over the PA before each game

     4. prayer initiated and led by a student at all home games

     5. prayers led by elected student undermines the protection of minority viewpoints

     6. Santa Fe case severely limits school-sanctioned prayer at public events

     7. in 2001, *Good News Club v. Milford Central School*

          a. provide space for an after-school Bible club for elementary students

          b. it could not be perceived that the school was endorsing the club

F. School discipline

     1. most states have statutes permitting teachers to use corporal punishment

     2. concept of *in loco parentis*

     3. in 1977, *Ingraham v. Wright*

     4. today twenty-four states still allow physical punishment

     5. in 1976, *Goss v. Lopez*

     6. entitled to a hearing if suspended for up to ten days

CHAPTER SUMMARY

Youths spend much of their time in school because education has become increasingly important as a determinant of social and economic success. Educational institutions are among the primary instruments of socialization, and as such they are bound to influence the amount of delinquent behavior by school-age children. There is a strong association between school failure and delinquency. Those who claim a causal link between school failure and delinquency cite two major factors: (1) academic failure, which arises from lack of aptitude, labeling, or class conflict and results in tracking, and (2) alienation from the educational experience, which is the result of the impersonal nature of schools, the passive role assigned to students, and students' perception of their education as irrelevant to their future lives.

Student misbehaviors, which may have their roots in the school experience, range from minor infractions of school rules (for example, smoking and loitering in the halls) to serious crimes, such as assault, arson, drug abuse, and vandalism. In summary, schools have the right to discipline students, but students are protected from unreasonable, excessive, and arbitrary discipline. Truancy is a significant educational problem. Some dissatisfied students drop out of school, and research has shown a decline in delinquency among those who do drop out. The school has also been the setting for important delinquency prevention efforts. Among the measures taken are security squads, electronic surveillance, and teacher training. Students do not lose their legal rights at the schoolhouse door. Among the most important legal issues facing students are the right to privacy, free speech, fair discipline, and freedom of religion.

KEY TERMS

academic achievement: Being successful in a school environment.

underachievers: Those who do not achieve success in school at the level of their expectations.

school failure: Failing to achieve success in school can result in frustration, anger, and reduced self-esteem, which may contribute to delinquent behavior.

tracking: Dividing students into groups according to their ability and achievement levels.

truant: Being out of school without permission.

Drop-out: To leave school before completing the required program of education.

zero tolerance policy: Mandating specific consequences or punishments for delinquent acts and not allowing anyone to avoid these consequences.

passive speech: A form of expression protected by the First Amendment but not associated with actually speaking words; examples include wearing symbols or protest messages on buttons or signs.

active speech: Expressing an opinion by speaking or writing; freedom of speech is a protected right under the First Amendment to the U.S. Constitution.

in loco parentis: In the place of the parent; rights given to schools that allow them to assume parental duties in disciplining students.

SELF TEST QUESTIONS

MULTIPLE CHOICE QUESTIONS

1. Which of the following descriptions best illustrates the hypothesis that school failure and delinquency share a common cause?
    A. Delinquency and school failure are associated with low self control.
    B. Academic failure leads to lower self esteem and this lower self-esteem leads to delinquency.
    C. Children who fail at school feel rejected and seek out like minded companions to engage in crime.
    D. Youths who get bad grades commit delinquent acts seek revenge

2. Today, more than _____ percent of school-aged children attend school, compared to only seven percent in 1890.
    A. 67   C. 90
    B. 77   D. 99

3. Only nine percent of the chronic offenders in Marvin Wolfgang's Philadelphia *Delinquency in a Birth Cohort* study graduated from high school, compared with _____ percent of non-offenders.
    A. 49   C. 69
    B. 59   D. 74

4. Which one of the following countries eighth-grade school students obtained the lowest average math achievement scores?
    A. Hungary   C. Malaysia
    B. United States   D. Slovak Republic

5. What does tracking refer to?
    A. schools monitor student performance to identify students who need help
    B. dividing students into groups according to ability and achievement level
    C. recording where students end up five years after graduation
    D. identifying patterns of delinquency and victimization inside schools

6. Siegel and Welsh note that there are _____ associations between school failure and delinquency.
    A. one   C. three
    B. two   D. four

7. Cohen contends that delinquency among lower class youths is a result of their poor preparation and socialization to function in schools; according to Cohen they essentially failed to live up to _____.
    A. middle class measuring rods   C. standards of decency
    B. working class yardsticks   D. white collar benchmarks

8. Siegel and Welsh note that over time the drop out rate overall is _____.
   A. increasing
   B. decreasing
   C. staying the same
   D. still not measured by US school officials

9. Some contend that the school experience is a(n) _____ of delinquent behavior; children who fail at school soon feel frustrated and rejected and believing they will never achieve success through conventional means, they seek out like-minded companions and together engage in antisocial behaviors.
   A. indirect cause
   B. direct cause
   C. related outcome of a third factor
   D. spurious cause

10. According to the text, who is most likely to bring a gun to schools?
    A. Drug abusers
    B. Those suffering from ADHD
    C. Those who have been the victims of crimes themselves and who hang with peers who carry weapons
    D. Youth who suffer from juvenile psychopathy and don't take their medication so they swing from one emotion to the other

11. According to the text, schools that experience which of the following traits have fewer behavior problems in the student body
    A. higher school taxes
    B. zero tolerance suspension policies, metal detectors, random searchers, and prayer in the schools.
    C. drug free environment, high achieving students, strong discipline, and involved parents
    D. all of the above

12. Schools can drug test student athletes according to the United States Supreme Court decision in _____.
    A. *Vernonia School District v. Acton*
    B. *Goss v. Lopez*
    C. *NJ v. T.L.O.*
    D. *Ingraham v. Wright*

13. In _____ (2001), the Supreme Court required an upstate New York school district to provide space for an after-school Bible club for elementary students; the Court ruled that it was a violation of the First Amendment's free speech clause to deny the club access to the school space on the ground that the club was religious in nature if the school routinely let secular groups use its space.

 A. *Ingraham v. Wright*
 B. *Vernonia School District v. Acton*
 C. *Goss v. Lopez*
 D. *Good News Club v. Milford Central School*

14. The United States Supreme Court ruled in _____ that prayers led by an "elected" student undermines the protection of minority viewpoints; such a system encourages divisiveness along religious lines and threatens the imposition of coercion upon those students not desiring to participate in a religious exercise.

 A. *Good News Club v. Milford Central School*
 B. *Vernonia School District v. Acton*
 C. *Santa Fe Independent School District, Petitioner v. Jane Doe*
 D. *Goss v. Lopez*

15. A form of expression protected by the First Amendment but not associated with actually speaking words is _____; examples include wearing symbols or protest messages on buttons or signs.

 A. active speech   C. interpretive speech
 B. passive speech   D. expressive speech

16. A form of expression protected by the First Amendment associated with spoken or written words is _____; examples include school speeches and articles in school newspapers.

 A. active speech   C. interpretive speech
 B. passive speech   D. expressive speech

17. Most researchers have looked at academic _____, dividing students into groups according to ability and achievement level, as a contributor to student delinquency.

 A. tracking   C. investiture
 B. prophecy   D. alienation

18. What legal doctrine gives the schools the right to assume some of the duties of parents, including discipline?

 A. investiture   C. *educatum primus*
 B. *in prayentis mantis*   D. *in loco parentis*

19. Which is the 1974 Act that restricts the disclosure of personal student information without parental consent?

 A. Taft Hartley Act
 B. Bartley-Fox Act
 C. Gramm-Newman Act
 D. Family Educational Rights and Privacy Act

20. Which of the following explanations best fits the view that the school experience is a direct cause of delinquent behavior?
    A. School problems are part of a generalized problem behavior syndrome.
    B. School problems lower self esteem and a lower self concept.
    C. School problems produce frustration, rejection, and negative attachments.
    D. Delinquents have a lower IQ, a turbulent family, and low self control.

21. Although school crime has declined in recent years, about how many rapes, sexual assaults, robberies, and aggravated assaults occur on or near school grounds?
    A. 50,000
    B. 75,000
    C. 125,000
    D. 150,000

22. Which of the following best describes the United States Supreme Court ruling in *Ingraham v. Wright* concerning corporal punishment in schools?
    A. The Eighth Amendment prohibits corporal punishment in schools.
    B. Neither the Eighth nor the Fourteenth Amendment was violated by a teacher's use of corporal punishment to discipline students.
    C. The court ruled that only reasonable discipline is allowed in schools.
    D. Corporal punishment in schools is legal in only three states.

23. The Supreme Court ruled in _____ that any time a student is to be suspended for up to ten days he or she is entitled to a hearing.
    A. *NJ v. TLO*   C. *Goss v. Lopez*
    B. *Vernonia School District v. Acton*   D. *Ingraham v. Wright*

24. In a 1988 case, *Hazelwood School District v. Kuhlmeier*, the Court extended the right of school officials to censor active speech when it ruled that the principal could censor articles in a student _____.
    A. student term paper
    B. school sponsored publication
    C. off campus website
    D. off campus billboard adjacent to campus

25. In 1986 in _____, the USSC upheld a school system's right to discipline a student who uses obscene or profane language and gestures.
    A. *Bethel School District No. 403 v. Fraser*
    B. *Vernonia School District v. Acton*
    C. *Goss v. Lopez*
    D. *Santa Fe Independent School District, Petitioner v. Jane Doe*

26. Freedom of speech is guaranteed in the First Amendment to the U.S. Constitution; the first of two categories involves _____, a form of expression not associated with actually speaking words; examples include wearing armbands or political protest buttons.

A. passive speech
B. active speech
C. divisive speech
D. inflammatory speech

27. Police need _____ before they can conduct a search, but educators can legally search students when there are reasonable grounds to believe the students have violated the law or broken school rules.

A. a hunch
B. mere suspicion
C. circumstantial evidence
D. probable cause

28. A _____ policy mandates specific consequences or punishments for delinquent acts and not allowing anyone to avoid these consequences.

A. zero tolerance
B. restorative
C. retributive
D. balanced

29. Which agency conducted an analysis of all 220 school-related shootings occurring between July 1, 1994 and June 30, 1999?

A. United States Marshals Service
B. Federal Bureau of Investigation
C. National School Safety Center
D. United States Secret Service

30. Which of the following causes of truancy is illustrated by drug and alcohol abuse, lack of understanding of attendance laws, lack of social competence, mental health difficulties, and poor physical health?

A. school variables
B. family variables
C. student variables
D. economic variables

TRUE/FALSE QUESTIONS:

1. While ninety percent of school aged youths today attend school, in 1890 only about seven percent attended school.

A. True
B. False

2. Siegel and Welsh note that the school has become a primary determinant of economic and social status; education is the key to a job that will mark its holder as successful.

A. True
B. False

3. Cross cultural comparisons show that the United States ranks at the top in math and science test scores.

A. True
B. False

4. Children who report that they do not like school and do not do well in school are more likely to self report delinquent acts than youths who like school and do well there.
    A. True
    B. False

5. Only nine percent of the chronic offenders in Wolfgang's Philadelphia cohort study graduated from high school, compared to 74 percent of non-offenders.
    A. True
    B. False

6. Siegel and Welsh note that the United States, the richest country in the world, devotes less of its resources to education than do many other nations; spending on elementary and secondary education (as a percentage of the U.S. gross domestic product) is less than that of other nations.
    A. True
    B. False

7. Siegel and Welsh note that tracking is an effective method for providing academic success to all students in a school.
    A. True
    B. False

8. Delinquency has been associated with low self-control and impulsivity, traits that also may produce school failure.
    A. True
    B. False

9. The adolescent who both fails at school and engages in delinquency may be experiencing drug use, depression, abuse, or disease—all symptoms of a troubled lifestyle.
    A. True
    B. False

10. School failure is a more robust predictor of delinquency than broken homes or race
    A. True
    B. False

11. Dropout rates have increased substantially over the last ten years: about twenty-seven percent of Americans ages sixteen to twenty-four have left school permanently without a diploma; of these more than one million withdrew before completing tenth grade.
    A. True
    B. False

12. Schools are often more safe than their surrounding communities; students who report being afraid in school are actually more afraid in parks, streets, and subways.
    A. True
    B. False

13. In the 1984 United States Supreme Court case *New Jersey v. T.L.O.*, the court ruled that students were protected against unreasonable searches and seizures, but that school personnel are not bound by the same restrictions as police officers.
    A. True
    B. False

14. According to the United States Supreme Court, to justify prohibiting a form of speech or expression of opinion, the school must be able to show that the forbidden conduct will substantially interfere with the discipline required to operate the school.
    A. True
    B. False

15. The 2000 United States Supreme Court case *Santa Fe independent School District, Petitioner v. Jane Doe* ruled that school prayers led by an elected student threatens the religious freedom of minority viewpoints and therefore is unconstitutional.
    A. True
    B. False

16. Siegel and Welsh note that the United States, the richest country in the world, devotes more of its resources to education than do many other nations; spending on elementary and secondary education (as a percentage of the U.S. gross domestic product) is more than double that of other nations.
    A. True
    B. False

17. Concerning the causes of truancy, student variables include school climate issues, such as school size and attitudes of teachers, other students, and administrators, and inflexibility in meeting the diverse cultural and learning styles of the students.
    A. True
    B. False

18. Concerning the causes of truancy, school factors include drug and alcohol abuse, lack of understanding of attendance laws, lack of social competence, mental health difficulties, and poor physical health.
    A. True
    B. False

19. Concerning the causes of truancy, family factors include employed students, single-parent homes, high mobility rates, parents who hold multiple jobs, and a lack of affordable transportation and child care.
    A. True
    B. False

20. Concerning the causes of truancy, economic influences include lack of guidance or parental supervision, domestic violence, poverty, drug or alcohol abuse in the home, lack of awareness of attendance laws, and differing attitudes toward education.
    A. True
    B. False

21. About 74 percent of all freshman graduate four years after they start high school.
    A. True
    B. False

22. When surveyed, most dropouts say they left school either because they did not like school or because they wanted to get a job.
    A. True
    B. False

23. Sherman Dorn, in *Creating the Dropout*, states that the relatively high dropout rate among minorities is the legacy of disciplinary policies instituted more than forty years ago when educational administrators opposed to school desegregation employed a policy of race-based suspension and expulsion directed at convincing minority students to leave previously all-White high school districts.
    A. True
    B. False

24. Those who claim a causal link between school failure and delinquency cite lack of vocational job prospects and single parent homes
    A. True
    B. False

25. Experts define bullying among children as repeated, negative acts committed by one or more children against another; these acts must be physical in nature to be considered bullying.
    A. True
    B. False

FILL IN ITEMS:

1. In a 1988 case, *Hazelwood School District v. Kuhlmeier*, the Court extended the right of school officials to censor _____ when it ruled that the principal could censor articles in a student publication.

2. Mandating specific consequences or punishments for delinquent acts and not allowing anyone to avoid these consequences is known as a _____ policy.

3. About _____ percent of high schools use random metal detectors.

4. In the 1977 case _____, the Court held that neither the Eighth nor the Fourteenth Amendment was violated by a teacher's use of corporal punishment to discipline students.

5. Under the concept of _____, discipline is one of the parental duties given to the school system.

6. In _____ v. *Milford Central School* (2001), the Supreme Court required an upstate New York school district to provide space for an after-school Bible club for elementary students; the Court ruled that it was a violation of the First Amendment's free speech clause to deny the club access to the school space on the ground that the club was religious in nature if the school routinely let secular groups use its space.

7. In a 1988 case, *Hazelwood School District v. Kuhlmeier*, the Court extended the right of school officials to censor active speech when it ruled that the principal could censor articles in a _____.

8. The most important U.S. Supreme Court decision concerning a student's right to passive speech was in 1969 in the case of _____ v. *Des Moines Independent Community School District*; this case involved the right to wear black armbands to protest the war in Vietnam

9. A 1974 federal law, the _____ and Privacy Act (FERPA), restricts disclosure of information from a student's education records without parental consent.

10. In 1995, the Supreme Court extended schools' authority to search by legalizing a random drug-testing policy for student _____.

11. One common strategy of school based delinquency prevention programs focus on _____ approaches, which seek to increase students' awareness about the dangers of drug abuse and delinquency.

12. One common strategy of school based delinquency prevention programs focus on _____ approaches, which seek to improve students' psychological assets and self image, giving them the resources to resist antisocial behavior.

13. In 1986 in *Bethel School District No. 403 v.* _____, the USSC upheld a school system's right to discipline a student who uses obscene or profane language and gestures.

14. It is possible that school-based crimes have _____ striking back against a weaker victim is a method of regaining lost possessions or self-respect.

15. In the 1984 United States Supreme Court case _____,
the court ruled that students were protected against unreasonable searches and seizures,
but that school personnel are not bound by the same restrictions as police officers.

ESSAY ITEMS:

1. Identify and discuss the three theoretical explanations of the delinquency and school
failure connection.

2. Discuss students' expectations of privacy while in school. What types of searches are
reasonable and what types of searches are unreasonable?

3. Should schools develop policies to drug test student athletes? What about drug testing
all students? What should be done if a student tests positive for a drug?

4. What factors can explain the declining position of the United States compared to other nations in respect to student achievement?

5. What would you recommend to reduce alienation among high school students?

ANSWER KEY

MULTIPLE CHOICE ITEMS

1. A	11. C	21. D
2. C	12. A	22. B
3. D	13. D	23. C
4. B	14. C	24. B
5. B	15. B	25. A
6. C	16. A	26. A
7. A	17. A	27. D
8. B	18. D	28. A
9. B	19. D	29. D
10. C	20. C	30. C

TRUE FALSE ITEMS

1. T	11. F	21. T
2. T	12. T	22. T
3. F	13. T	23. T
4. T	14. T	24. F
5. T	15. T	25. F
6. T	16. F	
7. F	17. F	
8. T	18. F	
9. T	19. F	
10. T	20. F	

FILL IN ITEMS

1. active speech
2. zero tolerance
3. 15
4. *Ingraham v. Wright*
5. *in loco parentis*
6. *Good News Club*
7. student publication
8. Tinker
9. Family Educational Rights
10. athletes
11. cognitive
12. affective
13. *Fraser*
14. survival value
15. *New Jersey v. T.L.O.*

Multiple Choice:

1. What percentage of school-age children attended school in 1890?
   A. 7
   B. 17
   C. 27
   D. 37

2. The average reading score of fourth-graders in 2003
   A. was significantly worse than it was in 1992.
   B. was significantly better than it was in 1992.
   C. was about the same as it as in 1992.
   D. was exactly the same as it was in 1992.

3. When compared to European and Asian high school students, American students
   A. perform significantly worse.
   B. perform significantly better.
   C. are about the same.
   D. score better than Asian but worse than European students.

4. About what percentage of American children are not familiar with the basic rules of print and writing?
   A. 8
   B. 18
   C. 28
   D. 38

5. What are the estimated costs to society of a student dropping out of high school?
   A. 43-88 thousand dollars
   B. 190-366 thousand dollars
   C. 243-388 thousand dollars
   D. 3430488 thousand dollars

6. What are the estimated costs to society of a student dropping out of high school if he or she turns to crime?
   A. .5-.7 million
   B. 1-1.4 million
   C. 1.3 to 1.5 million
   D. 1.5-2.0 million dollars

7. The USSC ruled in New Jersey v TLO that school officials may legally search students without consent if they reach which legal threshold?
    A clear and convincing evidence
    B. reasonable grounds
    C. probable cause
    D. strict scrutiny

8. What percentage of incarcerated felons did surveys reveal have 12 or more years of education?
    A. 20
    B. 30
    C. 40
    D. 50

9. Teachers are victims of how many non-fatal crimes in schools each year?
    A. 53,000
    B. 103,000
    C. 183,000
    D. 203,000

10. The US Secret Service found that most school shooters
    A. plan their attacks
    B. act on impulse when overwhelmed with emotion
    C. were unaffected by bullying
    D. were inner-city youth with single mothers

True False:

1. Having police undercover agents in schools has not been found to violate students' first and fourth amendment rights T F

2. The USSC has held that the fourth amendment against illegal search and seizure does not apply in schools. T   F

3. Zero tolerance policies in school are restricted to drug violations   T   F

4. The US Secret Service found that few school shooters were under the influence of illicit drugs or alcohol when the incidents occurred. T F

5. Bonds to school have insignificant effects upon delinquency T F

Multiple Choice:
1. a
2. c
3. a
4. b
5. c
6. c
7. b
8. c
9. c
10. a

True False:
1. T
2. F
3. F
4. T
5. F

CHAPTER TEN
DRUG USE AND DELINQUENCY

LEARNING OBJECTIVES

- Know which are the drugs most frequently abused by American youth.
- Understand the extent of the drug problem among American youth today.
- Be able to discuss how teenage drug use in this country has changed over time.
- Know the main explanations for why youths take drugs.
- Recognize the different behavior patterns of drug-involved youths.
- Understand the relationship between drug use and delinquency.
- Be familiar with the major drug-control strategies.
- Be able to argue the pros and cons of government using different drug-control strategies.

CHAPTER OUTLINE

Fernando's Story
1. 15 year old Latino takes drugs, skips school, and jumped out of father's car during argument
2. Fernando's father works overtime, drinks, and introduced son to alcohol and drugs.
3. Fernando's mother died in car accident three years earlier.
4. Fernando hazed due to speech defect and limp.
5. As a result of one of many police contacts, Fernando ordered by juvenile court to complete community service and individual counseling and is assessed for AOD [Alcohol and Other Drugs].
6. Counseling helps him deal with loss of mother and other issues. AOD use and delinquent activity reduced, but not eliminated

I. Introduction
    A. Survey data
        1. more than half of all high school–age kids have used drugs
        2. teen drug use is down from 5 and 10 years ago
        3. CASA study suggests that parents play an important role
    B. Vexing problem
        1. every city and town experiences adolescent drug use
        2. cross national studies indicate illicit drug use
        3. association between drug use and crime is troubling

II. Frequently Abused Drugs
    A. Marijuana and hashish
        1. commonly called pot or grass
        2. produced from the leaves of Cannabis sativa

   3. hash is a concentrated form of cannabis
     a. made from unadulterated resin from the female plant
   4. main active ingredient in both is tetrahydrocannabinol (THC)
   5. causes distortions in auditory and visual perception
     a. related to decreased activity
     b. overestimation of time and space
     c. increased food consumption
   6. marijuana is not physically addicting

B. Cocaine
   1. cocaine is an alkaloid derivative of the coca plant
   2. considered a medicinal
   3. controlled by the Pure Food and Drug Act of 1906
   4. cocaine is the most powerful natural stimulant
   5. produces euphoria, restlessness, and excitement
   6. crack is processed street cocaine

C. Heroin
   1. taken to desensitize from pain and free the mind of anxiety and emotion
   2. users become drowsy and may nod off
   3. street heroin is often only 1 to 4 percent pure
   4. probably the most dangerous commonly abused drug

D. Alcohol
   1. remains the drug of choice for most teenagers
   2. almost 70% of high school seniors reported using alcohol in the past year
   3. may be a factor in nearly half of all murders, suicides, and accidental deaths
   4. over 1.4 million drivers are arrested each year for DUI
   5. long-term use has been linked with depression and physical ailments

E. Anesthetic drugs
   1. are central nervous system (CNS) depressants
   2. most widely abused anesthetic drug is phencyclidine (PCP)
   3. effects of PCP can last up to two days

F. Sedatives and barbiturates
   1. depress the central nervous system into a sleeplike condition
   2. sedatives can be prescribed by doctors as sleeping pills

G. Tranquilizers
   1. reduce anxiety and promote relaxation
   2. used to combat anxiety, tension, fast heart rate, and headaches

H. Hallucinogens
   1. produce vivid distortions of the senses
   2. some produce hallucinations, and others cause psychotic behavior
   3. one common hallucinogen is mescaline
   4. mescaline produces vivid hallucinations and out-of-body sensations

       5. second group of hallucinogens are synthetic alkaloid compounds
           a. can be transformed into lysergic acid diethylamide
           b. commonly called LSD
           c. produces visual hallucinations and increased sensitivity

I. Stimulants
       1. synthetic drugs that stimulate action in the central nervous system
       2. methedrine is probably the most widely used and most dangerous amphetamine

J. Steroids
       1. use steroids to gain muscle bulk and strength
       2. health problems associated with their long-term use
       3. steroid users often share needles
       4.puts them at high risk for contracting HIV

K. Designer Drugs
       1. lab-created synthetics
       2. designed at least temporarily to get around existing drug laws
       3. most widely used designer drug is Ecstasy
       4. derived from speed and methamphetamine
       5. drug can also increase blood pressure and heart rate

L. Cigarettes
       1. about 25 countries prohibit the sale of cigarettes to minors
       2. states are required to reduce rates of illegal sales to minors
       3. 6 out of 10 high school seniors in America report having smoked

III. Drug Use Today
  A. Surveys
       1. show that marijuana continues to be the most widely used drug
       2. synthetic drugs such as Ecstasy have become more popular
       3. synthetics are cheap and produce a powerful, long-lasting high
       4. crack cocaine use has been in decline in recent years
           a. heavy criminal penalties
           b. tight enforcement
           c. social disapproval have helped to lower crack use
       5. most persistent teenage substance-abuse problem is alcohol
       6. well established that alcoholism runs in families

  B. Monitoring the Future (MTF) survey
       1. annual MTF survey conducted by the ISR
       2. 45,000 students located in 433 secondary schools participate in the survey
       3. drug use among American adolescents held steady in 2005
       4. declined from the recent peak levels reached in 1996 and 1997
       5. in 2005, 2.6 percent of tenth-graders reported use of Ecstasy
       6. significant drop in the use of alcohol by the youngest kids in the survey

nearly one-fifth of eighth-graders and almost half of twelfth-graders use alcohol-a 19 percent drop in annual rates in the last five years (from 41.9 percent in 2001 to 33.9 percent in 2005) and a 27 percent drop in the last ten years (from 46.5 percent in 1996).

    C. PRIDE survey

        1. National Parents' Resource Institute for Drug Education (PRIDE) survey

        2. findings from the PRIDE survey correlate highly with the MTF drug survey

        3. most recent data (2004-2005 school year) indicates little to no change over the previous school year, but a substantial decrease over the last ten years

    D. Are the survey results accurate?

        1. drug surveys must be interpreted with caution

        2. overly optimistic to expect heavy drug user cooperation

        3. students are likely to be absent from school during testing periods

        4. drug abusers are more likely to be absent

        5. most drug-dependent portion is omitted from the sample

        6. problems are consistent over time

            a. measurement of change or trends in drug usage

            b. validity of these surveys may be questioned

            c. probably reliable indicators of trends in substance abuse

IV. Why Do Youths Take Drugs?

    A. Social disorganization

        1. ties drug abuse to poverty, social disorganization, and hopelessness

        2. tied to the stress of living in a harsh urban environment

        3. data on class and crime is inconclusive

        drug use is higher among urban youths

        5. many drug-dealing youths had legitimate jobs at the time they were arrested

    B. Peer pressure

        1. adolescent drug abuse is highly correlated with the behavior of best friends

        2. friendships with other drug-dependent youths give them social support

        3. association with substance abusers increases the probability of drug use

        4. relationship is reciprocal

            a. adolescent substance abusers seek out friends who use drugs

            b. associating with drug abusers leads to increased levels of drug abuse

        5. peer networks are significant influence on long-term substance abuse

        6. youths become enmeshed in drug-use subculture

7. drug users have warm relationships with substance-abusing peers

C. Family factors
    1. drug users have a poor family life
    2. majority of drug users have had an unhappy childhood
    3. common to find substance abusers in large families
    4. substance abusers may have parents who are divorced, separated, or absent
    5. drug abuse patterns may also result from observation of parental drug use
        a. a more important cause of drug abuse than other family problems
        b. parental conflict over child-rearing practices
        c. failure to set rules
        d. unrealistic demands followed by harsh punishments
D. Genetic factors
    1. biological children of alcoholics reared by nonalcoholic adoptive parents
        a. more often develop alcohol problems than the natural children of the adoptive parents
    2. comparing alcoholism among identical and fraternal twins
        a. degree of concordance is twice as high among the identical twins
    3. future problems can be predicted by behavior as early as six years of age
E. Emotional problems
    1. linked drug use to emotional problems present in any economic class
    2.drugs help youths control or express unconscious needs
    3. introverted people may use drugs as an escape from feelings of inferiority
    4. drug abusers are also believed to exhibit psychopathic or sociopathic behavior
        a. addiction-prone personality
    5. presence of a significant degree of pathology
    6. half of all drug abusers may be diagnosed with antisocial personality disorder
F. Problem behavior syndrome
    1. one of many problem behaviors that begin early in life
        a. remain throughout the life course
    2. youths who abuse drugs:
        a. lack commitment to religious values
        b. disdain education
        c. spend most of their time in peer activities
G. Problem behaviors and substance abuse
    1. one of a constellation of social problems experienced by at-risk

youth

        2. drug users more likely to experience an array of social problems

            a. physical or sexual abuse associated with illicit drug use

        3. substance users are also more likely to have educational problems

            a. absent 10 plus days were more likely to report drug use

        4. association with substance user and serious behavioral and emotional problems

    H. Rational choice

        1. choose to use drugs:

            a. want to get high or relax

            b. improve their creativity

            c. escape reality

            d. increase their sexual responsiveness

V. Pathways to Drug Abuse

    A. Gateway drugs

        1. no single path to becoming a drug abuser

        2. most users start at a young age using alcohol as a gateway drug

        3. drinking with an adult present was a significant precursor of substance use

        4. little disagreement that serious users begin their involvement with alcohol

        5. though most recreational users do not progress to hard stuff

    B. Adolescents who distribute small amounts of drugs

        1. do not commit any other serious delinquent acts

        2. occasionally sell drugs to support their own drug use

        3. customers include friends, relatives, and acquaintances

    C. Adolescents who frequently sell drugs

        1. small number are high-rate dealers

        2. bridge the gap between adult drug distributors and the adolescent user

        3. frequent dealers often have adults who front for them

        4. teenagers distribute the drugs to friends and acquaintances

        5. frequent dealers are more likely to sell drugs in schools or other public places

        6. chance of apprehension is not significant, nor is the payoff substantial

        7.   Venklatest found that the average hourly earnings of drug dealers was between 2.50 to 7.10 an hour [much less than prior researchers]

    D. Teenage drug dealers who commit other delinquent acts

        1. distributes multiple substances and commits both property and violent crimes

        2. make up about 2 percent of the teenage population

            a. commit up to 40 percent of the robberies and assaults

            b. 60 percent of all teenage felony thefts and drug sales

           c. frequently are hired by older dealers to act as street-level drug runners

           d. supplier receives 50 to 70 percent of the drug's street value

E. Losers and burnouts

    1. commit unplanned crimes that increase their chances of arrest

    2. heavy drug use increases their risk of apprehension

        a. decreases their value for organized drug distribution networks

        b. not considered trustworthy or deft enough to handle drugs or money

F. Persistent offenders

    1. about 2/3 of substance-abusing youths continue to use drugs in adulthood

    2. about half desist from other criminal activities

    3. characteristics of those who persist:

        a. they come from poor families

        b. family members include other criminals

        c. do poorly in school

        d. started drugs and delinquency at an early age

        e. use multiple types of drugs and commit crimes frequently

        f. few opportunities to participate in legitimate adult activities

VI. Drug Use and Delinquency

A. Drug use and delinquency

    1. association has been established

    2. crime may be an instrument of the drug trade

        a. violence erupts when rival gangs

        b. use weapons to settle differences and establish territory

        c. between 35 and 40% of New York's homicides are drug-related

    3. drug users may also commit crimes to pay for their habits

        a. 573 narcotics users annually committed more than 200,000 crimes

    4. drug users may be more willing to take risks

        a. inhibitions are lowered by substance abuse

    5. ADAM program tracked trends in drug use among arrestees in urban areas

        a. almost 60% of juvenile males and 30% of juvenile females tested positive for marijuana

        b. prevalence was ten and six times higher than cocaine use for juvenile males and females respectively

    6. incarcerated youths are more likely to be involved in substance abuse

B. Drugs and chronic offending

    1. is possible that most delinquents are not drug users

        a. police are more likely to apprehend muddle-headed

substance abusers

        2. many criminals are in fact substance abusers
              a. less than 2% of the youths report using cocaine or heroin
              b. commit two or more index crimes each year
              c. drug-abusers accounted for 40 to 60% of all the index crimes reported in research by Johnson et al.
              d. one-quarter committed crimes solely to support a drug habit
    C. Explaining drug use and delinquency
        1. association established in a variety of cultures
        2. relationship is uncertain whether:
              a. drug use causes delinquency
              b. delinquency leads youths to engage in substance abuse
              c. both drug abuse and delinquency are functions of some other factor
        3. Huizinga and Menard used National Youth Survey data
              a. strong association between delinquency and drug use
              b. direction of the relationship is unclear
              c. drug abuse appears to be a type of delinquent behavior
              d. most youths involved in delinquency before drugs
              e. youths who abstain from alcohol almost never take drugs
              f. marijuana use is a cause of multiple drug use
              g. youths who commit felonies started off with minor delinquent acts

VII. Drug Control Strategies
    A. Law enforcement efforts
        1. aimed at reducing the supply of drugs and deterring users from drugs
        2. deter the sale of drugs through apprehension of large-volume drug dealers
        3. effort to cut off supplies of drugs by destroying overseas crops
        4. crop substitution and alternative development
        5. may result in a shift in production to another area or targeted crop
        6. efforts directed at interdicting drug supplies as they enter the country
              a. only one-third of all imports are being seized by law enforcement
              b. Operation Webslinger had shut down four Internet drug rings
              c. 115 arrests in 84 cities
              d. seized the equivalent of 25 million doses of GBH
        7. efforts have been made to bust large-scale drug rings
        8. police can intimidate and arrest street-level dealers and users
    B. Education strategies
        1. another approach relies on educational programs

2. overwhelming majority of public school districts include these components:
    a. teaching students about the causes and effects of substances
    b. teaching students to resist peer pressure
    c. referring students for counseling and treatment

C. Drug Abuse Resistance Education (D.A.R.E.)
    1. most widely known drug education program
    2. an elementary school course designed to give students skills resist peer pressure
    3. employs uniformed police
    4. program focuses on five major areas:
        a. providing accurate information about tobacco, alcohol, and drugs
        b. teaching students techniques to resist peer pressure
        c. teaching students to respect the law and law enforcers
        d. giving students ideas for alternatives to drug use
        e. building the self-esteem of students
    5. students need specific analytical and social skills to resist peer
    6. now taught in almost 80 percent of school districts
    7. Lynam found the program to be ineffective over both the short and long term
        a. D.A.R.E. had no effect on students' drug use through tenth grade
        b. at 20, no differences between D.A.R.E. grads and those who did not
        c. D.A.R.E. grads reported slightly lower levels of self-esteem
    8. to meet criticism D.A.R.E. began testing a new curriculum in 2001
    9. will work largely on changing social norms
    10. emphasis will shift from fifth-grade students to those in the seventh grade
    11. a booster program will be added in ninth grade

D. Community strategies
    1.two studies demonstrate the effectiveness of anti-drug messages
    2. community-based programs reach out to high-risk youths
        a. get them involved in after-school programs
        b. offer counseling
        c. delivering clothing, food, and medical care when needed
        d. encouraging school achievement
    3. Boys and Girls Clubs (BGCs) of America
        a. reading classes
        b. sports
        c. homework assistance
        d. SMART Moves (Self-Management and Resistance Training)
        e. evaluation results showed a reduction in substance abuse

E. Treatment strategies

1. more than 150,000 youths ages 12 to 17 are admitted to treatment facilities

2. over half being referred through the juvenile justice system

3. multisystemic treatment (MST) technique developed by Scott Henggeler

      a. direct attention to family, peer, and psychological problems

      b. focus on problem solving and communication skills

      c. program graduates were significantly less likely to recidivate

4. involve users in outdoor activities and wilderness training

5. more intensive efforts use group therapy

      a. leaders try to give users the skills and support

      b. based on the Alcoholics Anonymous model

6. residential programs are used with more heavily involved drug abusers

      a. detoxification units

      b. therapeutic communities

      c. hypnosis

      d. aversion therapy

      e. counseling

F. Harm reduction

1. lessening the harm caused to youth by drug use and overly punitive response to drug use

2. availability of drug treatment facilities staffed by health professionals

3. needle exchange programs to reduce transmission of HIV

4. drug [specialty] courts to divert chronic non-violent users to rehabilitation programs using the court as a therapeutic enterprise with wrap-around care, counseling, regular drug testing, phases, and aftercare.

VIII. What Does the Future Hold?

A. War on drugs

1. willing to go to great lengths to fight the drug war

2. all drug-control strategies are doomed to fail

      a. youths want to take drugs

      b. dealers find that their sale is a lucrative source of income

3. prevention, deterrence, and treatment strategies ignore core reasons for drugs

B. Legalization of drugs

1. short-term effect of reducing the association between drug use and crime

2. may have grave consequences

3. creating an overflow of unproductive people

4. dealers can earn more than the minimal wage

CHAPTER SUMMARY

Alcohol is the drug most frequently abused by American teens. Other popular drugs include marijuana; cocaine and its derivative, crack; and designer drugs such as Ecstasy. Self-report surveys indicate that more than half of all high school–age kids have tried drugs. Surveys of arrestees indicate that a significant proportion of teenagers are drug users and many are high school dropouts. The number of drug users may be even higher than surveys suggest, because these surveys may be missing the most delinquent youths. Although the national survey conducted by PRIDE shows that teenage drug use increased slightly in the past year, both it and the Monitoring the Future survey, also national, report that drug and alcohol use are much lower today than five and ten years ago.

There are many explanations for why youths take drugs, including growing up in disorganized areas in which there is a high degree of hopelessness, poverty, and despair; peer pressure; parental substance abuse; emotional problems; and suffering from general problem behavior syndrome. A variety of youths use drugs. Some are occasional users who sell to friends. Others are seriously involved in both drug abuse and delinquency; many of these are gang members. There are also "losers," who filter in and out of the justice system. A small percentage of teenage users remain involved with drugs into adulthood.

It is not certain whether drug abuse causes delinquency. Some experts believe there is a common cause for both delinquency and drug abuse—perhaps alienation and rage. Many attempts have been made to control the drug trade. Some try to inhibit the importation of drugs, others to close down major drug rings, and a few to stop street-level dealing. There are also attempts to treat users through rehabilitation programs and to reduce juvenile use by educational efforts. Some communities have mounted grassroots drives. These efforts have not been totally successful, although overall use of drugs may have declined somewhat. It is difficult to eradicate drug abuse because there is so much profit to be made from the sale of drugs. One suggestion: legalize drugs, but critics warn that such a step may produce greater numbers of substance abusers. Another option is to compel youths to participate in diversion programs such as specialty drug courts.

KEY TERMS

Substance abuse: Using drugs or alcohol in such a way as to cause physical harm to one-self.

Hashish: A concentrated form of cannabis made from unadulterated resin from the female cannabis plant.

Marijuana: The dried leaves of the cannabis plant.

Cocaine: A powerful natural stimulant derived from the coca plant.

Crack: A highly addictive crystalline form of cocaine containing remnants of hydrochloride and sodium bicarbonate; it makes a crackling sound when smoked.

Heroin: A narcotic made from opium and then cut with sugar or some other neutral substance until it is only 1 to 4 percent pure.

Addict: A person with an overpowering physical or psychological need to continue taking a particular substance or drug.

Alcohol: Fermented or distilled liquids containing ethanol, an intoxicating substance.

Anesthetic drugs: Nervous system depressants.

Inhalants: Volatile liquids that give off a vapor, which is inhaled, producing short-term excitement and euphoria followed by a period of disorientation.

Sedatives: Drugs of the barbiturate family that depress the central nervous system into a sleeplike condition.

Tranquilizers: Drugs that reduce anxiety and promote relaxation.

Hallucinogens: Natural or synthetic substances that produce vivid distortions of the senses without greatly disturbing consciousness.

Stimulants: Synthetic substances that produce an intense physical reaction by stimulating the central nervous system.

Anabolic steroids: Drugs used by athletes and body builders to gain muscle bulk and strength.

Designer drugs: Lab-made drugs designed to avoid existing drug laws.

Addiction-prone personality: The view that the cause of substance abuse can be traced to a personality that has a compulsion for mood-altering drugs.

Gateway drug: A substance that leads to use of more serious drugs; alcohol use has long been thought to lead to more serious drug abuse.

Multisystemic treatment (MST): Addresses a variety of family, peer, and psychological problems

Drug courts: specialty courts that compel users to participate in rehabilitation programs

Legalization of drugs: Decriminalizing drug use to reduce the association between drug use and crime.

MULTIPLE CHOICE

1. _____ is the most powerful natural stimulant; its use produces euphoria, restlessness, and excitement, while overdoses can cause delirium, violent manic behavior, and respiratory failure.
    A. amphetamines   C. LSD
    B. cocaine   D. PCP

2. Which drug is associated with distortions in auditory and visual perception, decreased activity, overestimation of time and place, and increased food consumption?
    A. PCP   C. LSD
    B. marijuana   D. amphetamines

3. _____ is a concentrated form of cannabis made from unadulterated resin from the female *Cannabis sativa*.
    A. cocaine   C. hashish
    B. opium   D. marijuana

4. _____ is produced from the leaves of *Cannabis sativa*.
    A. marijuana   C. opium
    B. hashish   D. cocaine

5. _____ produce(s) insensibility to pain and free the mind of anxiety and pain; users experience relief from fear, release of tension, elevated spirits, and apathy following periods of euphoria.
    A. Cocaine   C. Inhalants
    B. Marijuana   D. Narcotics

6. Crack is processed street cocaine; its manufacture involves using _____ to remove hydrochlorides to create a crystaline form of cocaine that can be smoked.
    A. calcium phosphate   C. thiamine mononitrate
    B. sodium phosphate   D. sodium bicarbonate

7. _____ is the most used narcotic in the United States; it is produced from opium.
    A. Tobacco   C. Heroin
    B. Alcohol   D. Marijuana

8. What is the main active ingredient in marijuana?
    A. erythorbic acid   C. sodium benzoate
    B. tetrahydrocannabinol   D. phosphoric acid

9. The most widely abused anesthetic drug is phencyclidine, also known as _____; it was originally developed as an animal tranquilizer.
    A. PCP   C. LSD
    B. MDMA   D. crack

10. Which of the following was noted as a problem of school-based adolescent drug surveys?
    A. the under representation of rural schools
    B. the inclusion of high risk substance abusers
    C. the over representation of hard drug users in the survey
    D. the exclusion of the most drug prone users

11. _____ are central nervous system depressants, and they produce loss of sensation, stupor, and unconsciousness.
    A. Cocaine   C. Anesthetics
    B. Inhalants   D. Stimulants

12. A substance that leads to the use of more serious drugs is called a _____; alcohol and marijuana has been thought to lead to more serious drug use.
    A. illicit entry   C. precipitating factor
    B. gateway drug   D. precursor drug

13. Methedrine is the most widely used and most dangerous _____.
    A. amphetamine   C. tranquilizer
    B. sedative   D. inhalant

14. Amyl nitrite is a commonly used volatile liquid packaged in capsule form, and it is a type of _____.
    A. tranquilizer   C. hallucinogen
    B. sedative   D. inhalant

15. _____ are the most commonly used drugs of the barbiturate family, and they depress the central nervous system into a sleep-like condition.
    A. Hallucinogens   C. Sedatives
    B. Inhalants   D. Tranquilizers

16. According to Siegel and Welsh, _____ may be a factor in nearly half of all murders, suicides, and accidental deaths.
    A. cocaine   C. alcohol
    B. tobacco   D. sleep deprivation

17. According to Siegel and Welsh, the most widely used illicit drug is _____.
    A. methamphetamine   C. heroin
    B. marijuana   D. crack

18. One study conducted in Miami found that 573 narcotics users annually committed more than
    A. 50,000 crimes
    B. 100,000 crimes
    C. 200,000 crimes
    D. 250,000 crimes

19. The most widely used designer drug is ecstasy, which is derived from which two drugs?
    A. LSD and PCP
    B. heroin and cocaine
    C. marijuana and cocaine
    D. speed and methamphetamine

20. _____ are lab-created synthetic drugs which are designed to at least temporarily get around existing drug laws.
    A. Designer drugs
    B. Steroids
    C. Inhalants
    D. Tranquilizers

21. A great effort has been made to cut off supplies of drugs by destroying overseas crops and arresting members of drug cartels; this approach is known as _____.
    A. border control
    B. street level enforcement
    C. tertiary prevention
    D. source control

22. According to the text, many adolescents who sell small amounts of drugs
    A. become chronic recidivists
    B. sell to friends, relatives, and acquaintances
    C. sell in bulk to finance their party lifestyle
    D. are in tightly organized super gangs

23. Siegel and Welsh note that sixty-four percent of all admissions to treatment facilities in the United States involved _____ as the primary drug of abuse.
    A. marijuana
    B. cocaine
    C. tobacco
    D. codeine

24. The D.A.R.E. approach has been adopted so rapidly since its founding in 1983 that it is now taught in almost _____ of school districts nationwide and in fifty-four other countries.
    A. 25 percent
    B. 45 percent
    C. 60 percent
    D. 80 percent

25. The ten-year follow-up at age twenty found the only difference was that those who had participated in D.A.R.E. reported _____ at age twenty.
    A. a greater willingness to just say no to anything
    B. slightly lower levels of self-esteem
    C. moderately higher tolerance levels for alcohol
    D. moderately higher perceptions of the police

26. Natural or synthetic substances that produce vivid distortions of the senses without greatly disturbing consciousness are known as _____.
      A. hallucinogens   C. sedatives
      B. inhalants   D. anesthetics

27. Volatile liquids that give off a vapor which is inhaled that produces short-term excitement and euphoria followed by a period of disorientation are known as _____.
      A. anesthetics   C. sedatives
      B. tranquilizers   D. inhalants

28. Research in Miami found the pathway to drug use included
      A. experimenting with alcohol at age 7, getting drunk at age 8, having alcohol with an adult present at age 9, becoming a regular drinker by age 11, and later becoming a crack user.
      B. experimenting with marijuana at age 6, drinking with gang members at age and crack use at age 12.
      C. experimenting with designer drugs at age 11 and selling crack by age 14
      D. experimenting with marijuana at age 6, drinking at age 9 with a parent, and selling crack by age 11.

29. The _____ technique was developed by Scott Henggeler, and it directs attention to family, peer, and psychological problems by focusing on problem solving and communication skills.
      A. multisystemic treatment   C. milieu therapy
      B. electric shock   D. behavior modification

30. _____therapy involves getting users to associate drugs with unpleasant sensations, such as nausea.
      A. Multisystemic treatment   C. Milieu therapy
      B. Electric shock   D. Aversion

TRUE/FALSE

1. According to Siegel and Welsh, alcoholism runs in families.
      A. True
      B. False

2. According to Siegel and Welsh, heavy steroid use can lead to flashbacks
      A. True
      B. False

3. Heroin is cut with neutral substances so that it is only one to four percent pure.
      A. True

B. False

4. Heroin is cut with neutral substances so that it is only eighty to eighty-five percent pure.
   A. True
   B. False

5. According to Siegel and Welsh, heroin is the most dangerous commonly used drug.
   A. True
   B. False

6. Recent survey results indicate that drug use among adolescents today is lower than in 1996 and 1997.
   A. True
   B. False

7. According to Siegel and Welsh, marijuana is the drug most commonly used by teenagers.
   A. True
   B. False

8. Although marijuana is not physically addictive, smoking pot presents some health risks, including increased risks of lung cancer, chronic bronchitis, and fertility problems.
   A. True
   B. False

9. Siegel and Welsh note that findings from the PRIDE survey are negatively correlated with the MTF drug survey.
   A. True
   B. False

10. High school surveys may be excluding some of the most drug-prone young people in the population.
    A. True
    B. False

11. According to the National Youth Survey, a longitudinal survey by Delbert Elliot and associates, there is little if any association between drug use and social class.
    A. True
    B. False

12. Research indicates that drug users have warm relationships with substance abusing peers.
    A. True
    B. False

13. Research indicates that drug users have relationships that are cold, brittle, and distant with substance abusing peers.
    A. True
    B. False

14. Self-report surveys indicate that half of high school seniors have tried drugs, and three-quarters have used alcohol.
    A. True
    B. False

15. Self-report surveys show that drug abusers are more likely to become delinquents than are non-abusers.
    A. True
    B. False

16. Research indicates that between 5 and 8 percent of all juvenile male arrestees in some cities test positive for cocaine.
    A. True
    B. False

17. Alcohol may be a factor in nearly half of all murders, suicides, and accidental deaths; alcohol-related deaths number one hundred thousand a year, far more than all other illegal drugs combined.
    A. True
    B. False

18. Concerning high school surveys, although the validity of these surveys may be questioned, they are probably reliable indicators of trends in substance abuse.
    A. True
    B. False

19. Robert MacCoun and Peter Reuter found that drug dealers make about $30 per hour when they are working and clear on average about $2,000 per month.
    A. True
    B. False

20. Drinking with an adult present can be a significant precursor of substance abuse and delinquency.
    A. True
    B. False

21. According to the problem behavior syndrome model, substance abuse may be one of a constellation of social problems experienced by at-risk youth.
    A. True
    B. False

22. About seventy-one percent of high school seniors report having smoked cigarettes over their lifetime; however, in recent years, cigarette use by high school students has been on the decline.
>   A. True
>   B. False

23. The most widely abused anesthetic drug is phencyclidine, known as PCP, and it was originally developed as an animal tranquilizer.
>   A. True
>   B. False

24. Research shows that biological children of alcoholics raised by non-alcoholic adoptive parents more often develop alcohol problems than the natural children of adoptive parents.
>   A. True
>   B. False

25. New York City authorities estimate that 35-40 percent of homicides are drug related
>   A. True
>   B False

FILL IN

1. _____ is associated with distortions in auditory and visual perception, decreased activity, overestimation of time and place, and increased food consumption.

2. _____ is the most powerful natural stimulant; its use produces euphoria, restlessness, and excitement, while overdoses can cause delirium, violent manic behavior, and respiratory failure.

3. _____ is the most used narcotic in the United States; it is produced from opium.

4. Cutting off the supply of drugs by destroying overseas crops and arresting members of the drug cartels is known as _____.

5. The most widely known drug education program is called _____; it is an elementary school course designed to give students the skills for resisting peer pressure to use drugs.

6. Methedrine is the most widely used and most dangerous _____.

7. MDMA is also known as _____.

8. Heroin is cut with neutral substances so that it is only _____ percent pure.

9. MacCoun and Reuter contend that adolescent drug dealers make about _____ a month.

10. Amyl nitrite is a commonly used volatile liquid packaged in capsule form, and it is a type of _____.

11. Research by _____ indicates that many drug-dealing youths had legitimate jobs at the time they were arrested for drug trafficking.

12. _____ therapy involves getting users to associate drugs with unpleasant sensations, such as nausea.

13. According to Siegel and Welsh, _____ may be a factor in nearly half of all murders, suicides, and accidental deaths.

14. _____ is a concentrated form of cannabis made from unadulterated resin from the female plant.

15. The main active ingredient in both marijuana and hashish is _____, a mild hallucinogen.

ESSAY

1. Discuss the drug-delinquency connection.

2. Discuss issues of reliability and validity for school based substance abuse surveys.

3. Identify and discuss the various approaches to control drug use.

4. If program evaluation results for DARE have not been overly positive, what are some reasons to explain the continued interest in the program?

5. What are some reasons juveniles use drugs? How can these reasons influence policies and programs to curb adolescent drug use?

ANSWER KEY

MULTIPLE CHOICE

1. B	11. C	21. D
2. B	12. B	22. B
3. C	13. A	23. A
4. A	14. D	24. D
5. D	15. C	25. B
6. D	16. C	26. A
7. C	17. B	27. D
8. B	18. C	28. A
9. A	19. D	29. A
10. D	20. A	30. D

TRUE FALSE

1. T	11. T	21. T
2. F	12. T	22. F
3. T	13. F	23. T
4. F	14. T	24. T
5. T	15. T	25: T
6. T	16. T	
7. T	17. T	
8. T	18. T	
9. F	19. T	
10. T	20. T	

FILL IN

1. marijuana
2. cocaine
3. heroin
4. source control
5. DARE
6. amphetamine
7. ecstasy
8. 1 to 4
9. $2000
10. inhalant
11. the Rand Corporation
12. aversion
13. alcohol
14. Hashish
15. tetrahydrocannabinol

Multiple Choice

1. More than _____ Americans are estimated to be problem drinkers?
    A. 10 million
    B. 20 million
    C. 24 million
    D. 28 million

2. Just over _____ drivers are arrested each year for driving under the influence?
    A. 1 million
    B. 1.4 million
    C. 1.8 million
    D. 2 million

3. Phencyclidine (PCP), or angel dust,
    A. is a central nervous system enhancers
    B. lasts about 12 hours on humans
    C. rarely leads to an overdose such as with heroin
    D. can cause heavy users to engage in violent acts

4. Sedatives
    A. often create hallucinations such as those common with LSD usage
    B. are often mixed with heroine to create freebase
    C. depress the central nervous system into a sleeplike condition
    D. cannot be legally prescribed by physicians in most states

5. Hallucinogens
    A. like tranquilizers, can lead to addiction and withdrawal
    B. can scramble sensations so users hear colors and smell music
    C. should be legal since Dr. Timothy O'Leary reported how mind-expanding they are during his many university and other tours in the 1960's and 70's
    D. never lead to flashbacks years later and cannot create birth defects

6. Methamphetamines
    A. are created from natural products
    B. are used in Jewish and Native American religious practices
    C. when produced create dangers to "cookers" and others who are present
    D. should be legalized since alcohol is legal

7. Designer drugs such as Ecstasy
    A. are rarely used in rave parties
    B. are rarely used as date-rape drugs
    C. last only a few hours
    D. can cause heat stroke as the drug causes dehydration

8. Although drug usage has been stable or dropped for most drugs since the 1990's, which three drugs showed significant increased use in 2005?
    A. sedatives, Oxytocin, and inhalants.
    B. heroin, valium, and cigarettes
    C. alcohol, speed, and cocaine
    D. methamphetamines, Ecstasy, and PCP

9. Heavy drinking is defined as
    A. having five or more alcoholic drinks on the same occasion on at least five different days in the past week.
    B. having five or more alcoholic drinks on the same occasion on at least five different days in the past 30 days.
    C. having four or more alcoholic drinks on the same occasion on at least five different days in the past 3 weeks.
    D. having four or more alcoholic drinks on the same occasion on at least five different days in the past 30 days.

10. Recent data from the National Survey on Drug Use and Health (NSDUH, formerly called the National Household Survey on Drug Abuse) report that
    A. illicit drug use of girls declined at approximately the same rate as boys
    B. girls are closing the gap with boys in using marijuana, alcohol, and cigarettes
    C. more boys than girls use alcohol
    D. girls often use drugs to get the courage to commit crimes, not due to depression and anxiety.

True False

1. In 1989 The United States invaded Panama to stop it from trafficking in cocaine
    T F

2. Since the war on terrorism in Afghanistan, drug production in that country has declined   T F

3. Global rates of interception of cocaine indicate that one-quarter to one-third of all imports are seized by law enforcement. T F

4 Drug Courts compel youths to participate in rehabilitation programs   T F

5 Evaluations have concluded that Drug Abuse Resistance Education has shown excellent results in the short run, but without follow-up, adolescents resume their drug habit   T F

Answer Key

Multiple Choice

1. b
2. b
3. d
4. c
5. b
6. c
7. d
8. a
9. b
10. b

Web True False Answer Key

1. T
2. F
3. T
4. T
5. F

CHAPTER ELEVEN
THE HISTORY AND DEVELOPMENT OF JUVENILE JUSTICE

LEARNING OBJECTIVES

- Understand the major social changes leading to creation of the first modern juvenile court in Chicago in 1899.
- Be familiar with some of the landmark Supreme Court decisions that have influenced present-day juvenile justice procedures.
- Be able to comment on the nature of delinquency cases being processed in juvenile court.
- Know how children are processed by the juvenile justice system, beginning with investigation and arrest and concluding with reentry into society.
- Understand the conflicting values in contemporary juvenile justice.
- Recognize key similarities and differences between the adult and juvenile justice systems.
- Be able to argue the pros and cons of the juvenile justice system's goal to treat rather than punish and assess if this goal is being met today.
- Understand the need for and be aware of the key elements of a comprehensive juvenile justice strategy to deal with juvenile delinquency.
- See the difference between prevention and intervention efforts to reduce juvenile delinquency.
- Be able to identify and comment on pressing issues in the future of juvenile justice

CHAPTER OUTLINE

Jennifer's story
1. Jennifer is a bright sixteen year old without adjustment problems.
2. When Jennifer confronts her boyfriend's other lover, words lead to punches being thrown; she is referred to Youth Court, a diversion program in which the jury is composed of teenagers.
3. Jennifer agrees to counseling and drug and alcohol preassessment and to write a paper about how to control her anger.
4. Jennifer completes Youth court, her record is cleared, and serves on future juries in Youth Court and continues as an "excellent volunteer with great leadership potential"

I. Juvenile Justice in the Nineteenth Century
   A. Nineteenth century
      1. delinquent, neglected, and runaway children were treated like adult offenders
      2. they received harsh sentences similar to those imposed on adults
      3. legislation introduced to humanize criminal procedures for children
      4. probation designed to help young people avoid imprisonment
      5. no special facilities existed for the care of youths in trouble with

the law
B. Urbanization
    1. United States experienced rapid population growth due to
        a. an increased birthrate
        b. expanding immigration
    2. rural poor and immigrant groups were attracted to urban commercial centers
    3. nature of growth
        a. in 1790, 5% of the population lived in cities
        b. in 1920, 51% of the population lived in cities
        c. NYC quadrupled its population between 1825 and 1855
    4. people overwhelmed the existing system of work and training
    5. many question the family's ability to exert control over children
    6. work began to center around factories, not the home
    7. wealthy families could no longer absorb vagrant youth as apprentices or servants
    8. chronic poverty became an American dilemma
        a. affluent voiced concern over the dangerous classes
        b. segments of the population susceptible to decaying environment
C. Child-saving movement
    1. Society for the Prevention of Pauperism
        a. formed in 1817 by prominent New Yorkers
        b. attacked taverns, brothels, and gambling parlors
        c. concerned about the inadequate moral training of children of dangerous classes
    2. activists became known as child savers
    3. influenced state legislatures giving courts the power to commit children to specialized institutions
        a. runaways or criminal offenders
    4. House of Refuge opened in New York in 1825
        a. founded on the concept of protecting potential criminal youths
        b. taking them off the streets
        c. reforming them in a family-like environment
        d. youths were required to do piecework
        e. institution was run like a prison with strict discipline and absolute separation of the sexes
        f. concept enjoyed expanding popularity
    5. House of Reformation founded in Boston in 1826
    6. Similar institutions were opened in Massachusetts and New York in 1847

    7. philosophy of *parens patriae*
        a. duty of the state to act on behalf of the child

b. provide care and protection equivalent to that of a parent

c. refuge programs given parental control over a committed child

D. Were they really child savers?

    1. debate continues over the true objectives of the early child savers

    2. Anthony Platt reappraised the child-saving movement

        a. representatives of the ruling class

        b. galvanized by urban poor to take action to preserve their way of life

    3. motivated more by self-interest than by benevolence

    4. most cases petitioned to the juvenile court were for petty crimes and status offenses

    5. basic legal rights of children were violated

E. Development of juvenile institutions

    1. state intervention in the lives of children continued into the twentieth century

    2. child savers helped create reform schools

    3. state institutions opened in Westboro, Massachusetts, in 1848, and in Rochester, New York, in 1894

    4.institutional programs began in Ohio in 1850 and in Maine, Rhode Island, and Michigan in 1906

        a. subject to harsh working conditions

        b. taught a trade where possible

        c. received some basic education

        d. racially and sexually segregated

        e. discipline was harsh

        f. physical care was poor

    4. Children's Aid Society created by Charles Loring Brace in 1853

        a. rescued youths from the harsh environment of the city

        b. provided them with temporary shelter

        c. placing-out plan

        d. sent children to western farms where they could be cared for

        e. placed on orphan trains

        f. 150,000 children were placed in rural homesteads

    5. Society for the Prevention of Cruelty to Children (SPCC)

        a. the first SPCC created in New York in 1874

        b. concerned that

            i. abused boys would become lower-class criminals

            ii. mistreated young girls might become sexually promiscuous women

        c. protected children subjected to cruelty and neglect at home and at school

        d. criminal penalties were created for negligent parents

        e. provisions were established for removing children from the home

II. A Century of Juvenile Justice
    A. Reforms
        1. children committed under the doctrine of *parens patriae* without due process
        2. several key questions posed on due process protections
    B. Increasing delinquency rates
        1. hastened the development of a juvenile court
        2. by 1850, delinquency was fastest growing component of the local crime problem
    C. Illinois Juvenile Court Act and Its Legacy
        1. child-saving movement culminated in passage of Illinois Juvenile Court Act passed in 1899
            a. children should not be held as accountable as adult transgressors
            b. objective is to treat and rehabilitate rather than punish
            c. disposition should be predicated on youth's needs
            d. system should avoid the trappings of the adult criminal process
        2. child savers believed that children were influenced by their environments
        3. Illinois Juvenile Court Act established juvenile delinquency as a legal concept
        4. distinction made between neglected children and delinquents
        5. delinquents were those under the age of sixteen who violated the law
        6. key provisions of the act were these:
            a. a separate court was established for delinquent and neglected children
            b. procedures developed to govern the adjudication of juvenile matters
            c. children separated from adults in courts and in institutional programs
            d. probation programs developed to assist the court in making decisions
        7. by 1917, juvenile courts had been established in all but three states
        8. juvenile court jurisdiction
            a. based primarily on a child's non-criminal actions and status
            b. *parens patriae* philosophy predominated
            c. court's process was paternalistic rather than adversarial
            d. attorneys were not required
            e. hearsay evidence was admissible in adjudication hearings
            f. verdicts were based on a preponderance of the evidence
            g. non-criminal behavior added to the jurisdiction of juvenile courts

9. conditions exacerbated by rapid growth in the juvenile institutional population

D. Reforming the system

    1. reform of the system was slow in coming

    2. in 1912, the U.S. Children's Bureau was formed

        a. first federal child welfare agency

        b. investigated the state of juvenile institutions

        c. status offenders commonly were housed with delinquents

        d. status offenders given sentences more punitive than delinquents

E. Due process

    1. juvenile court system denied children procedural rights available to adults

    2. reform efforts begun in earnest in the 1960s

    3. in 1962, New York passed legislation creating a family court system

    4. legislation established the PINS classification

    5. many juvenile courts had to improve their social services

    6. U.S. Supreme Court radically altered the juvenile justice system

        a. established the right of juveniles to receive due process of law

        established that juveniles had the same rights as adults

F. Federal commissions

    1. *President's Commission on Law Enforcement and the Administration of Justice* organized by President Lyndon Johnson in 1967 suggested

        a. juvenile justice system must provide underprivileged youths with opportunities for success, including jobs and education

        b. recognized need to develop effective law enforcement procedures to control hard-core offenders while at the same time granting them due process

        c. was a catalyst for the passage of the federal *Juvenile Delinquency Prevention and Control (JDP) Act of 1968* which

            i. created Youth Development and Delinquency Prevention Administration which concentrated on helping states develop new juvenile justice programs

        d. Congress passed the *Omnibus Safe Streets and Crime Control Act* in 1968

            i. Title I of this law established the Law Enforcement Assistance Administration (LEAA) to provide federal funds for improving the adult and juvenile justice systems

            ii. In 1972, Congress amended the JDP to allow the LEAA to focus its funding on juvenile justice and delinquency-prevention programs

    2. *National Advisory Commission on Criminal Justice Standards and*

Goals established in 1972 by the Nixon administration
    a. identified strategies of
        i. preventing delinquent behavior
        ii. developing diversion activities
        iii. establishing dispositional alternatives
        iv. providing due process for all juveniles
        v. controlling violent and chronic delinquents
    b. recommendations formed the basis for the *Juvenile Justice and Delinquency Prevention Act of 1974*
        i. eliminated the Youth Development and Delinquency Prevention Administration
        ii. replaced it with the Office of Juvenile Justice and Delinquency Prevention (OJJDP) within the LEAA
3. LEAA phased out in 1980 and OJJDP became an independent agency in the Department of Justice
    a. in 1970s, its most important goals were
        i. removing juveniles from detention in adult jails
        ii. eliminating the incarceration of delinquents and status offenders together
4. *Violent Crime Control and Law Enforcement Act of 1994*
    a. largest piece of crime legislation in U.S. history
    b. provided for 100,000 new police officers and billions of dollars for prisons and prevention programs for both adult and juvenile offenders
G. Leading constitutional cases in juvenile justice
    1. *Oklahoma Publishing Co. v. District Court* (1977)
        a. concerns information obtained in an open juvenile proceeding
        b. violation of the First Amendment to prohibit publication
    2. *Smith v. Daily Mail Publishing Co.* (1979)
        a. publication of the identity of a juvenile suspect
        b. USSC declared the statute unconstitutional
        c. juvenile proceedings are meant to be private and confidential
        d. violations do not justify the use of a criminal statute
    3. *Fare v. Michael C.* (1979)
        a. request for lawyer is immediate revocation of right to silence
        b. child requested to see his probation officer at the time of interrogation
        c. probation officer cannot be expected to offer the same type of advice
    4. *Schall v. Martin* (1984)
        a. upheld preventive detention before adjudication
    5. *New Jersey v. T.L.O.* (1984)
        a. determined that the Fourth Amendment applies to school

searches

    b. USSC adopted a "reasonable suspicion" standard

  6. *Thompson v. Oklahoma* (1988)

    a. concerned capital punishment for a 15 year old juvenile murderer

    b. USSC ruled it violated the Eighth Amendment

  7. *Stanford v. Kentucky* and *Wilkins v. Missouri* (1989)

    a. imposition of the death penalty on 16-18 year old juveniles

    b. was not unconstitutional

  8. *Vernonia School District v. Acton* (1995)

    a. suspicionless drug testing of all students in interscholastic athletics

    b. testing does not constitute unreasonable search

  9. *United States v. Lopez* (1995)

    a. federal Gun-Free School Zone Act was unconstitutional

III. Juvenile Justice Today

 A. Jurisdiction

  1. exercises jurisdiction over delinquents and status offenders

  2. have jurisdiction involving conduct directed at juveniles

    a. parental neglect

    b. deprivation

    c. abandonment

    d. abuse

  3. states have also set different maximum ages for jurisdiction

  4. today's juvenile justice system exists in all states by statute

 B. Juvenile justice process

  1. most children come into the justice system as a result of contact with police

  2. less serious offenses may require police action

  3. more than 70% of all children arrested are referred to the juvenile court

  4. police investigation

    a. police have the authority to investigate the incident

    b. decide whether to release the youths or formally charge

    c. juveniles have constitutional rights similar to those of adults

  5. detention

    a. child is referred to juvenile court

    b. question whether to place in a detention facility or shelter care

    c. detention hearing is held

  6. pretrial procedures

    a. begins with a hearing

    b. juveniles are informed of their rights

    c. plea bargaining may also occur at any stage of the

proceedings

  d. adjudication hearing is scheduled if plea is not reached

  e. if specific criteria are met youth may be waived to adult court

 7. adjudication

  a. trial stage of the juvenile court process

  b. court hears evidence on the allegations in the delinquency petition

  c. trial on the merits (dealing with issues of law and facts) and rules of evidence similar to those of criminal proceedings generally apply

  d. juvenile is entitled to many of the procedural guarantees like adults

 8. disposition

  a. if the adjudication process finds the child delinquent, the court must decide what should be done to treat the child

  b. most juvenile court acts require a bifurcated process, or two stage decision

  c. disposition imposed in light of the offense, the youth's prior record, and his or her family background

 9. treatment

  a. offenders may be placed in some form of correctional treatment

  b. probation is the most commonly used formal sentence

  c. most severe of the statutory dispositions available is commitment

  d. child may be sent to a training school or a residential treatment facility

  e. some jurisdictions have juvenile aftercare or parole

  f. juveniles have a legal right to treatment

 10. conflicting values in juvenile justice

  a. often-conflicting values at the heart of the system

  b. treatment consistent with the doctrine of *parens patriae*

  c. guarantee constitutional due process

C. Criminal justice versus juvenile justice

 1. components of the adult and juvenile criminal processes are similar but the juvenile system has a separate organizational structure

 2. juvenile court movement made certain that the stigma attached to a convicted offender would not be affixed to youth in juvenile proceedings

 3. language and concepts different from adult criminal court

 4. juveniles have a petition filed against them instead of being indicted for a crime

 5. criminal trial is called a hearing in the juvenile system

D. Similarities and differences between juvenile and adult justice systems

 1. discretion in decision making in both the adult and the juvenile systems

2. Miranda warnings apply to both juveniles' interrogation, for an offense that would be a criminal violation if they were adults, and to adults

3. both are protected from prejudicial lineups

4. both have the right to counsel at most key stages of the court process

5. standard in both is proof beyond a reasonable doubt

6. juveniles and adults can be kept in detention without bail if they are considered dangerous

E. Differences

1. primary purpose of juvenile procedures is protection and treatment

2. primary purpose of adult procedures is punish the guilty

3. juveniles can be apprehended for status offenses

4. adult courts are more formal and are open to the public

5. juveniles have no constitutional right to a jury trial.

6. juveniles can be searched in school without probable cause

IV. Comprehensive Juvenile Justice Strategy

A. Comprehensive strategy

1. increased prevention of delinquency

2. enhanced responsiveness from the juvenile justice system

3. greater accountability on the part of youth

4. decreased costs of juvenile corrections

5. a more responsible juvenile justice system

6. more effective juvenile justice programs

7. less delinquency

8. fewer delinquents becoming serious, violent, and chronic offenders

9. fewer delinquents becoming adult offenders

B. Prevention

1. early childhood services may prevent delinquency

2. low intelligence and school failure are important risk factors

3. home-visiting programs target families at risk for child abuse

C. Intervention

1. designed to ward off involvement in more serious delinquency

a. Big Brother/Big Sister program

b. Juvenile Mentoring Program (JUMP)

c. Job Corps and YouthBuild U.S.A

2. improve the chances of young people obtaining jobs in the legal economy

D. Graduated sanctions

1. include immediate sanctions for nonviolent offenders

2. secure institutions are reserved for repeat serious offenders and violent offenders

E. Institutional programs

1. juvenile incarceration is overused

2. warehousing juveniles without treatment does little to deter criminal behavior

F. Alternative courts

      1.provide special services to youth and helps alleviate case flow problems

      2. place nonviolent first offenders into intensive treatment programs

G. Drug courts

      1.special court with jurisdiction over the burgeoning number of cases involving substance abuse and trafficking

            a. in 2003, there were 285 juvenile drug courts (with another 110 in the planning process) with 12,500 juveniles enrolled

H. Teen courts

      1. young people rather than adults determine the disposition in a case

      2.typically involve young juveniles with no prior arrest records

      3. charged with minor law violations

      4. some teen courts require offenders to write formal apologies to their victims

      5. adults supervise the courtroom activities

      6. desire for peer approval and the reaction to peer pressure

      7. learn more about the legal system

      8. four potential benefits

            a. accountability

            b. timeliness

            c. cost savings

            d. community cohesion

      9. more than 900 of these courts in operation

      10. evaluation study indicated favorable results for teen courts:

            a. in three of the four jurisdictions six-month recidivism rates were lower

            b. six-month recidivism rates were under 10 percent

V. Future of Juvenile Justice

    A. Debated future

      1. criminalizing of the juvenile court

      2. reality of treating juveniles closely resembles punishing adult criminals

      3. some have made it easier to waive children to the adult courts

    B. Getting tough

      1. primary motivation for moving cases to the adult criminal justice system

      2.criminalizing acts that would be under the jurisdiction of the juvenile court

      3. once an adult, always an adult

    C. Reforms

      1. efforts to reduce the use of secure detention and secure confinement

      2. growing public support for prevention and intervention programs.

CHAPTER SUMMARY

Urbanization created a growing number of at-risk youth in the nation's cities. The juvenile justice system was established at the turn of the twentieth century after decades of efforts by child-saving groups. These reformers sought to create an independent category of delinquent offender and keep their treatment separate from adults. Over the past four decades, the U.S. Supreme Court and lower courts have granted procedural safeguards and the protection of due process in juvenile courts. Major court decisions have laid down the constitutional requirements for juvenile court proceedings. In years past the protections currently afforded to both adults and children were not available to children.

For both violent and property offenses, more than half of all formally processed delinquency cases in 2002 resulted in the youth being adjudicated delinquent. The juvenile justice process consists of a series of steps: the police investigation, the intake procedure in the juvenile court, the pretrial procedures used for juvenile offenders, and the adjudication, disposition, and postdispositional procedures. There are conflicting values in juvenile justice. Some experts want to get tough with young criminals, while others want to focus on rehabilitation. The adult and juvenile justice systems have a number of key similarities and differences. One of the similarities is the right to receive Miranda warnings; this applies to juveniles as well as adults. One of the differences is that juvenile proceedings are not considered criminal, while adult proceedings are.

There has been a movement to toughen the juvenile justice system, and because of this many view the importance of treatment as having been greatly diminished. Proponents of treatment argue that it is best suited to the developmental needs of juveniles. Critics contend that treatment simply serves to mollycoddle juveniles and reduces the deterrent value of the juvenile court. A comprehensive juvenile justice strategy has been developed to preserve the need for treatment services for juveniles while at the same time using appropriate sanctions to hold them accountable for their actions. Elements of this strategy include delinquency prevention, intervention programs, graduated sanctions, improvement of institutional programs, and treating juveniles like adults.

New courts, such as drug courts and teen courts, are now in place. Prevention efforts are targeted at children and teens in an effort to prevent the onset of delinquency. Intervention efforts are targeted at children and teens considered at higher risk for delinquency and are designed to ward off involvement in more serious delinquent behavior. The future of the juvenile justice system is in doubt. A number of state jurisdictions are now revising their juvenile codes to restrict eligibility in the juvenile justice system and remove the most serious offenders. At the same time there are some promising signs, such as public support for prevention and intervention programs and some states beginning to incorporate research-based initiatives to guide juvenile justice programming and policy.

KEY TERMS

House of Refuge: A care facility developed by the child savers to protect potential criminal youths by taking them off the street and providing a family-like environment.

Children's Aid Society: Child-saving organization that took children from the streets of large cities and placed them with farm families on the prairie.

orphan train: A practice of the Children's Aid Society in which urban youths were sent west for adoption with local farm couples.

Society for the Prevention of Cruelty to Children (SPCC): First established in 1874, these organizations protected children subjected to cruelty and neglect at home or at school.

Law Enforcement Assistance Administration (LEAA): Unit in the U.S. Department of Justice established by the Omnibus Crime Control and Safe Streets Act of 1968 to administer grants and provide guidance for crime prevention policy and programs.

Office of Juvenile Justice and Delinquency Prevention (OJJDP): Branch of the U.S. Justice Department charged with shaping national juvenile justice policy through disbursement of federal aid and research funds.

juvenile justice process: Under the *parens patriae* philosophy, juvenile justice procedures are informal and nonadversarial, invoked for juvenile offenders rather than against them; a petition instead of a complaint is filed; courts make findings of involvement or adjudication of delinquency instead of convictions; and juvenile offenders receive dispositions instead of sentences.

detention hearing: A hearing by a judicial officer of a juvenile court to determine whether a juvenile is to be detained or released while proceedings are pending in the case.

adjudicatory hearing: The fact-finding process wherein the juvenile court determines whether there is sufficient evidence to sustain the allegations in a petition.

bifurcated process: The procedure of separating adjudicatory and dispositionary hearings so different levels of evidence can be heard at each.

disposition: For juvenile offenders, the equivalent of sentencing for adult offenders; juvenile dispositions should be more rehabilitative than retributive.

petition: Document filed in juvenile court alleging that a juvenile is a delinquent, a status offender, or a dependent and asking that the court assume jurisdiction over the juvenile.

drug courts: Courts whose focus is providing treatment for youths accused of drug-related acts.

systematic review: rigorous methods for locating, apprising, and synthesizing evidence of prior evaluation studies

meta-analysis: a statistical technique that synthesizes and integrates findings from prior

teen courts: generally handle first time offenders with misdemeanor offenses; peers prosecute, defend, and determine sanctions for youths who admit to their guilt.

SELF TEST QUESTIONS

MULTIPLE CHOICE

1. A meta analysis
    A. is a longitudinal study usually spanning 12 – 18 months.
    B. examines the five most prominent studies in the field.
    C. reviews a number of studies that examined a phenomena.
    D. Usually, due to budgetary constraints, uses only secondary source statistical analysis.

2. Juvenile drug courts
    A. have been researched extensively.
    B. have shown some success, but further research is required.
    C. have higher recidivism rates than traditional courts.
    D. are being phased out.

3. According to the Illinois Juvenile Court Act of 1899, which of the following is a principle consideration of the legislation?
    A. The system should emphasize rules and procedures to provide an orderly environment to process cases.
    B. The system should avoid the adult criminal process with all its rules and procedures.
    C. The system should emphasize rules and procedures to teach delinquents to respect the law.
    D. The system should emphasize rules and procedures so that delinquents will know what to expect once they 'graduate' to the adult system.

4. According to the Illinois Juvenile Court Act of 1899, which of the following is a principle consideration of the legislation?
    A. Dispositions should rely on determinant sentencing models.
    B. Juveniles, regardless of their needs, should receive identical dispositions.
    C. Disposition should be predicated on analysis of the youth's special circumstances and needs.
    D. Prosecutors shall have unbridled discretion in choosing dispositions.

5. Brace and the Children's Aid Society devised the _____ to send these children to western farms where they could be cared for and find a home; youths were placed on what became known as orphan trains, which made preannounced stops in western farming communities.
    A. placing-out plan   C. urban dispersal plan
    B. frontier resettlement plan   D. wilderness survival program

6. In the _____ the US Supreme Court radically altered the juvenile justice system when it issued a serious of decisions that established the right of juveniles to receive due process of law.

A. 1950s   C. 1970s

B. 1960s   D. 1980s

7. According to Siegel and Welsh, what were children's legal rights during the period of the Child Savers?

A. Child rights were strictly enforced.

B. Children enjoyed greater protections of their legal rights than adults.

C. Children's rights were not protected during the legal process.

D. There were many court cases which clarified and expanded juvenile legal rights.

8. In their study of the early juvenile court Memphis, Tennessee, Shelden and Osborne noted that more than ninety-six percent of the actions with which females were charged were _____.

A. drug related offenses   C. violent crime

B. property offenses   D. status offenses

9. What type of labor was performed by juveniles housed in the House of Refuge?

A. They attended college prep courses.

B. They worked on the GED.

C. They performed piece work manufacturing.

D. They learned management and organizational principles.

10. Prior to the creation of the juvenile court, how were juveniles who violated the law treated?

A. They were simply released once their identity was established.

B. We don't know, since no records were kept that far back in time.

C. They were treated more harshly than adults to teach other youths.

D. They were treated as adults.

11. Which of the following is offered as a potential benefit of teen courts?

A. Reduction of caseload of regular courts

B Increased criminal procedure

C. Increased punitiveness

D. Enhanced control of youths by the juvenile justice system

12. Juvenile aftercare is similar to _____ for adults.

A. probation   C. incarceration

B. treatment   D. parole

13. Adults plea bargain, while the term used in the juvenile justice system is _____.

A. brokerage   C. an adjustment

B. advocacy   D. a substitution

14. If the youth is adjudicated delinquent, the court must decide an outcome or treatment approach; this decision is made during the _____.
      A. adjudication hearing   C. disposition hearing
      B. pretrial conference   D. arraignment

15. A _____ for a juvenile is similar to a criminal trial for an adult.
      A. adjudicatory hearing   C. disposition hearing
      B. bifurcated process   D. sentencing hearing

16. Adult offenders are labeled "criminals"; the comparable term for a juvenile is a "_____."
      A. adolescent transgressor   C. delinquent child
      B. youthful offender   D. thug

17. Which theory supports the use of alternative terms for indictment, jail, and trial?
      A. Control theory   C. Strain theory
      B. Conflict theory   D. Labeling theory

18. The authors describe which program as a delinquency prevention program by minimizing early risk
      A. Olweus' bullying program.
      B. Comprehensive Education and Training Program.
      C. Head Start.
      D. DARE .

19. According to the text, increased juvenile violent crime and family disintegration have overwhelmed the system and led crime control advocates to call for
      A. the abolition of the juvenile court.
      B. the reduction of juvenile court jurisdiction over juveniles charged with serious crimes.
      C. greater use of boot camps.
      D. reduction in procedural protections for juveniles charged with serious crimes.

20. Which of the following best describes the goals of the Illinois Juvenile Court Act of 1899?
      A. Disposition should consider the youth's special circumstances and needs.
      B. The system should deter, punish, and treat juveniles.
      C. Children should be treated as adult criminals.
      D. The juvenile system should mirror the adult system in formality and process.

21. The first Society for the Prevention of Cruelty to Children was created in 1874, and by 1900 _____.
      A. it had ceased to exist
      B. it had merged with the SPCA
      C. there were 300 such societies in the US
      D. there were 27 such societies in the US

22. About how many youths were placed out in rural homesteads by the Children's Aid Society by 1930?
    A. 5,000   C. 47,000
    B. 27,000   D. 150,000

23. The doctrine of _____ allowed justice officials to place youths in restrictive settings, for the youth's own good, and without the legal protections afforded by the adult criminal justice system.
    A. *pluribus unum*   C. *in forma pauperis*
    B. *parens patriae*   D. *in loco parentis*

24. The most prominent of the care facilities developed by the child savers was the _____, opened in 1825; it was founded on the concept of protecting potential criminal youths by taking them off the street and reforming them in a family like environment.
    A. The Oliver Twist House   C. Home for Little Wanderers
    B. Hull House   D. House of Refuge

25. From the court's creation in 1899 until the late 1960s, what was the burden of proof in a juvenile court case?
    A. beyond a reasonable doubt   C. absolute certainty
    B. preponderance of the evidence D. 80% probability

26. In 1817 prominent New Yorkers formed the _____; the group attacked taverns, brothels, and gambling, but they also viewed the moral training of youths from the dangerous classes as inadequate.
    A. Society for the Prevention of Pauperism   C. Society of Moral Righteousness
    B. Coalition for City Wide Improvement   D. Institute for Social Betterment

27. In 1790 only five percent of the population lived in cities, and by 1920 it was _____ percent.
    A. 15   C. 51
    B. 35   D. 83

28. Which state was the first to develop probation as a disposition of the court?
    A. New York   C. Massachusetts
    B. California   D. Pennsylvania

29. Which of the following was seen as the primary purpose of the original juvenile justice system?
    A. incapacitation   C. retribution
    B. deterrence   D. rehabilitation

30. The first modern juvenile court was created in _____ in Chicago.
    A. 1829   C. 1899
    B. 1849   D. 1914

TRUE/FALSE

1. Juveniles have the right to a jury trial, counsel, and Miranda warnings the same as adults.
 A. True
 B. False

2 The objective of the first juvenile court act was to provide greater procedural protection to juveniles within a therapeutic milieu.
 A. True
 B. False

3. The *National Advisory Commission on Criminal Justice Standards and Goals* was established in 1973 by the Nixon administration, and it called for a complete dissolution of the juvenile justice system.
 A. True
 B. False

4. Siegel and Welsh note that the oldest age for original juvenile court jurisdiction in delinquency cases is the same for all states.
 A. True
 B. False

5. If the child denies the allegation of delinquency, an adjudicatory hearing or trial is scheduled.
 A. True
 B. False

6. According to the Illinois Juvenile Court Act of 1899, the objective of the juvenile justice system is to punish rather than treat and rehabilitate.
 A. True
 B. False

7. According to the Illinois Juvenile Court Act of 1899, disposition should be predicated on analysis of the youth's special circumstances and needs.
 A. True
 B. False

8. According to the Illinois Juvenile Court Act of 1899, the objective of the juvenile justice system is to treat and rehabilitate rather than punish.
 A. True
 B. False

9. According to the Illinois Juvenile Court Act of 1899, children should not be held as accountable as adult transgressors.
 A. True
 B. False

10. For both violent and property crime, more than half of all formally processed delinquency cases in 2002 resulted in the youth being adjudicated delinquent.
    A. True
    B. False

11. In 1817, prominent New Yorkers formed the Society for the Prevention of Pauperism. Although they concerned themselves with attacking taverns, brothels, and gambling parlors, they also were concerned that the moral training of children of the dangerous classes was inadequate.
    A. True
    B. False

12. New York more than quadrupled its population in the thirty-year stretch between 1825 and 1855, from 166,000 in 1825 to 630,000 in 1855.
    A. True
    B. False

13. Adults have a constitutional right to counsel, but juveniles do not have this right.
    A. True
    B. False

14. Although some states allow it, juveniles do not have a constitutional right to a jury trial.
    A. True
    B. False

15. Siegel and Welsh note that teen courts can alleviate some of the crowding in the formal juvenile justice system.
    A. True
    B. False

16. Siegel and Welsh note that juveniles are not indicted for a crime; they have a petition filed against them.
    A. True
    B. False

17. In the 1990s most states made transfers to adult court easier.
    A. True
    B. False

18. Juveniles like adults are protected from prejudicial lineups and other identification procedures.
    A. True
    B. False

19. Juveniles, unlike adults, do not have rights to appeals.
   A. True
   B. False

20. Juveniles cannot be placed in pretrial detention facilities barring life and death circumstances.
   A. True
   B. False

21. From its origin, the juvenile court granted youths the right to a jury trial, right to counsel, and the protection against self-incrimination.
   A. True
   B. False

22. The child savers and the early juvenile court were more concerned with sex related status offenses of female youths than they were of male youths.
   A. True
   B. False

23. About 150,000 abused, neglected, and delinquent urban youths were relocated to Western farming communities between 1854 and 1930.
   A. True
   B. False

24. Significant attention and resources were devoted to insuring the protection of the rights of juveniles by the child savers.
   A. True
   B. False

25. Prior to the creation of the juvenile justice system, the poor, the insane, the diseased, and vagrant and destitute children were commonly housed in the same institutions.
   A. True
   B. False

FILL IN

1. The first modern juvenile court was created in 1899 in _____.

2. Juvenile Court judges may transfer, or _____, juvenile offenders who are deemed untreatable from the jurisdiction of the juvenile court to the adult criminal justice system.

3. _____ opened in 1825 in New York City; it was founded on the principles of reformation through hard work, manual labor, and strict discipline.

4. Juveniles can be taken into custody for acts that would not be criminal if they were committed by an adult; these offenses are called _____-___.

5. The concept of _____ refers to the power of the state to act in behalf of the child and provide care and protection equivalent to that of a parent.

6. _____ were used to ship urban youths to Western farm communities between 1854 and 1930.

7. While adults are arrested, juveniles are _____.

8. In 1817 prominent New Yorkers formed the _____; the group attacked taverns, brothels, and gambling, but they also viewed the moral training of youths from the dangerous classes as inadequate.

9. From the court's creation in 1899 until the late 1960s, _____ was the burden of proof in a juvenile court case.

10. The _____ was the largest piece of crime legislation in the history of the United States, providing funds to prevent and control delinquency.

11. _____ focus on providing treatment for youths accused of drug-related acts.

12. A _____ is a statistical technique that synthesizes and integrates findings from prior evaluation studies

13. _____ are diversionary courts in which peers determine sanctions for youths who admit to their guilt.

14. If the child denies the allegation of delinquency, a(n) _____ hearing or trial is scheduled.

15. Siegel and Welsh note that juveniles are not "indicted" for a crime; they have a _____ filed against them.

ESSAY

1. Describe the social, political, and economic events that led to the creation of the juvenile justice system.

2. What values are reflected in the philosophy of the juvenile court? What interests and values are being addressed?

3. Discuss the similarities and differences between the adult criminal justice system and the juvenile justice system.

4. Are there still enough significant differences and a pressing social need to justify having a juvenile justice system?

5. What is procedural due process and how was it introduced into the juvenile court?

ANSWER KEY

MULTIPLE CHOICE

1. A	11. A	21. C
2. B	12. D	22. D
3. B	13. C	23. B
4. C	14. C	24. D
5. A	15. A	25. B
6. B	16. C	26. A
7. C	17. D	27. C
8. D	18. C	28. C
9. C	19. A	29. D
10. D	20. A	30. C

TRUE FALSE

1. F	11. T	21. F
2. F	12. T	22. T
3. F	13. F	23. T
4. F	14. T	24. F
5. T	15. T	25. T
6. F	16. T	
7. T	17. T	
8. T	18. T	
9. T	19. F	
10. T	20. F	

FILL IN

1. Chicago
2. waive
3. House of Refuge
4. status offenses
5. *parens patriae*
6. orphan trains
7. take into custody
8. Society for the Prevention of Pauperism
9. preponderance of the evidence
10. Violent Crime Control and law Enforcement Act of 1994
11. drug courts
12. meta-analysis
13. teen courts
14. adjudicatory
15. petition

Multiple Choice

1. According to Anthony Platt, the Child Savers
    A. were primarily motivated to help youth who were facing, without sufficient familial or governmental assistance, the ills of urbanization.
    B. felt threatened by and wanted to control the poor ethnic working classes.
    C. were in favor of greater due process in the juvenile court.
    D. were interested in furthering the autonomy of immigrant youth.

2. The procedure of separating adjudicatory and dispositionary hearings so different levels of evidence can be heard at each is called
    A. transfer/waiver.
    B. bifurcated process.
    C. blended sentencing.
    D. intermediate sanctions.

3. Between 1992 and 1995, _____ states and the District of Columbia changed their transfer statutes to make it easier to waive juveniles to adult courts.
    A. 20
    B. 30
    C. 40
    D. 50

4. Siegel and Welsh point out that
    A. a get-tough approach may suppress some crimes, but the benefits are offset by increased costs of secure placement.
    B. econometric logarithms show that incarcerating youth saves money.
    C. although it costs about the same to incarcerate as to adjudicate them for new crimes if they are released and recidivate, it is unethical if it can be avoided.
    D. there is general agreement that incarceration deters crime.

5. Although terms such as CHINS and PINS were ostensibly applied to prevent labeling, according to the text they also,
    A. allowed for provision of medical care by allowing third party payment.
    B. allowed youth to be sent to regular schools while in hostels.
    C. allowed juvenile courts to expand their role as social service agencies.
    D. allowed for all the procedural protections of adult court.

6 .The maximum age below which children fall under the jurisdiction of the juvenile court
    A. was determined In re Gault (1967) to be 18.
    B. usually is less than 18 years of age.
    C. usually is 16 years old.
    D. varies from state to state.

7. Which factors determine if a policeman will file a petition or not arrest even if he or she has probable cause to do so?
    A. seriousness of the offense
    B. child's past contact with the police
    C. child's denial of offense
    D. all of the above

8. According to the text, when the police do have probable cause,
    A. 80 percent of the time they will file a formal charge.
    B. in many cases they will refer the child to a community service agency instead of filing a formal charge.
    C. the police will in 70 percent of the cases verbally warn the child but take no further action.
    D. they immediately call the department of social services to obtain guidance on whether an arrest or diversion is the most appropriate disposition.

9. In the adjudication procedure, juvenile delinquents have the constitutional right to
    A. to counsel.
    B. be their own lawyers.
    C. jury trial.
    D. counsel from a probation officer.

10. The most common form of disposition in juvenile court is
    A. civil commitment.
    B. half way houses.
    C. boot camp.
    D. probation.

True False
1. In the last twenty years there has been a growing consensus that the juvenile court system should be abolished T F

2. The Child Savers were civil libertarians T   F

3. Most states have the same age of criminal responsibility and eligibility for transfer to adult court T F

4. Drug courts help juveniles obtain treatment while under close supervision of the court T F

5. Juveniles are usually deterred from committing any future crimes once they have been processed through the system. T   F

Answer Key

Multiple Choice

1. b
2. b
3. c
4. a
5. c
6. d
7. d
8. b
9. a
10. d

True False

1. F
2. F
3. F
4. T
5. F

CHAPTER TWELVE
POLICEWORK WITH JUVENILES

LEARNING OBJECTIVES

- Identify key historical events that have shaped juvenile policing in America today.
- Understand key roles and responsibilities of the police in responding to juvenile offenders.
- Be able to comment on the organization and management of police services for juveniles.
- Be aware of major court cases that have influenced police practices.
- Understand key legal aspects of policework, including search and seizure and custodial interrogation, and how they apply to juveniles.
- Be able to describe police use of discretion and factors that influence discretion.
- Understand the importance of police use of discretion with juveniles and some of the associated problems.
- Be aware of the major policing strategies to prevent delinquency.
- See the pros and cons of police using different delinquency prevention strategies.

CHAPTER OUTLINE

Rico's story
    1. One of twelve children in Harlem.
    2. Mother struggled daily to provide for family, however, father heavily involved in criminal activity and drifts in and out of the picture
    3. Rico attended large public school where violence, sexual assaults, and drugs were common
    4. Rico was a brilliant student who aspired to go to college
    5. Rico is involved in fight in school, but policemen assigned to the school use discretion and issue warning only
    6. Rico graduates high school and then attends the University of Cincinnati and becomes a member of the US Boxing team.
    7. Rico graduates with a BA and attends medical school.
    8. Today Rico, or Dr. Richard Larkin, is an assistant professor.

I. History of Juvenile Policing
    A. Origin of police agencies
        1. specialized police services for juveniles is a recent phenomenon
        2. individuals were entrusted with policing themselves with pledge system
        3. watch system was created to police larger communities
    B. Industrial revolution
        1. first organized police force was established in London in 1829
        2. in the America, sheriff became the most important police official
        3. reform efforts
            a. Wickersham Commission of 1931

b. International Association of Chiefs of Police

c. August Vollmer, police chief in Berkeley, California

4. outside influences

a. U.S. Supreme Court handed down decisions

b. LEAA funded justice-related programs

C. Role of the juvenile police officer

1. specialized juvenile police programs are more the norm

2. many police programs involve prevention components

3. programs address child abuse, domestic violence, and missing children

II. Police and Juvenile Offenders

A. Primary responsibility

1. police primary responsibility is to protect the public

2. police work is substantially different from its fictional glorification

B. Redefined mission

1. police role should be to maintain order

2. be a visible and accessible component of the community

3. aggressive action by police can help reduce the incidence of repeat offending

4. little evidence for adding police or skills to reduce crime

5. improving police and community relationships is critical

6. percentage of youth who believe police are honest varies by race: 57 percent of European Americans, 51 percent of Asian Americans, 31 percent of Hispanic Americans, 30 percent of Native Americans, and 15 percent of African Americans.

C. Police roles

1. juvenile officers operate as specialists as part of the juvenile unit

2. most officers regard the violations of juveniles as non-serious

3. serious juvenile offenders are small minority of the offender population

4. juvenile offenders can produce major role conflicts for police

a. 73% of all juvenile arrests are referred to juvenile court

b. 20% of all juvenile arrests are handled informally

5. police may adopt law enforcer or delinquency prevention worker role

D. Police and violent juvenile crime

1. crimes of homicide, rape, robbery, aggravated assault, and kidnapping

2. justice agencies experiment with different methods of controlling violent youth

a. increased directed patrols in street-corner hot spots of crime

b. proactive arrests of serious repeat offenders

c. problem-oriented policing

3. improving communications between the police and the community

4. policing programs that work

        a. increased directed patrols in street-corner hot spots of crime

        b. proactive arrests of serious repeat offenders

        c. proactive arrests of drunk drivers

        d. arrests of employed suspects for domestic assault

        e. problem-oriented policing

    5. what does not work

        a. neighborhood block watch

        b. arrests of juveniles for minor offenses

        c. arrests of unemployed suspects for domestic assault

        d. drug market arrests

        e. community policing that is not targeted at risk factors

        f. adding extra police in cities with no regard to assignment

III. Police and the Rule of Law

    A. Arrest procedure

        1. police decide whether to release him or make a referral to juvenile court

        2. cases involving serious crimes are often referred to court

        3. less serious cases are often diverted from court action

        4. most states require the law of arrest be the same for both adults and juveniles

        5. to make a legal arrest:

            a. officer must have probable cause to believe that an offense took place

            b. the suspect is the guilty party

            c. probable cause is between a mere suspicion and absolute certainty

        6. misdemeanor cases

            a. the police officer must personally observe the crime

        7. felony cases

            a. can be made based on probable cause

        8. statutes are designed to give the police the authority to *act in loco parentis*

        9. juvenile is not arrested but rather taken into custody

    B. Search and seizure

        1. fourth amendment protections

            a. protected against unreasonable searches and seizures

            b. warrants issued based on probable cause

            c. particularity requirement of searches and seizures

        2. pretrial motion to suppress the evidence illegally obtained evidence

            a. person may be searched after a legal arrest

            b. automobile search based on probable cause

            c. suspect's outer garments may be frisked if police are suspicious

        3. warrantless searches

            a. stop-and-frisk-pat down of a suspect's outer garments

b. search incident to arrest- body search after a legal arrest

c. vehicle search based on probable cause

d. consent search based on knowingly and voluntarily consent

e. plain view- seize suspicious objects seen in plain view

f. electronic surveillance based on expectation of privacy

C. Custodial interrogation

1. Supreme Court placed constitutional limitations on police interrogation

a. 1966 *Miranda v. Arizona*

2. specific rights

a. they have the right to remain silent

b. any statements they make can be used against them

c. they have the right to counsel

d. if they cannot afford counsel, it will be furnished at public expense

3. Miranda warning has been made applicable to children taken into custody

4. parents or attorneys need not be present for children for rights waiver

5. California case: *People v. Lara*

a. waiver determined by the totality of the circumstances doctrine

6. most controversial legal issues addressed in the state courts

a. *Fare v. Michael C.*

b. *California v. Prysock*

IV. Discretionary Justice

A. Discretion

1. police rely on their discretion to choose an appropriate course of action

2. low-visibility decision making

3. informality that has been built into the system

4. discretion may permit the law to discriminate against particular groups

5. procedures of juvenile personnel are rarely subject to judicial review

6. problem of discretion is one of extremes

7. Project on Policing Neighborhoods

a. police still use discretion

b. 13% of police encounters with juveniles resulted in arrest

c. search or interrogation of suspects in 24% of the encounters

8. three-quarters of all juvenile arrests are referred to juvenile court

9. police are much more likely to take formal action when:

a. the crime is serious

b. reported by a victim who is a respected member of the community

c. offender is well known to them

B. Environmental factors
    1. norms of the community affect the decision
    2. perception of community alternatives to police intervention
C. Police policy
    1. policies and customs of the local police department
    2. galvanize the local media to demand police action
    pressure from supervisors
D. Situational factors
    1. specific traits of offenders
    2. dress, attitude, speech, and level of hostility toward the police
    3. recent research challenges the influence of demeanor on decision making
    4. important variables in the police discretionary process
        a. attitude of the complainant
        b. type and seriousness of the offense
        c. race, sex, and age of the offender
        d. attitude of the offender
        e. offender's prior contacts with the police
        f. perceived willingness of the parents to assist
        g. setting or location in which the incident occurs
        h. if the offender denies the actions or insists on a court hearing
        i. likelihood that a child can be served by a community agency
E. Bias and police discretion
    1. phrase "Driving While Black" has been coined
    2. law enforcement policy that disproportionately affects African-Americans
        a. law-abiding African Americans are more often victims of crimes, therefore over policing may be necessary
    3. Bishop and Frazier found that race can have a direct effect on decisions
        a. African Americans more likely recommended for formal processing,
        b. referred to court,
        c. adjudicated delinquent, and
        d. given harsher dispositions for comparable offenses
F. Gender bias
    1. some research support for various forms of gender bias
    2. police are less likely to process females for delinquent acts
    3. discriminate against females by arresting them for status offenses
    4. female status offenders are arrested for less serious offenses than boys
    5. double standard in court for males and females
G. Organizational bias
    1. policies may result in biased practices

2. bureaucratized and unprofessional departments
      a. likely to be insulated from the communities they serve
3. administrators may have stereotyped view of the urban poor
      a. troublemakers and needing control
4. lower-class neighborhoods experience much greater police scrutiny
5. Sampson's research indicates police officers
      a. may not discriminate on an individual level
      b. class and racial bias in the police processing of delinquent youth

V. Police Work and Delinquency Prevention
    A. Aggressive law enforcement
        1. aggressive patrolling targeted at specific patterns of delinquency
        2. tactics which have not proven to be effective against gangs
            a. saturation patrol
            b. targeting gang areas
            c. arresting members for any law violations
        3. making aggressive enforcement of curfew and truancy laws
    B. Police in schools
        1. more than 14,000 full-time police working as school resource officers
        a. develop recreational programs for juveniles
        b. develop delinquency prevention programs
        2. Gang Resistance Education and Training (G.R.E.A.T.) program
        a. to reduce gang activity
        b. teach students the negative consequences of gang membership
        c. evaluations of G.R.E.A.T. show mixed results
        3. Community Outreach Through Police in Schools Program
        a. better understand the way their feelings affect their behavior
        b. develop constructive means of responding to violence and trauma
        c. change their attitudes toward police
    C. Community policing
        1. emergence of the community policing model is important change
            a. gain the trust and assistance of concerned citizens
            b. to increase feelings of community safety
        2. Youth Firearms Violence Initiative (YFVI)
        a. education and intervention programs related to handgun safety
        b. community-based programs on youth handgun violence
        c. assist families in addressing youth handgun problems
    D. Problem-oriented policing
        1. involves a systematic analysis of problems
        2. response to the problems or conditions underlying criminal incidents

3. more proactive than incident-driving policing
4. four-step model, often referred to as S.A.R.A
    a. scanning involves identifying a specific crime problem through data
    b. analysis involves in-depth analysis of the crime problem
    c. response- partners respond to problem based on analysis
    d. assessment- response to the problem as evaluated

E. Boston's Operation Ceasefire
1. intervention strategies are also important
    a. specific delinquency prevention strategies
    b. juvenile justice sanctions
    c. public information campaign on consequences of gun violence
2. aims to reduce youth homicide victimization and youth gun violence
    a. implemented in Boston
    b. police program with juvenile and criminal justice and social agencies
3. program has two main elements
    a. focus on illicit gun traffickers who supply youth with guns
    b. attempt to generate a strong deterrent to gang violence
    c. track and seize illegal guns and targeting traffickers
    d. pull every deterrence lever available
    e. 63% reduction in mean monthly number of youth homicide victims
    f. significant decreases in gun assaults and gang violence

CHAPTER SUMMARY

Modern policing developed in England at the beginning of the nineteenth century. The Industrial Revolution, recognition of the need to treat children as a distinguishable group, and growing numbers of unemployed and homeless youths were among some of the key events that helped shape juvenile policing in America. The contemporary role of juvenile officers is similar to that of officers working with adult offenders: to intervene if the actions of a citizen produce public danger or disorder. Juvenile officers must also have a thorough knowledge of the law, especially the constitutional protections available to juveniles. Juvenile officers operate either as specialists in a police department or as part of the juvenile unit of a police department.

Through the *Miranda v. Arizona* decision, the U.S. Supreme Court established a clearly defined procedure for custodial interrogation. Most courts have held that the Fourth Amendment ban against unreasonable search and seizure applies to juveniles and that illegally seized evidence is inadmissible in a juvenile trial. Most courts have concluded that parents or attorneys need not be present for children effectively to waive their right to remain silent. Discretion is a low-visibility decision made in the administration of adult and juvenile justice. Discretionary decisions are made without guidelines from the police administrator. Numerous factors influence the decisions police make about juvenile offenders, including the seriousness of the offense, the harm inflicted on the victim, and the likelihood that the juvenile will break the law again. Discretion is essential in providing individualized justice but problems such as discrimination, unfairness, and bias toward particular groups of juveniles must be controlled.

Police have taken the lead in delinquency prevention. Major policing strategies to prevent delinquency include aggressive law enforcement, police in schools, community policing, and problem-oriented policing. The ever-changing nature of juvenile delinquency calls for further experimentation and innovation in policing strategies to prevent delinquency. Tailoring policing activities to local conditions and engaging the community and other stakeholders are important first steps.

KEY TERMS

Pledge system: English system in which neighbors protected each other from thieves and warring groups.

Watch system: Replaced the pledge system in England; watchmen patrolled urban areas at night to provide protection from harm.

Community policing: Police strategy that emphasizes fear reduction, community organization, and order maintenance rather than crime fighting.

Juvenile officers: Police officers who specialize in dealing with juvenile offenders; they may operate alone or as part of a juvenile police unit in the department.

Role conflicts: Conflicts police officers face that revolve around the requirement to perform their primary duty of law enforcement and a desire to aid in rehabilitating youthful offenders.

Informants: individuals who have access to criminal networks and who, under conditions of anonymity, provide information to authorities in exchange for money or special treatment.

Problem-oriented policing: Law enforcement that focuses on addressing the problems underlying incidents of juvenile delinquency rather than the incidents alone.

Arrest: Taking a person into the custody of the law to restrain the accused until he or she can be held accountable for the offense in court proceedings.

Probable cause: Reasonable ground to believe the existence of facts that an offense was committed and that the accused committed that offense.

search and seizure: The U.S. Constitution protects citizens from any search and seizure by police without a lawfully obtained search warrant; such warrants are issued when there is probable cause to believe that an offense has been committed.

custodial interrogation: Questions posed by the police to a suspect held in custody in the prejudicial stage of the juvenile justice process; juveniles have the same rights against self-incrimination as adults when being questioned.

Miranda warning: Supreme Court decisions require police officers to inform individuals under arrest of their constitutional rights; warnings must also be given when suspicion begins to focus on an individual in the accusatory stage.

Discretion: Use of personal decision making and choice in carrying out operations in the criminal justice system, such as deciding whether to make an arrest or accept a plea bargain.

Procedural justice: describes in detail the methods and procedures to be used in determining and enforcing the rights and duties of persons toward each other under substantive law, which is the part of law that creates, defines, and regulates rights

SELF TEST QUESTIONS

MULTIPLE CHOICE

1. Before the Norman conquest of England, the _____ assumed that neighbors would protect each other from thieves and warring groups.
    A. constable   C. national militia
    B. posse   D. pledge system

2. By the thirteenth century, the _____ was created to police larger communities; men were organized in church parishes to patrol areas at night and guard against disturbances and breaches of the peace.
    A. watch system   C. national militia
    B. posse   D. pledge system

3. By the seventeenth century, the _____, the justice of the peace, and the night watchman formed the nucleus of the police system.
    A. constable   C. national militia
    B. posse   D. pledge system

4. When the industrial revolution brought thousands of people from the countryside to work in factories, the need for police protection increased; as a result, the first organized police force was organized in _____.
    A. Boston in 1854   C. London in 1829
    B. New York in 1779   D. New York in 1899

5. The most famous police reformer of the 1930s was _____; as the police chief of Berkeley, CA, he instituted numerous reforms, including university training, modern management techniques, prevention programs, and juvenile aid bureaus.
    A. O.W. Wilson   C. Peel
    B. Vollmer   D. Parker

6. Many police departments adopted the concept that the police role should be to maintain order and be a visible and accessible component of the community; this movement, referred to as _____, argues that police efforts can be successful only when conducted in partnership with concerned citizens.
    A. problem oriented policing   C. militaristic model policing
    B. traditional policing   D. community policing

7. Juveniles account for about _____ percent of all violent crime arrests.
    A. 16   C. 36
    B. 26   D. 46

8. Handling juvenile offenders can produce major _____ for police; they may experience a tension between their desire to perform what they consider their primary duty, law enforcement, and the need to aid in the rehabilitation of youthful offenders.

    A. role conflicts   C. moral ambiguity
    B. role strain   D. legal dilemmas

9. It is estimated that _____ percent of all juvenile arrests are handled informally within the police department or are referred to a community service agency.

    A. 5   C. 30
    B. 20   D. 64

10. _____ was the most common disposition of police encounters with juveniles.

    A. Release   C. Command/threaten
    B. Search/interrogate   D. Arrest

11. _____ is law enforcement that is focused on addressing the problems underlying incidents of juvenile delinquency rather than the incidents only.

    A. Community policing   C. Traditional policing
    B. Problem oriented policing   D. Militaristic policing

12. Which of the following is *not* one of the programs identified as policing programs that work?

    A. increased directed patrols in street-corner hot spots of crime
    B. proactive arrests of serious repeat offenders
    C. neighborhood block watch
    D. problem-oriented policing

13. _____ is reasonable grounds to believe that an offense was committed and that the accused committed that offense.

    A. Preponderance of the evidence   C. Reasonable doubt
    B. Reasonable suspicion   D. Probable cause

14. Which of the following is the legal standard in order that police can make an arrest for felonies that they do not witness?

    A. reasonable suspicion   C. probable cause
    B. hunch   D. absolute certainty

15. _____ is taking a person into the custody of the law to restrain the accused until he or she can be held accountable for the offense in court proceedings.

    A. Bail   C. Arrest
    B. Detention   D. Waiver

16. The _____ amendment states the right of the people to be secure in their persons, houses, papers, and effects, against unreasonable searches and seizures.

    A. First   C. Fifth
    B. Fourth   D. Sixth

17. Which of the following statements is not part of the Miranda warnings?
    A. They have the right to remain silent.
    B. Any statements they make can be used against them.
    C. Failing to talk to the police can be used against them.
    D. They have the right to counsel.

18. The authors note that research indicates that there are a number of effective policing practices, including: increased directed patrols in street-corner hotspots of crime, proactive arrests of serious repeat offenders, and _____.
    A. problem oriented policing   C. hiring more police
    B. gun buy back programs   D. saturation patrols

19. Juveniles can waive their Miranda rights, but the validity of the waiver is determined by the circumstances of each case to include his or her age, his or her education level, his or her knowledge of the charges, whether he or she was allowed to consult with family, and the method of interrogation; this illustrates the _____ test.
    A. wait and see   C. IQ waiver
    B. Liar, Liar pants on fire test   D. totality of the circumstances

20. Most juvenile codes provide broad authority for the police to take juveniles into custody; such statutes are designed to give the police the authority to act _____.
    A. *in loco policius*   C. *in forma paupera*
    B. *in loco parentis*   D. *in domino padre*

21. In _____, the court ruled that the question of a child's waiver is to be determined by the totality of the circumstances doctrine.
    A. *People v. Lara*   C. *Miranda v. Arizona*
    B. *People v. Dukes*   D. *California v. Prysock*

22. In _____, the Court ruled that a youth's asking to speak to his probation officer was not the equivalent of asking for an attorney; consequently, statements he made to the police absent legal counsel were admissible in court.
    A. *Schall v. Martin*   C. *California v. Prysock*
    B. *Fare v. Michael C.*   D. *People v. Dukes*

23. Police _____ is selective enforcement of the law by authorized police agents; it gives officers a choice among possible courses of action within the limits on their power.
    A. bias   C. discretion
    B. discrimination   D. absolute power

24. The norms of the community affect discretion; some officers work in communities that tolerate a fair amount of personal freedom, while others work in more conservative communities that expect a no-nonsense approach to law enforcement. Which source of discretion do these points illustrate?
    A. environmental factors   C. situational factors
    B. police policy   D. officer characteristics

25. Recent research has challenged the influence of suspect's demeanor on police decision making, suggesting that it is delinquent behavior and actions that occur during police detention that influence the police decision to take formal action. Which source of discretion does this point illustrate?

    A. environmental factors   C. situational factors

    B. police policy   D. officer characteristics

26. Which of the following statements concerning gender bias in the juvenile justice system is false?

    A. Police tend to be more lenient toward females than males with regard to acts of delinquency.

    B. Females seem to be referred to juvenile court more often than males for minor or status offenses.

    C. Younger female offenders are treated by police in a harsher manner than older ones.

    D. Police tend to be more lenient toward males than females with regard to acts of delinquency.

27. Boston's _____ had two main elements: a direct law-enforcement focus on illicit gun traffickers that supply youths with guns, and an attempt to generate a strong deterrent to gang violence.

    A. Operation Gladiola   C. Project Hope

    B. Operation Ceasefire   D. Civil Liberties Task Force

28. The G.R.E.A.T. program

    A. works in conjunction with drug courts to force non-violence drug users to treatment.

    B. has had no effect upon gangs.

    C. is a community organization rather than school approach.

    D. like DARE, has trained police come into the classrooms.

29. A recent study in Indianapolis, as part of Project on Policing neighborhoods, found that _____ of police encounters with juveniles resulted in arrest?

    A. 13

    B. 23

    C. 33

    D. 43

30. Who found that African Americans are more likely than European Americans to be recommend for formal processing, referred to court, adjudicated delinquent, and given harsher dispositions for comparable offenses?

    A. Kennedy

    B. Bishop and Frazier

    C. Van De Haag

    D. Loeber and Loeber

TRUE/FALSE

1. According to the LEMAS survey, eighty-two percent of local police officers were employed by a department that had full time community policing officers.
    A. True
    B. False

2. Police are much less likely to refer juvenile offenders to courts; it is estimated that eighty-eight percent of all juvenile arrests are handled informally within the police department or are referred to a community service agency.
    A. True
    B. False

3. The systematic nature of problem oriented policing is characterized by its adherence to a four-step model, often referred to as DAWN.
    A. True
    B. False

4. Most states require that the law of arrest be the same for both adults and juveniles.
    A. True
    B. False

5. It is estimated that 70 percent of all juvenile arrests are referred to juvenile court, whereas just over 20 percent of all juvenile arrests are handled informally within the police department or are referred to a community-service agency.
    A. True
    B. False

6. Boston's Operation Ceasefire involved the police and social service agencies of the greater Boston area.
    A. True
    B. False

7. The three factors mentioned in the text as most salient in shaping police discretion include race, policies and customs of the police dept, and class of the offender
    A.   True
    B.   False

8. Juveniles typically account for about forty-five percent of all violent crime arrests.
    A. True
    B. False

9. Juveniles typically account for about sixteen percent of all violent crime arrests.
    A. True
    B. False

10. Traditional professional policing is law enforcement that is focused on addressing the problems underlying incidents of juvenile delinquency rather than the incidents only.
    A. True
    B. False

11. Problem-oriented policing is law enforcement that is focused on addressing the problems underlying incidents of juvenile delinquency rather than the incidents only.
    A. True
    B. False

12. In misdemeanor cases, the police officer must personally observe the crime to place a suspect in custody for the offense.
    A. True
    B. False

13. For a felony, the police officer may make a legal arrest without having observed the crime if the officer has probable cause to believe that an offense took place and the person being arrested committed it.
    A. True
    B. False

14. For a misdemeanor, the police officer may make a legal arrest without having observed the crime if the officer has probable cause to believe that an offense took place and the person being arrested committed it.
    A. True
    B. False

15. Most juvenile codes provide broad authority for the police to take juveniles into custody; such statutes are designed to give the police the authority to act *in loco parentis*.
    A. True
    B. False

16. The Fifth Amendment states that the right of the people to be secure in their persons, houses, papers, and effects, against unreasonable searches and seizures, shall not be violated, and no warrants shall issue, but upon probable cause, supported by oath or affirmation, and particularly describing the place to be searched, and the persons or things to be seized.
    A. True
    B. False

17. The Fourth Amendment states the right of the people to be secure in their persons, houses, papers, and effects, against unreasonable searches and seizures, shall not be violated, and no warrants shall issue, but upon probable cause, supported by oath or affirmation, and particularly describing the place to be searched, and the persons or things to be seized.
    A. True
    B. False

18. Most courts have held that the Fourth Amendment ban against unreasonable search and seizure applies to juveniles, and that illegally seized evidence is inadmissible in a juvenile trial.
   A. True
   B. False

19. As a general rule, juveniles can waive their rights to protection from self-incrimination, but the validity of the waiver is determined by the circumstances of each case.
   A. True
   B. False

20. As a general rule, juveniles can waive their rights to protection from self-incrimination, but the validity of the waiver is determined by the suspect's age.
   A. True
   B. False

21. In *Fare v. Michael C*, the Court ruled that a youth's asking to speak to his probation officer was not the equivalent of asking for an attorney; consequently, statements he made to the police absent legal counsel were admissible in court.
   A. True
   B. False

22. Traditionally, it was believed that police officers rely heavily on the demeanor and appearance of the juvenile in making the decision to arrest; recent research has challenged the influence of suspect's demeanor on police decision making, suggesting that it is delinquent behavior and actions that occur during police detention that influence the police decision to take formal action.
   A. True
   B. False

23. Minority representation in arrest statistics indicates that African-American youths make up almost half of the juvenile arrests for homicide.
   A. True
   B. False

24. Sampson found that teenage residents of neighborhoods with low socioeconomic status have a significantly greater chance of acquiring police records than youths living in higher socioeconomic areas, regardless of the actual crime rates in these areas.
   A. True
   B. False

25. Goldman's research found that 64 percent of juveniles were handled informally by the police.
   A. True
   B. False

FILL IN:

1. Before the Norman conquest of England, the _____ system assumed that neighbors would protect each other from thieves and warring groups.

2. By the thirteenth century, the _____ system was created to police larger communities; men were organized in church parishes to patrol areas at night and guard against disturbances and breaches of the peace.

3. By the seventeenth century, the _____, the justice of the peace, and the night watchman formed the nucleus of the police system.

4. The most famous police reformer of the 1930s was _____; as the police chief of Berkeley, CA, he instituted numerous reforms, including university training, modern management techniques, prevention programs, and juvenile aid bureaus.

5. Many police departments adopted the concept that the police role should be to maintain order and be a visible and accessible component of the community; this movement, referred to as _____ policing, argues that police efforts can be successful only when conducted in partnership with concerned citizens.

6. In _____, the Court ruled that a youth's asking to speak to his probation officer was not the equivalent of asking for an attorney; consequently, statements he made to the police absent legal counsel were admissible in court.

7. Handling juvenile offenders can produce major _____ for police; they may experience a tension between their desire to perform what they consider their primary duty, law enforcement, and the need to aid in the rehabilitation of youthful offenders.

8. The _____ or paternalism hypothesis holds that police are likely to act paternally toward young girls and not arrest them.

9. _____ policing is law enforcement that is focused on addressing the problems underlying incidents of juvenile delinquency rather than the incidents only.

10. _____ is reasonable grounds to believe that an offense was committed and that the accused committed that offense.

11. Most juvenile codes provide broad authority for the police to take juveniles into custody; such statutes are designed to give the police the authority to act_____.

12. _____ is taking a person into the custody of the law to restrain the accused until he or she can be held accountable for the offense in court proceedings.

289

13. The _____ Amendment states that the right of the people to be secure in their persons, houses, papers, and effects, against unreasonable searches and seizures, shall not be violated, and no warrants shall issue, but upon probable cause, supported by oath or affirmation, and particularly describing the place to be searched, and the persons or things to be seized.

14. _____ is defined as questions posed by the police to a suspect held in custody in the prejudicial stage of the juvenile justice process.

15. In *People v.* _____, the US Supreme Court ruled that the question of a child's waiver is to be determined by the totality of the circumstances doctrine.

ESSAY

1. Contrast community policing, problem oriented policing, and traditional policing.

2. Identify and discuss the areas affecting police discretion.

3. Discuss custodial interrogations of juveniles. Under what circumstances can juveniles legally waive their rights against self-incrimination?

4. Identify the requirements for a lawful arrest.

5. Discuss an integrated, community-policing strategy identified in the chapter.

ANSWER KEY

MULTIPLE CHOICE

1. D	11. B	21. A
2. A	12. C	22. B
3. A	13. D	23. C
4. C	14. C	24. A
5. B	15. C	25. C
6. D	16. B	26. D
7. A	17. C	27. B
8. A	18. A	28 D
9. B	19. D	29 A
10. C	20. B	30 B

TRUE FALSE

1. T	11. T	21. T
2. F	12. T	22. T
3. F	13. T	23. T
4. T	14. F	24. T
5. T	15. T	25 T
6. T	16. F	
7. F	17. T	
8. F	18. T	
9. T	19. T	
10. F	20. F	

FILL IN

1. pledge	11. *in loco parentis*
2. watch	12. arrest
3. constable	13. fourth
4. Vollmer	14. custodial interrogation
5. community	15. *Lara*
6. *Fare v. Michael C.*	
7. role conflicts	
8. chivalry	
9. problem orientated	
10. probable cause	

Multiple Choice

1. August Vollmer instituted all of the following except:
   A. modern management techniques
   B. prevention programs
   C. juvenile bureaus
   D. NCIC

2. Which of the following acts was a catalyst for developing hundreds of new police programs and enhancing police services for children?
   A. Law Enforcement Assistance Association
   B. Kerner Commission
   C. Omnibus Crime Bill
   D. All of the following were catalysts for developing hundreds of new police programs and enhancing police services for children.

3. Which of the following is not an example of a specialized juvenile police program?
   A. DARE
   B. Gang control
   C. Juvenile court
   D. Zero tolerance policing

4. Which of the following is not true about community policing?
   A. it is based on partnership with citizens and citizen's groups in the community
   B. it rejects crime control as basic to policing
   C. it seeks to reach out to diverse elements of the community
   D. it has been credited by some for recent reductions in crime

5. Which group of juvenile's overwhelmingly believe that the police are not honest?
   A. Native Americans
   B. African Americans
   C. Asian Americans
   D. Hispanic Americans

6. The chapter began with Rico's story. Why did he credit the NYPD for his success in college and career?
   A. They forced him to change by arresting him.
   B. They referred him to drug court.
   C. They referred him to counseling and anger management.
   D. They encouraged him, rather than arrest him after his fight.

7. What percentage of juvenile arrestees are referred to juvenile court?
   A. 30
   B. 40
   C. 60

D. 70

8. Role conflicts of police officers when dealing with juvenile offenders
   A. exist due to many situations with no clear solution and limited options.
   B. interfere with effective and efficient policing and can be eradicated.
   C. are increased with community policing due to the influence of many groups.
   D. make obtaining convictions almost impossible and lead to cases being thrown out of court.

9. According to the text, during a stop-and-frisk the police
   A. can conduct a full body search.
   B. may pat down a suspect's outer garments.
   C. may search a car.
   D. may search the trunk in a car.

10. According to the text, Miranda warnings must be made when a juvenile
    A. is subject to custodial interrogation.
    B. stopped-and-frisked.
    C. is asked to identify himself.
    D. all of the above.

True-False
1. It is settled that police are more deferential to female than male offenders T F

2. According to the text, role conflicts can be reduced by passing more rules and regulations T F

3. To make a lawful arrest with juveniles, reasonable suspicion rather than probable cause is the legal threshold T F

4. Collaborating with community organizations is at the heart of community policing efforts to reduce juvenile delinquency. T F

5. The requirements to invoke Miranda warnings are noncustodial interrogation T F

Multiple Choice
1. D
2. A
3. D
4. B
5. B
6. D
7. D
8. A
9. B
10. A

True False
1. F
2. F
3. F
4. T
5. F

CHAPTER THIRTEEN
JUVENILE COURT PROCESS: PRETRIAL, TRIAL, AND SENTENCING

LEARNING OBJECTIVES

- Understand the roles and responsibilities of the main players in the juvenile court.
- Be able to discuss key issues of the preadjudicatory stage of juvenile justice, including detention, intake, diversion, pretrial release, plea bargaining, and waiver.
- Be able to argue the pros and cons of waiving youths to adult court.
- Understand key issues of the trial stage of juvenile justice, including constitutional rights of youths and disposition.
- Be familiar with major U.S. Supreme Court decisions that have influenced the handling of juveniles at the preadjudicatory and trial stages.
- Know the most common dispositions for juvenile offenders.
- Be able to argue the pros and cons of confidentiality in juvenile proceedings and privacy of juvenile records.

CHAPTER OUTLINE

Cliff's story
    1. Cliff is a 16 year old European-American raised by grandparents in a rural community
    2. He and his sisters were removed from the parents when he was 7 due to domestic violence and parental drug abuse
    3. Cliff does poorly in school and has been charged with disorderly conduct and threatening to assault his grandfather, and is suspected of taking drugs
    4. He has threatened suicide and has been diagnosed with bipolar disorder
    5. Cliff received juvenile probation and functional family treatment
    6. Functional family treatment involves the entire community in dealing with his problems. A year long follow-up establishes that he has exhibited fewer problematic and criminal behaviors

I. Juvenile Court and Its Jurisdiction
    A. Organization
        1. juvenile court can be part of a criminal trial court or probate court
        2. Independent juvenile court is a specialized court for children
        3. two often incompatible goals
            a. acting in the best interest of the child
            b. acting in the best interest of public protection
    B. Court case flow
        1. 1.6 million delinquency cases are adjudicated annually
        2. case flow decreased 11 percent since 1997
        3. downward trend comes after steady increase beginning in the mid-1980's

4.   74% of delinquency cases involved a male
5.   29% of delinquency cases involved African-American youths
C. Actors in the juvenile courtroom
    1. defense attorney
        a. delinquent youth have right of counsel at state trials
        b. courts must provide counsel to indigent defendants
        c. defense attorney helps outline the child's position
        d. detention hearings and bail
        e. attorney represents the child at adjudication
        f. play a critical role in the disposition hearing
        g. protects the child's right to treatment
        h. many juvenile offenders do not trust their attorney
        i. court-appointed attorneys work for the system
        j. effective participation of the juvenile as a defendant
        k. understanding of the lawyer's advocacy role
        l. confidential nature of the attorney-client relationship
    2. guardian ad litem
        a. when there is a question of a need for a particular treatment
        b. guardian ad litem acts in child's best interests
    3. court appointed special advocates
        a. volunteers who advise the court about child placement
        b. they would investigate the needs of children
    4. public defender services for children
        a. states have expanded public defender services
        b. an all-public defender program
        c. an appointed private-counsel system
        d. combination system of public defenders and private attorneys
    5. Public defender issues
        a. many juveniles still go to court unrepresented
        b. lawyers work on more than 500 cases per year
        c. half leave their jobs in under two years
        d. lack investigatory support and other resources
    6. prosecutor
        a. responsible for bringing the state's case against the juvenile
        b. selected by political appointment or popular election
        c. adversary process inconsistent with treatment
        d. prosecutor not part of the original juvenile court model
        e. prosecutors control over intake and waiver decisions
        f. have broad discretion in the exercise of their duties
    7. juvenile court judge
        a. rule on pretrial motions
        b. make decisions about the continued detention
        c. make decisions about plea-bargaining agreements
        d. handle trials
        e. holding disposition hearings

f. handle waiver proceedings

g. handle appeals where allowed by statute

h. extensive influence over other agencies of the court

i. exercise considerable leadership to juvenile justice problems

II. Juvenile Court Process

    A. Release or detain?

        1. decision whether to detain will be made

        2. detention can be a traumatic experience

        3. variety of youths in detention

            a. neglected and dependent, runaways, or homeless

            b. others have had a trial but have not been sentenced

            c. some are awaiting the imposition of their sentence

            d. some may have violated probation

            e. some are adjudicated youths awaiting transfer to a training school

        4. effort to remove status offenders from detention facilities

        5. juveniles detained in 20% of all delinquency cases

            a. violent 25%

            b. property 17%

            c. drugs 20%

            d. public order 21%

            e. 329,800 youths in detention

        6. typical delinquent detainee

            a. male

            b. over sixteen years of age

            c. charged with a violent crime

        7. most youths are released to their parents or guardians

        8. detained if the police believe they are inclined to run away

        9. are likely to commit an offense

        10. dangerous to the parent

        11. formal petition should be filed within twenty-four hours

        12. facilities should provide youth with:

            a. education, visitation, and private communications

            b. counseling and continuous supervision

            c. health care, nutrition, recreation, and reading

    B. Detention Diversion Advocacy Program

        1. employs laypersons to advocate for youthful offenders at disposition hearings

        2. relies on a case-management strategy

        3.identifying youths likely to be detained pending their adjudication

        4. restricted to youth currently held, or likely to be held, in secure detention

        5. DDAP case managers present a release plan to the judge

6. emphasis is placed on allowing the youth to live at home

7. frequent and consistent support and supervision to the children

8. evaluations indicate that it is very successful:

    a. lower overall recidivism rate

    b. lower percentage of youths with two or more subsequent referrals

    c. lower percentage returned to court on a violent crime charge

    d. lower percentage with two or more subsequent petitions

C. Adult jails

    1. significant problem in juvenile justice is placing youths in adult jails

    until recently, placing juveniles in adult facilities was common

    2. JJDPA amended to require states to remove all juveniles from adult lockups

    3. state could lose federal juvenile justice funds

    4. adults neither have contact nor share programs or staff

    5. debate whether the initiative has succeeded

    6. OJJDP made deinstitutionalization of status offenders a cornerstone of policy

        a. prohibits the placement of status offenders in secure detention facilities

        b. reduces interaction with serious offenders

        c. insulates status offenders from stigma of being a detainee

    8. should juvenile court be stripped of jurisdiction over status offenders

D. Bail for children

    1. adults retain the right to reasonable bail in non-capital cases

        a. contained in the Eighth Amendment to the Constitution

    2. most states refuse juveniles the right to bail

    3. juvenile proceedings are civil, not criminal

    4. statutory provisions allow children to be released into parental custody

    5. U.S. Supreme Court has never decided the issue of juvenile bail

E. Preventive detention

    1. state has a right to detain dangerous youth until their trial

        a. *Schall v. Martin*

        b. upheld the state of New York's preventive detention statute

        c. most states allow "dangerous" youths to be held indefinitely before trial

        d. robbery, assault, and criminal possession of a weapon

        e. arrested at 11:30 P.M. and lied about his residence

        f. Martin was found to be a delinquent

        g. sentenced to two years' probation

        h. filed a class action for all youths subject to preventive detention

2. U.S. Supreme Court upheld state's right for preventive detention

3. pretrial detention need not be considered punishment

4. preventive detention deprives offenders of their freedom

    a.   their guilt has not been proven

F. Intake process

1.screening of cases by the juvenile court system

2.determine whether the services of the juvenile court are needed

3. process reduces demands on court resources

4. enables assistance from community agencies without court intervention

5. 16% of all delinquency cases in 2002 were dismissed at intake

6. 26% were processed informally

7. enter into consent decrees with juveniles without filing petitions

    a. consent decree is a court order authorizing disposition of the case

    b. without a formal label of delinquency

8. few formal criteria for selecting children for such alternatives

G. Diversion

1. important alternatives chosen at intake is non-judicial disposition

2. involves abandoning efforts to apply coercive measures to a defendant

3. employ a particular formula for choosing youths

4. created to remove non-serious offenders from the justice system

5. provide them with non-punitive treatment services

6. help them avoid the stigma of a delinquent label

7. widening the net

    a. use diversion for youths ordinarily turned loose at intake

    b. find diversion a more attractive alternative

8. diversion has also been criticized as ineffective

9. some challenge the net-widening concept as naive

H. Petition

1. report to the court to initiate the intake process

2. formal complaint that initiates judicial action against a juvenile

3. petition includes basic information:

    a. name, age, and residence of the child;

    b. the parents' names; and

    c. facts alleging the child's delinquency

4. if the child does not admit to the facts in the petition

    a. date is set for a hearing on the petition

5. if after being given the right to counsel

    a. child admits the allegation in the petition

    b. hearing scheduled to make admission before the court

    c. information is gathered to develop a treatment plan

6. the court may issue a summons

7. some require petition be filed under oath

    a. or an affidavit accompany the petition

b. while other states proceed by petition alone

I. Plea and plea bargaining

    1. more than 90 percent of all adult defendants plead guilty

    2. exchange of prosecutorial and judicial concessions for guilty pleas

    3. court determines an appropriate disposition

        a. If the child admits to the facts

    4. plea bargaining seen as unnecessary since no jury trials or long sentences

    5.court must dispose of cases in the best interests of the child

    6. some hold that plea bargaining with juveniles is unregulated and unethical

    7. plea negotiations generally involve the following:

        a. reduction of a charge

        b. elimination of possible waiver to the criminal court

        c. change in proceedings from delinquency to a status offense

        d. agreements regarding dispositional programs

    8. 20% of cases processed in Philadelphia resulted in a negotiated plea

III. Transfer to the Adult Court

    A. Waiver

        1. transferring a juvenile from the juvenile court to the criminal court

        2. cases waived to criminal court has actually declined 46% to 7,100 cases

        3. less than 1% of the formally processed cases waived to adult court

    B. Waiver procedures

        1. concurrent jurisdiction

            a. prosecutor has the discretion of filing charges in either court

            b. case has jurisdiction in both courts

        2. statutory exclusion

            a. certain offenses are automatically excluded from juvenile court

        3. judicial waiver

            a. hearing is held before a juvenile court judge

    C. Due process in transfer proceedings

        1. standards for transfer procedures are set by state statute

        2. exclude certain serious offenses from juvenile court jurisdiction

        3. response to the current demand to get tough on crime

        4. prosecutor discretion may be more effective transfer mechanism

    D. *Kent v. United States*

        1. Kent arrested at age 16

            a. charges of housebreaking, robbery, and rape

        2. detained at the receiving home for almost a week

        3. there was no arraignment or hearing

        4. motion requesting a hearing on the waiver was filed

5. judge made no finding and gave no reasons for his waiver decision
6. judge denied motions for a hearing,
    a. recommendations for hospitalization for psychiatric observation
    b. requests for access to the social service file
    c. offers to prove Kent was fit for rehabilitation under the juvenile court
7. sentenced to serve a period of thirty to ninety years on his conviction
8. *parens patriae* is not designed to allow procedural unfairness
9. court set up criteria concerning waiver of the jurisdictions
    a. seriousness of the alleged offense to the community
    b. offense committed in an aggressive, violent, or willful manner
    c. whether the offense was committed against persons or property
    d. prosecutive merit of the complaint
    e. sophistication and maturity of the juvenile
    f. record and previous history of the juvenile
    g. prospects for adequate protection of the public
    h. the likelihood of reasonable rehabilitation

E. *Breed v. Jones*
1. alleged to have, if committed by an adult, committed robbery
2. juvenile court found that the allegations were true and sustained the petition
3. at which point Jones was found unfit for treatment in the juvenile court
4. held for criminal trial, was tried and found guilty
5. violated double-jeopardy clause of Fifth Amendment
    a. as applied to the states through the Fourteenth Amendment
    b. double jeopardy refers to potential risk of trial and conviction
6. prohibits trying a child in an adult court if prior adjudicatory proceeding
7. different judge is often required for each hearing
    a. same evidence is often used in both transfer hearing and trial
8. states that have transfer hearings provide a legitimate transfer hearing
    a. sufficient notice to the child's family and defense attorney
    b. the right to counsel
    c. statement of the reason for the court order regarding transfer

F. Should youths be transferred to adult court?
1. most experts oppose waiver because it clashes with the rehabilitative ideal

2. advanced the criminalization of the juvenile court

3. waiver can also create long-term harm

4. labels children as adult offenders early in life

5. waived juveniles have higher recidivism rate than those kept in juvenile court

6. transferred felons are not more likely to be sentenced to prison

7. many transferred juveniles were repeat property offenders

8. 39% of all waived youth are African Americans

9. not all experts challenge the waiver concept

10. is consistent with the get tough policy that is currently popular

11. 27% of juveniles tried in criminal court were sent to prison

12. more likely than adults to be charged with a violent felony

13. waiver is superior to alternative methods for handling serious offenders

IV. Juvenile Court Trial
    A. Adjudication hearing
        1. case will be brought for trial in the juvenile court
        2. judge is required to make a finding based on the evidence
        3. the standard of proof used—beyond a reasonable doubt is same as adults
        4. adjudication hearing is comparable to an adult trial
        5. state vary with regard to basic requirements of due process and fairness
        6. most juvenile courts have bifurcated hearings
        7. most state juvenile codes provide specific rules of procedure
            a. written petition be submitted to the court
            b. ensure the right of a child to have an attorney
            c. adjudication proceedings be recorded
            d. allow the petition to be amended
            e. seeks assurance that the plea is voluntary
        8. informal alternatives are used
        9. continuing the case without a finding for a period of time
        10. delinquency finding is not the same thing as a criminal conviction
    B. Constitutional rights at trial
        1. application of constitutional due process standards to the juvenile trial
            a. legal counsel
            b. an open and fair hearing
            c. opportunity to confront those making accusations against him
        2. for many years, juvenile rights were deemed unnecessary
        3. *Gault* decision reshaped the constitutional nature of the juvenile court system
            a. made it similar to the adult system
        4. *In re Winship*
            a. concerned proof required in juvenile delinquency

adjudications

        b. beyond a reasonable doubt

        c. equal to the requirements in the adult system

    5. *McKeiver v. Pennsylvania*

        a. concerned trial by jury in a juvenile court's adjudicative stage

        b. ruled it is not a constitutional requirement

    6. once an adjudicatory hearing has been completed

        a. court is normally required to enter a judgment against the child

C. *In re Gault*

    1. Gault was fifteen years of age

    2. taken into custody for making an obscene telephone call

    3. his parents were not informed that he was being taken into custody

    4. Gault was under probation for stealing a wallet

    5. the complainant was not at the hearing

    6. neither the boy nor his parents were advised of any constitutional rights

    7. there was no transcript or recording of the proceedings

    8. Gault was committed to the state industrial school for the period of his minority

        a. to remain in the state school until he reached the age of twenty-one

    9. Gault's attorneys filed a *writ of habeas corpus*

    10. denied by the Superior Court of the State of Arizona

    11. Court ruled Gault was denied the following basic due process rights

        a. notice of the charges with respect to their timeliness and specificity

        b. right to counsel

        c. right to confrontation and cross-examination

        d. privilege against self-incrimination

        e. right to a transcript of the trial record

        f. right to appellate review

    12. Court agreed that Gault's constitutional rights had been violated

    13. established that a child has the due process constitutional rights listed above

    14. remains the single most significant case in juvenile justice

D. Disposition

    1. orders treatment for the juvenile

    2. dispositions should be in the best interest of the child

    3. while at the same time meeting society's needs for protection

    4. adjudication and disposition hearings are bifurcated

E. Predisposition report

    1. judge orders probation department to complete a predisposition report

2. helps the judge decide which disposition is best for the child

3. aids probation in developing treatment programs

4. helps the court develop a body of knowledge about the child for treatment

5. probation department recommends a disposition to the presiding judge

6. court follows 90% of all probation-department recommendations

F. Dispositions

    1. informal consent decree

        a. minor or first offenses

        b. informal hearing is held

        c. judge will ask the youth and guardian to agree to a treatment program

        d. no formal trial or disposition hearing is held

    2. probation

        a. youth required to obey a set of probation rules

        b. participate in a treatment program

    3. home detention

        a. child is restricted to his or her home in lieu of a secure placement

        b. rules include regular school attendance and curfew observance

    4. court-ordered school attendance

        a. judge may order mandatory school attendance

    5. financial restitution

        a. judge can order the juvenile offender to make financial restitution

    6. fines

        a. some states allow fines to be levied against juveniles aged 16 and over

    7. community service

        a. require juveniles to spend time in the community working off their debt

    8. outpatient psychotherapy

        a. youths who are diagnosed with psychological disorders

        b. may be required to undergo therapy at a local mental health clinic

    9. drug and alcohol treatment

    10. commitment to secure treatment

        a. a training school, camp, ranch, or group home

    11. commitment to a residential community program

        a. youths who commit crimes of a less serious nature but who still need structured program

    12. foster home

    13. employ a graduated sanction program for juveniles

        a. immediate sanctions for nonviolent offenders

   b. intermediate sanctions for repeat minor offenders

   c. secure care for repeat serious offenders and violent offenders

  14. probation is the disposition of choice

G. Juvenile sentencing structures

  1. states have used the indeterminate sentence in juvenile court

  2. place the offender with the state department of juvenile corrections

   a. correctional authorities determine when the youth is ready to return

   b. or held until the youth reaches legal majority

  3. current trend to change from indeterminate to a determinate sentence

  4. certain penalty be set in all cases on conviction for a specified offense

H. Sentencing reform

  1. goal has been to reduce judicial discretion

  2. create mandatory periods of incarceration for serious crimes

  3. Washington's Juvenile Justice Reform Act of 1977

   a. based on the principle of proportionality

I. Blended sentences

  1. imposition of juvenile and adult sanctions for juvenile offenders

   a. adjudicated in juvenile court or convicted in criminal court

   b. adult sentence is revoked no further violation is recorded

J. History of the death penalty for juveniles

  1. 366 juvenile offenders executed since 1642

  2. 22 juveniles executed from 1976-2003

  3. as of 2003, twenty-one states permitted the juvenile death penalty

  4. Texas accounted for thirteen of twenty-two executions since 1976

  5. *Thompson v. Oklahoma* (1988)

   a. USSC prohibited the execution of persons under age sixteen

   b. left open the age at which execution would be legally appropriate

  6. *Wilkins v. Missouri* and *Stanford v. Kentucky* (1989)

   a. states free to impose death penalty for murderers

   b. who committed their crimes after they reached age 16 or 17

  7. Roper v Simmons (2005).

   death penalty for anybody who committed a crime when he or she was less than 18 years of age was declared unconstitutional, as a violation of the 8th amendment's provision against cruel and unusual punishment and the 14th amendment

K. Child's right to appeal

  1. normally restrict appeals to cases where juvenile seeks review of a final order

  2. law does not recognize a federal constitutional right of appeal

  3. each jurisdiction determines for itself what method of review will be used

a. direct appeal

b. collateral attack of a case

L. Confidentiality in juvenile proceedings

    1. open versus closed hearings

    2. *Davis v. Alaska*

        a. any injury resulting from the disclosure of a juvenile's record

        b. outweighed by right to completely cross-examine an adverse witness

    3. *Oklahoma Publishing Co. v. District Court*

        a. state court was not allowed to prohibit the publication of information

        b. obtained in an open juvenile proceeding

        c. Supreme Court ruled that it violated the First Amendment

    4. *Smith v. Daily Mail Publishing Co*

        a. publication of the identity of juvenile suspect in violation of state law

        b. ruled unconstitutional because state's interest in protecting child of not such magnitude to justify the use of criminal statute

    5. privacy of juvenile records

        a. for most of the twentieth century, juvenile records were confidential

        b. today, open by court order in many jurisdictions by statutory exception

CHAPTER SUMMARY

Prosecutors, judges, and defense attorneys are the key players in the juvenile court. The juvenile prosecutor is the attorney responsible for bringing the state's case against the accused juvenile. The juvenile judge must ensure that the children and families who come before the court receive the proper help. Defense attorneys representing children in the juvenile court play an active part in virtually all stages of the proceedings. Many decisions about what happens to a child may occur prior to adjudication. Key issues include detention, intake, diversion, pretrial release, plea bargaining, and waiver. Because the juvenile justice system is not able to try every child accused of a crime or a status offense due to personnel limitations, diversion programs seem to hold greater hope for the control of delinquency. As a result, such subsystems as statutory intake proceedings, plea bargaining, and other informal adjustments are essential ingredients in the administration of the juvenile justice system.

Each year, thousands of youths are transferred to adult courts because of the seriousness of their crimes. This process, known as waiver, is an effort to remove serious offenders from the juvenile process and into the more punitive adult system. Most juvenile experts oppose waiver because it clashes with the rehabilitative ideal. Supporters argue that its increased use can help get violent juvenile offenders off the street, and they point to studies that show that, for the most part, transfer is reserved for the most serious cases and the most serious juvenile offenders. Most jurisdictions have a bifurcated juvenile code system that separates the adjudication hearing from the dispositional hearing. Juveniles alleged to be delinquent have virtually all the rights given a criminal defendant at trial—except possibly the right to a trial by jury. In addition, juvenile proceedings are generally closed to the public.

In re Gault is the key legal case that set out the basic requirements of due process that must be satisfied in juvenile court proceedings. The major categories of dispositional choice in juvenile cases are community release, out-of-home placements, fines or restitution, community service, and institutionalization. Although the traditional notion of rehabilitation and treatment as the proper goals for disposition is being questioned, many juvenile codes do require that the court consider the least restrictive alternative.

Since Roper v Simmons in 2005, individuals cannot be executed for crimes they committed before they were 18 years of age. Many state statutes require that juvenile hearings be closed and that the privacy of juvenile records be maintained to protect the child from public scrutiny and to provide greater opportunity for rehabilitation. This approach may be inconsistent with the public's interest in taking a closer look at the juvenile justice system.

KEY TERMS

Juvenile defense attorneys: Represent children in juvenile court and play an active role at all stages of the proceedings.

Guardian ad litem: A court-appointed attorney who protects the interests of the child in cases involving the child's welfare.

Public defender: An attorney who works in a public agency or under private contractual agreement as defense counsel to indigent defendants.

Juvenile prosecutor: Government attorney responsible for representing the interests of the state and bringing the case against the accused juvenile.

Juvenile court judge A judge elected or appointed to preside over juvenile cases whose decisions can only be reviewed by a judge of a higher court.

Shelter care: A place for temporary care of children in physically unrestricting facilities.

Bail: Amount of money that must be paid as a condition of pretrial release to ensure that the accused will return for subsequent proceedings; bail is normally set by the judge at the initial appearance, and if unable to make bail the accused is detained in jail.

Preventive detention: Keeping the accused in custody prior to trial because the accused is suspected of being a danger to the community.

Intake: Process during which a juvenile referral is received and a decision made to file a petition in juvenile court to release the juvenile, to place the juvenile under supervision, or to refer the juvenile elsewhere.

Diversion: Officially halting or suspending a formal criminal or juvenile justice proceeding at any legally prescribed processing point after a recorded justice system entry, and referral of that person to a treatment or care program or a recommendation that the person be released.

Widening the net: Phenomenon that occurs when programs created to divert youths from the justice system actually involve them more deeply in the official process.

Complaint: Report made by the police or some other agency to the court that initiates the intake process.

Plea bargaining: The exchange of prosecutorial and judicial concessions for a guilty plea by the accused; plea bargaining usually results in a reduced charge or a more lenient sentence.

Transfer process: Transferring a juvenile offender from the jurisdiction of juvenile court to adult criminal court.

Due process: Basic constitutional principle based on the concept of the primacy of the individual and the complementary concept of limitation on governmental power; safeguards the individual from unfair state procedures in judicial or administrative proceedings; due process rights have been extended to juvenile trials.

Least detrimental alternative: Choosing a program that will best foster a child's growth and development.

Indeterminate sentence: Does not specify the length of time the juvenile must be held; rather, correctional authorities decide when the juvenile is ready to return to society.

Determinate sentence: Specifies a fixed term of detention that must be served.

Mandatory sentences: Sentences are defined by a statutory requirement that states the penalty to be set for all cases of a specific offense.

Final order: Order that ends litigation between two parties by determining all their rights and disposing of all the issues.

Appellate process: Allows the juvenile an opportunity to have the case brought before a reviewing court after it has been heard in juvenile or family court.
Writ of habeus corpus: Judicial order requesting that a person detaining another produce the body of the prisoner and give reasons for his or her capture and detention.

Confidentiality: Restricting information in juvenile court proceedings in the interest of protecting the privacy of the juvenile.

SELF TEST QUESTIONS

MULTIPLE CHOICE

1. In 2002 US juvenile courts process an estimated _____ delinquency cases (cases involving juveniles charged with criminal law violations) each year.
    A. 650,000   C. 1.6 million
    B. 800,000   D. 3.7 million

2. The number of delinquency cases handled by juvenile courts _____ percent from 1997 until 2002.
    A. declined 5   C. increased 11
    B. declined 11   D. increased 19

3. Due process is contained in which amendments?
    A. First and Fifth   C. Fifth and Sixth
    B. Fifth and Eight   D. Fifth and Fourteenth

4. In 2002 _____ percent of juvenile delinquency cases involved a female.
    A. 16   C. 21
    B. 26   D. 31

5. The constitutionality of the death penalty
    A. depends on the individual state constitution.
    B. has been upheld since Roper v Simmons.
    C. depends on if it is implemented with due process.
    D. is unconstitutional in the United States.

6. Approximately what share of juveniles were adjudicated delinquent of the 934,9000 cases brought before a judge in 2002?
    A. one-quarter   C. one-half
    B. one-third   D. two-thirds

7. About _____ percent of the juvenile court population was comprised of African-American youth, although they make up about 16 percent of the general population.
    A. 8   C. 29
    B. 15   D. 5

8. As the result of a series of Supreme Court decisions, the right of delinquent youth to have counsel at state trials has become a fundamental part of the juvenile justice system; today, courts must provide counsel to _____ defendants who face the possibility of incarceration.
    A. hapless   C. possibly guilty
    B. indigent   D. all

9. The _____ helps outline the child's position regarding detention hearings, bail hearings, explores the possibility for informal adjustment of the case, represents the child at adjudication, and represents the youth at the disposition hearing.

    A. juvenile court judge   C. juvenile defense attorney

    B. juvenile's parent   D. *guardian ad litem*

10. A _____ is appointed by the court and advocates on behalf of the youth's best interest; they fulfill many roles, ranging from legal advocate to concerned individual who works with parents and human service professionals in developing a proper treatment plan that best serves the interests of the minor child.

    A. *guardian ad litem*   C. district attorney

    B. court appointed defense attorney   D. jail house lawyer

11. _____ are volunteers who advise the juvenile court about child placement; they investigate the needs of children and provide a vital link between the judge, the attorneys, and the child in protecting the juvenile's right to a safe placement.

    A. *Guardian ad litem*   C. Court appointed special advocate

    B. Court appointed defense attorney   D. Child welfare specialist

12. Which of the following was not identified as one of the three alternatives for providing children with legal counsel?

    A. an all-public defender program

    B. an appointed private counsel system

    C. law school intern program

    D. combination system of public defenders and appointed private attorneys

13. The authors note that the _____ is the central character in a court of juvenile or family law.

    A. defense counsel   C. juvenile court judge

    B. *guardian ad litem*   D. bailiff

14. Alternatives to detention centers, such as temporary foster homes, detention boarding homes, and programs of neighborhood supervision, have been developed; these alternatives, referred to as _____, enable youths to live in a more home-like setting while the courts dispose of their case.

    A. intermediate sanctions   C. shock incarceration

    B. shelter care   D. diversion

15. Despite an on-going effort to limit detention, juveniles are still being detained in about _____ percent of all delinquency cases.

    A. 5   C. 40

    B. 20   D. 65

16. _____ is responsible for bringing the state's case against the accused juvenile.

    A. district attorney   C. *guardian ad litem*

    B. juvenile court judge   D. defense attorney

17. Which of the following is not a characteristic of the DDAP approach?
   A. restricted to youths currently held or likely to be held in secure detention
   B. coordinates with tutors, drug counselors, and family counselors
   C. provides a get tough approach for juveniles typically released home pending trial
   D. requires daily contact between program staff and the juvenile

18. Which of the following is not one of the findings of the DDAP evaluation study?
   A. overall recidivism rate of the DDAP group was 34%, compared with 60% for the control group
   B. 14% of the DDAP group had 2 or more subsequent referrals, compared to 50% for the control group
   C. 59% of the DDAP group returned on a violent crime charge, compared with 25% for the control group
   D. 9% of the DDAP group returned on a violent crime charge, compared with 25% for the control group

19. The JJDPA of 1974 was amended in 1989 to require that the states _____.
   A. prohibit smoking in juvenile justice facilities
   B. prohibit corporal punishment within juvenile detention facilities
   C. remove all juveniles from the adult jails and lockups
   D. waive more juveniles to the adult system

20. Adults retain the right, via the _____ amendment to the Constitution, to reasonable bail in non-capital cases.
   A. first   C. fifth
   B. fourth   D. eighth

21. In _____, the United States Supreme Court ruled that the state has a right to detain dangerous youth until their trial, a practice called preventive detention.
   A. *Schall v. Martin*   C. *In re Gault*
   B. *Berg v. City of Long Beach*   D. *Breed v. Jones*

22. The term _____ refers to the screening of cases by the juvenile court system to determine whether the services of the juvenile court are needed.
   A. intake   C. petition
   B. diversion   D. waiver

23. About _____ percent of all delinquency cases in 2002 were dismissed at intake, often for lack of legal sufficiency.
   A. 7   C. 39
   B. 16   D. 48

24. In 2002, about _____ percent of delinquency cases were processed informally, with the juvenile voluntarily agreeing to the recommended disposition (for example, probation).

    A. 7   C. 39

    B. 26   D. 48

25. The _____ is a court order authorizing disposition of the case without a formal label of delinquency; it is based on an agreement between the intake department of the court and the juvenile who is the subject of the complaint.

    A. consent decree   C. discretion

    B. waiver   D. unilateral transformation

26. Juvenile _____ is the process of placing youths suspected of law violating behavior into treatment orientated programs prior to formal trial and disposition to minimize the stigma and labeling of the juvenile justice system.

    A. diversion   C. unilateral transformation

    B. intake   D. displacement

27. The most damaging criticism of diversion programs has been that it involves children in the juvenile justice system who would have been released without official notice without the diversion program; this is called _____.

    A. widening the net   C. displacement tendency

    B. most restrictive alternative   D. funneling tendency

28. In the case of _____, the United States Supreme Court articulated the basic requirements of due process that must be satisfied in juvenile court proceedings.

    A. *In re Gault*   C. *Breed v. Jones*

    B. *Kent v. United States*   D. *Schall v. Martin*

29. The authors note that more than _____ percent of all adult defendants plead guilty.

    A. 30   C. 75

    B. 50   D. 90

30. A hearing is held before a juvenile court judge, who then decides whether jurisdiction should be waived and the case transferred to criminal court; this is referred to as _____.

    A. judicial waiver   C. concurrent jurisdiction

    B. direct file   D. excluded offenses

TRUE FALSE

1. There are distinct gender-based differences in the juvenile court population; about three quarters (74%) of all juvenile arrests in 2002 involved a male.

    A. True

    B. False

2. The number of delinquency cases handled by juvenile courts increased 11 percent between 1997 and 2002.
     A. True
     B. False

3. In the text Franklin Zimring's position on juvenile transfer can be summarized as demanding virtually complete abolishment.
     A. True
     B. False

4. The Least Restrictive Alternative doctrine holds that if a youth is not needing secure confinement, she or he should be sent to a less secure facility (even if a greater amount of services are often found in more secure facilities).
     A. True
     B. False

5. Approximately 30 percentage of youth are detained in delinquency cases.
     A. True
     B. False

6. About 29 percent of the juvenile court population was comprised of African-American youth, although they make up only about 16 percent of the general population.
     A. True
     B. False

7. In Maryland juvenile court defense lawyers work on about 360 cases per year,
     A. True
     B. False

8. For the first 60 years of its existence, the juvenile court did not include a prosecutor, because the concept of an adversary process was seen as inconsistent with the philosophy of treatment.
     A. True
     B. False

9. For the first 60 years of its existence, the prosecutor was the central actor in the juvenile court because the state's interest in justice, deterrence, and retribution were the central philosophies of the court.
     A. True
     B. False

10. The authors note that in Pennsylvania about 94 percent of juvenile defense attorneys do not have access to independent investigators or social workers.
     A. True
     B. False

11. The authors note that removing status offenders from secure facilities serves two purposes: it reduces interaction with serious offenders, and it insulates status offenders from the stigma associated with being a detainee in a locked facility.
    A. True
    B. False

12. The authors note that detention is used in about 20% of all delinquency cases.
    A. True
    B. False

13. According to federal guidelines, all juveniles in state custody must be separated from adult offenders or the state could lose federal juvenile justice funds.
    A. True
    B. False

14. The authors note that most states refuse juveniles right to bail because they argue that juvenile proceedings are civil, not criminal, and rehabilitative, not punitive.
    A. True
    B. False

15. The court ruled in *McKeiver v. Pennsylvania* that trial by jury in a juvenile court's adjudicative stage is not a constitutional requirement.
    A. True
    B. False

16. The United States Supreme Court has never decided the issue of whether juveniles have the constitutional right to bail.
    A. True
    B. False

17. In *New York v. The Delinquent Child*, the United States Supreme Court decided juveniles do not have the constitutional right to bail.
    A. True
    B. False

18. In *Schall v. Martin*, the United States Supreme Court ruled that the state has a right to detain dangerous youth until their trial, a practice called preventive detention.
    A. True
    B. False

19. Juvenile diversion is the process of placing youths suspected of law-violating behavior into treatment programs prior to formal trial and disposition to minimize their penetration into the justice system and thereby avoid stigma and labeling.
    A. True
    B. False

20. The petition is the formal complaint that initiates judicial action against a juvenile charged with delinquency or a status offense.
    A. True
    B. False

21. Blended sentencing allows the imposition of juvenile and adult sanctions for juvenile offenders adjudicated in juvenile court or convicted in criminal court.
    A. True
    B. False

22. In *Breed v. Jones*, the US Supreme Court declared that youths are granted the protection of the double-jeopardy clause of the Fifth Amendment; once found to be delinquent, the youth can no longer be tried as an adult for the same offense.
    A. True
    B. False

23. The authors note that about 35 percent of all waived youth are African Americans, even though they represent 29 percent of the juvenile court population.
    A. True
    B. False

24. Rules of evidence in adult criminal proceedings generally apply in juvenile court, and the standard of proof used-beyond a reasonable doubt- is the same as that used in adult court.
    A. True
    B. False

25. The authors note that most states grant juveniles the right to bail because they argue that juvenile proceedings are criminal, not civil, and punitive, not rehabilitative.
    A. True
    B. False

FILL IN

1. As the result of a series of Supreme Court decisions, the right of delinquent youth to have counsel at state trials has become a fundamental part of the juvenile justice system; today, courts must provide counsel to _____ defendants who face the possibility of incarceration.

2. The juvenile _____ helps outline the child's position regarding detention hearings, bail hearings, explores the possibility for informal adjustment of the case, represents the child at adjudication, and represents the youth at the disposition hearing.

3. A _____ is appointed by the court and advocates on behalf of the youth's best interest; they fulfill many roles, ranging from legal advocate to

concerned individual who works with parents and human service professionals in developing a proper treatment plan that best serves the interests of the minor child.

4. _____ are volunteers who advise the juvenile court about child placement; they investigate the needs of children and provide a vital link between the judge, the attorneys, and the child in protecting the juvenile's right to a safe placement.

5. Adults retain the right, via the _____ Amendment to the Constitution, to reasonable bail in non-capital cases.

6. In _____, the United States Supreme Court ruled that the state has a right to detain dangerous youth until their trial, a practice called preventive detention.

7. The term "_____" refers to the screening of cases by the juvenile court system to determine whether the services of the juvenile court are needed.

8. Alternatives to detention centers, called _____, allow youths to live in a home like setting such as temporary foster homes, detention foster homes, and neighborhood based programs while the court decides their case.

9. The _____ is a court order authorizing disposition of the case without a formal label of delinquency; it is based on an agreement between the intake department of the court and the juvenile who is the subject of the complaint.

10. The most damaging criticism of diversion programs has been that it involves children in the juvenile justice system who would have been released without official notice without the diversion program; this is called _____.

11. A _____ is the report made by the police or some other agency to the court to initiate the intake process.

12. The _____ is the formal document that initiates judicial action against a juvenile charged with delinquency or a status offense.

13. In the case of _____, the United States Supreme Court articulated the basic requirements of due process that must be satisfied in juvenile court proceedings.

14. _____ is the exchange of prosecutorial and judicial concessions for guilty pleas.

15. A hearing is held before a juvenile court judge, who then decides whether jurisdiction should be waived and the case transferred to criminal court; this is referred to as _____-___.

317

ESSAY

1. Discuss the significance of the US Supreme Court case *In re Gault*.

2. Identify and discuss three mechanisms used to transfer juvenile cases to the adult criminal justice system.

3. Identify and discuss the roles of the central actors in the juvenile justice system.

4. Identify and discuss the significance of the Juvenile Justice and Delinquency Prevention Act of 1974.

5. Discuss the changes made to the Juvenile Justice and Delinquency Prevention Act of 1974 since it was enacted.

MULTIPLE CHOICE

1. C	11. C	21. A
2. B	12. C	22. A
3. D	13. C	23. B
4. B	14. B	24. B
5. D	15. B	25. A
6. D	16. A	26. A
7. C	17. C	27. A
8. B	18. C	28. A
9. C	19. C	29. D
10. A	20. D	30. A

TRUE FALSE

1. T	11. T	21. T
2. F	12. T	22. T
3. F	13. T	23. T
4. T	14. T	24. T
5. F	15. T	25. F
6. T	16. T	
7. T	17. F	
8. T	18. T	
9. F	19. T	
10. T	20. T	

FILL IN

1. indigent
2. defense attorney
3. *guardian ad litem*
4. court appointed special advocate
5. Eighth
6. *Schall v. Martin*
7. intake
8. shelter care
9. consent decree
10. widening the net
11. complaint
12. petition
13. *In re Gault*
14. plea bargaining
15. judicial waiver

Multiple Choice
1. Which of the following does not hamper juvenile defense attorneys from providing their indigent clients' an adequate defense?
   A. large caseloads
   B. high turnover
   C. low salaries
   D. income requirements for clients

2. A balanced approach
   A. stresses rehabilitation, resocialization, and reintegration.
   B. stresses retribution, just deserts, and incapacitation.
   C. stresses community service, restitution, and day fines.
   D. emphasizes enforcement, prosecution, detention of serious offenders, and evidence-based treatment interventions.

3. A recent study in New Jersey found ___ percent of youth were inappropriately placed in detention instead of hospitals, foster care homes, or other non-custodial settings.
   A. 15
   B. 20
   C. 25
   D. 30

4. To detain a juvenile, what standard is applied?
   A. reasonable suspicion and drug use
   B. probable cause and evidence of flight risk
   C. probable cause and suspicion of gang involvement
   D. clear and convincing evidence

5. The Office of Juvenile Justice and Delinquency Prevention Act of 1974
   A. has the force of constitutional law to require the removal of juveniles from adult facilities
   B. has the force of statutory law to require the removal of juveniles from adult facilities
   C. has the force of case law to require the removal of juveniles from adult facilities
   D. uses financial incentives to obtain compliance

6. Which of the following is not an objective of juvenile intake?
   A. drug testing under the Arrestee Drug Abuse monitoring system (ADAM)
   B. facilitate diversion to community resources
   C. screen out cases that are not within the court's jurisdiction
   D. determine if juvenile court services are needed

7. The purpose of diversion programs is to
   A. widen the net so more state control is implemented on at-risk populations
   B. refer youth to treatment without stigmatization
   C. bring the jail to the community so money is saved while monitoring predatory youth
   D. increase supervision and control

8. Due process
   A. was first applied to juveniles in the Winship case
   B. is referred to in the 9th amendment
   C. refers to the rules and procedures to protect individual rights
   D. does not apply in juvenile court since the objective of the court is to help youth

9. An indeterminate sentence
   A. specifies specific date of release, but the treatment models are to be determined by treatment staff
   B. leaves for a great deal of adjustment to length of sentence to processes after the disposition is meted out in court
   C. is much more appropriate for deterrence and retribution than rehabilitation
   D. is synonymous with incapacitation in prison.

10. Plea bargaining in juvenile court
    A. occurs at the same frequency as it does in adult court
    B. occurs much less frequently than in adult court
    C. is unconstitutional
    D. violates due process

True False

1. The get tough approach has led to juvenile court proceedings that are virtually indistinguishable from adult proceedings T   F

2. The conservative policies of the last 10 years have brought about an increase in transfer to adult court T F

3. Whereas transfer to adult court has significantly decreased in the last eleven years, from 1985-2002, the number of youths placed on formal probation increased dramatically

4. Youth transferred to adult court usually are incarcerated about twice as much as those under similar circumstances who are not transferred

5. A predisposition report goes beyond simply describing the offense for which the youth was adjudicated.

Answer Key

Multiple Choice
1. D
2. D
3. C
4. B
5. D
6. A
7. B
8. C
9. B
10. B

Web True False Answer Key
1. F
2. F
3. T
4. F
5. T

CHAPTER 14
JUVENILE CORRECTIONS: PROBATION,
COMMUNITY TREATMENT, AND INSTITUTIONALIZATION

LEARNING OBJECTIVES

- Be able to distinguish between community treatment and institutional treatment for juvenile offenders.
- Be familiar with the disposition of probation, including how it is administered and by whom and recent trends in its use compared with other dispositions.
- Be aware of new approaches for providing probation services to juvenile offenders and comment on their effectiveness in reducing recidivism.
- Be able to describe the range of residential community treatment programs that serve as alternatives to incarceration and discuss the pros and cons of residential community treatment for juvenile offenders.
- Understand key historical developments of secure juvenile corrections in this country, including the principle of least restrictive alternative.
- Be familiar with recent trends in the use of juvenile institutions for juvenile offenders and how their use differs across states.
- Understand key issues facing the institutionalized juvenile offender, including minority overrepresentation and gender discrimination.
- Be able to identify the various juvenile correctional treatment approaches that are in use today and comment on their effectiveness in reducing recidivism.
- Understand the concept of right to treatment for institutionalized juveniles and the ongoing struggles to uphold minimum standards and ensure basic civil rights for institutionalized juveniles.
- Know the nature of aftercare for juvenile offenders and comment on recent innovations in these programs.

CHAPTER OUTLINE
A. Karen Gilligan

Age 16, oldest of four, lives with parents in small rural community
1. mother works two jobs, father unemployed, both alcoholics
2. high school attendance sporadic
3. Karen starts to drink alcohol and vandalizes local businesses
4. Karen is ordered to house arrest, attend school, attend Alcohol and Other Drug (AOD program), and participate in family therapy
5. after missing appointments and skipping school, she is placed on intensive supervision
6. Karen is ordered to attend daily counseling and tutoring at community center.
7. Individual and family counseling pays off as she develops insight into her negative thinking, aggression, and AOD problems. She stops delinquent behaviour, pays restitution, attends school and improves communication with her parents.

I. Juvenile Probation
    A. Probation
        1. non-punitive legal disposition for delinquent youths
        2. emphasizing treatment without incarceration
        3. primary form of community treatment
        4. offender is not a danger to the community
        5. community treatment maximizes the liberty of the individual
        6. vindicates the authority of the law and protects the public
        7. promotes rehabilitation by maintaining normal community contacts
        8. avoids the negative effects of confinement
        9. reduces the financial cost to the public
    B. Historical development
        1. recorded as early as 1820
        2. by 1890 probation had become a mandatory part of the court structure in MA
        3. probation is cornerstone in the development of the juvenile court system
    C. Expanding community treatment
        1. 30 – 40 percent of adult prison inmates had prior experience with the juvenile court
        2 . probation is still the backbone of community-based corrections
        3. almost 385, 400 juveniles were on formal probation in 2002
        4, 62% of all juvenile dispositions
    D. Contemporary juvenile probation
        1. probation represents an appropriate disposition.
        2. court can tailor a program to each juvenile offender
        3. confidence in rehabilitation and accommodating public protection
        4.probation is often the disposition of choice, particularly for status offenders
        5. probation sentence implies a contract between the court and the juvenile
        6. court promises to hold a period of institutionalization in abeyance
        7. juvenile promises to adhere to a set of rules mandated by the court
        8. status reviewed regularly to ensure that a juvenile is not kept on probation needlessly
    E. Conditions of probation
        1. restitution or reparation
        2. intensive supervision
        3. intensive counseling
        4. participation in a therapeutic program
        5. participation in an educational or vocational training program
        6. insist that probationers lead law-abiding lives
        7. maintain a residence in a family setting
        8. refrain from associating with certain types of people
        9. remain in a particular area unless they have permission to leave
        10. court can revoke probation if a youth violates the conditions

F. Organization and administration
       1. organization varies across states
       2. some administered by the local juvenile court
       3. some split jurisdiction: juvenile court and a state executive
       4. some have statewide office of juvenile probation

G. Duties of juvenile probation officers
       1. they screen complaints by deciding to adjust the matter at intake
       2. participate in release or detention decisions at predisposition stage
       3. assist the court in reaching its dispositional decision at post adjudication stage
       4. they supervise juveniles placed on probation
       5. provide direct counseling and casework services
       6. interview and collect social service data
       7. make diagnostic recommendations
       8. maintain working relationships with law enforcement agencies
       9. use community resources and services
       10. direct volunteer case aides
       11. write predisposition or social investigation reports
       12. work with families of children under supervision
       13. provide specialized services, such as group therapy
       14. supervise specialized caseloads involving children with special problems
       15. make decisions about revocation of probation and its termination

II. Probation Innovations
    A. Community corrections
       1. traditionally emphasized offender rehabilitation
       2. primary job is to help the offender adjust to society
       3. recent efforts add a control dimension to community corrections

    B. Intensive supervision
       1. treat offenders who would normally be sent to a secure treatment facility
       2. primary goal of JIPS is decarceration
       3. maintaining community ties and reintegration
       4. intensive probation programs get mixed reviews
       5. failure rate is high because supervised more closely
       6. intensive supervision was found to be less cost-effective than treatments studied

    C. Electronic monitoring
       1. house arrest often coupled with electronic monitoring
       2. monitored through random phone calls, visits, or electronic devices
       3. fitted with an unremovable monitoring device
       4. recidivism rates are no higher than in traditional programs
       5. costs are lower
       6. Institutional overcrowding is reduced
       7. existing systems can be affected by faulty telephone equipment
       8. most house arrest programs do not provide rehabilitation services

D.	Restorative Justice
1. non-punitive strategy for delinquency control that attempts to address the issues that produce conflict between two parties (offender and victim) and reconcile them
2. victim and community central to justice process
3. first priority of justice is to assist victims
4. second priority is to restore the community
5. offender has the responsibility to victims and to the community
6. restorative justice helps offender develop competency and insight
7. stakeholders share responsibilities through partnerships
8. successful programs had enhanced victim satisfaction and reduced victim retaliation
E. Balanced probation
1. integrate community protection
2. accountability of the juvenile offender
3. individualized attention to the offender
4. California 8% Solution program based on balanced model
a. an outside school for students in junior and senior high school
b. transportation to and from home
c. counseling for drug and alcohol abuse
d. employment preparation and job placement services
e. at-home, intensive family counseling for families
F. Restitution
1. victim restitution is a widely used community treatment
2. reimburse the victim of the crime or donate money to a charity or public cause
3. required to provide some service directly to the victim
4. method of informal adjustment at intake
5. benefit in offering monetary compensation or service to crime victims
6. offender can take a step toward becoming a productive member of society
7. most evaluations have shown that it is reasonably effective
8. Finkelstein found about 73.5 % of youths successfully completed their orders
9. foster involuntary servitude
F. Residential community treatment
1. variations in perception of the value of institutional care
2. large training schools have not proved to be effective
G. Group homes
1. non-secure residences that provide treatment opportunities and family living
2. generally house twelve to fifteen youngsters
3. institutional quality of the environment is minimized

H.   Family group homes
        1. juveniles are placed in a group home that is run by a family instead of a professional staff
I. Foster care programs
        1. involve one or two juveniles who live with a family
        2. quality of the foster home experience depends on the foster parents
        3. multidimensional treatment foster care (MTFC)
J. Rural programs
        1. include forestry camps, ranches, and farms
        2. provide recreational activities or work for juveniles

III. Secure Corrections
    A. History of juvenile institutions
        1. previously neglected, dependent, delinquent children confined in adult prisons
        2. New York House of Refuge was established in 1825
        3. first reform school was Lyman School for Boys, Westborough, MA
        4. early reform schools were generally punitive in nature
        5. cottage system
            a. housed in compounds of cottages
            b. each of which could accommodate twenty to forty children
            c. set of "parents" ran each cottage creating a homelike atmosphere
    B. Twentieth century developments
        1. reform schools began to adopt a militaristic style after World War I
        2. camps run by the Civilian Conservation Corps started in the 1930s
            a. Los Angeles County
            b. placed these offenders in conservation camps
            c. paid them low wages
            d. released them when they had earned enough money to return home
        3. in 1930s the U.S. Children's Bureau sought to reform juvenile corrections
        4. American Law Institute's Model Youth Correction Authority Act
        5. decarceration policy
            a. courts use least restrictive alternative for status offenders
        6. states prohibited from placing status offenders in separate facilities
            a. that are similar in form and function to those used for delinquent offenders
        7.1994 report issued by OJJDP
            a. crowding, inadequate health care, and lack of security problematic
            b. poor control of suicidal behavior
            c. overcrowding prevalent

IV. Juvenile Institutions Today: Public And Private
    A. Population trends
        1. most juveniles are housed in public institutions administered by state agencies
        2. private institutions are relatively small facilities holding fewer than thirty youths
        3. 80 percent of public and 20 percent of private facilities are high- secure facilities
        4. almost 97,000 juveniles held in public (69%) and private (31%) facilities in USA
        5. most status offenders are held in private facilities
        6. District of Columbia followed by Wyoming make the greatest use of custodial treatment
        7. data does not include minors incarcerated as adults
    B. Physical conditions
        1. physical plans of juvenile institutions vary in size and quality
        2. individual living areas also vary
        3. new facilities usually try to provide a single room for each individual
        4. 36% of the 2,964 facilities that reported information were overcrowded

V. Institutionalized Juvenile
    A. Typical resident
        1. seventeen-year-old White male
        2. incarcerated for an average stay of 3.5 months in a public facility
            a. or 4 months in a private facility
        3.   65 percent suffer from mental health problems
        4. minority youths are incarcerated 2 to 4 times that of White youths
            a. minority youths are less likely to be diverted from the court system
            b. more than 6 in 10 juveniles in custody belong to racial or ethnic minorities
            c. 7 in 10 youths held in custody for a violent crime are minorities
    B. Male inmates
        1. males make up the great bulk of institutionalized youth
            a. accounting for 6 out of 7 juvenile offenders in residential placement
        2. inmate value system:
            a. exploit whomever you can
            b. don't play up to staff
            c. don't rat on your peers
            d. don't give in to others
        3. inmates scheme to manipulate staff and take advantage of weaker peers

C. Female inmates

    1. between 1991-2003 the number of females in custody increased by 52 percent, now accounting for 15 percent of all juvenile offenders

    2. girls are more likely than boys to be incarcerated for status offenses

    3. institutions for girls are generally more restrictive than those for boys

    4. institutions fewer educational and vocational programs and fewer services

    5. numerous allegations of emotional and sexual abuse by correctional workers

    6. most incarcerated in single-sex institutions that are isolated in rural areas

    7. girls' institutions tend to be smaller than boys' institutions

        a. lack the money to offer as many programs and services

    8. recommended changes

        a. promote, and support effective gender-specific and

        b. developmentally sound, culturally sensitive practices with girls

        c. promote an integrated system of care for at-risk and delinquent girls

        d. and their families based on their competencies and needs

        e. assess the adequacy of services to meet the needs of delinquent girls

        f. review practices to assess the gender impact of decision making

VI. Correctional Treatment for Juveniles

    A. Treatment

        1. nearly all juvenile institutions implement some form of treatment program

            a. counseling

            b. vocational and educational training

            c. recreational programs

            d. religious counseling

        2. purpose of these programs is to rehabilitate youths

        3. one large study found 10% lower recidivism rate for treated juveniles than untreated juveniles

        4. best programs reduced recidivism up to 40 percent

        5. common problems is the lack of well-trained staff members

        6. problem with treatment programs is that they are not administered as intended

    B. Individual treatment techniques: past and present

        1. combine of psychotherapy, reality therapy, and behavior modification

        2. individual counseling is one of the most common treatment approaches

        3. professional counseling may be based on psychotherapy

        4. another frequently used treatment is reality therapy

            a. stress that offenders are completely responsible for their own actions

        5. behavior modification is used in many institutions

        6. current behavior can be shaped through rewards and punishments

C. Group treatment techniques
  1. group therapy is more economical than individual therapy
  2. individuals derive hope from other members of the group
  3. group members can monitor each other's progress and deviance
  4.some group members may need more individualized treatment
  5. some individuals may dominate group interaction
  6. Guided Group Interaction (GGI) is a fairly common method of group treatment
  7. version of GGI is called positive peer culture (PPC)
  8. milieu therapy makes all aspects of the inmates' environment part of their treatment
  9. group counseling often focuses on drug and alcohol issues
    a. appropriate expressions of anger
D. Educational, vocational, and recreational programs
  1. educational programs are probably the best-staffed programs in training schools
    a. mentally challenged
    b. learning disabilities
    c. far behind their grade levels in basic academics
    d. dislike school
  2. institutions should allow the inmates to attend a school in the community
  3. vocational training has long been used as a treatment technique
  4. common drawback of vocational training programs is sex-typing
  5. need to acquire kinds of skills that will give them hope for advancement
  6. recreational activity is also important in helping relieve adolescent aggressions
E. Wilderness programs
  1. programs involve troubled youths in outdoor activities
  2. mechanism to improve their social skills, self-concept, and self-control
  3. few programs evaluated for their effects on recidivism
  4.MacKenzie concludes that these programs do not work
F. Juvenile boot camps
  1. camps combine get-tough elements of adult programs with treatment
  2. rehabilitate juvenile offenders is one goal
  3. second goal is to reduce the number of beds needed in secure institutional programs
  4. boot camp youths report more positive attitudes to their environment
  5. staff at boot camps report more favorable working conditions
  6. ineffective correctional approach to reducing recidivism
  7. little in the way of therapy or treatment to correct offending behavior
  8. 51 state-run boot camps are in operation in more than 30 states

VII. Legal Right to Treatment
 A. Primary goal
  1. help youths reenter the community successfully
  2. origins of the concept in mental health field

a. individuals who are deprived of their liberty because of a mental illness

b. entitled to treatment to correct that condition

3. *Inmates of the Boys' Training School v. Affleck* in 1972

    a. due process guarantees are violated without rehabilitation

    b. juveniles have a statutory right to treatment

4. minimum conditions

    a. room equipped with lighting sufficient for an inmate to read until 10pm

    b. sufficient clothing to meet seasonal needs

    c. bedding to be changed once a week

    d. personal hygiene supplies

    e. a change of undergarments and socks every day

    f. minimum writing materials: pen, pencil, paper, and envelopes

    g. prescription eyeglasses, if needed

    h. equal access to all books and periodicals

    i. daily showers

    j. daily access to medical facilities

    k. general correspondence privileges

5. *Nelson v. Heyne* in 1974

    a. juveniles have a right to treatment

    b. condemned the use of corporal punishment in juvenile institutions

6. *Pena v. New York State Division for Youth*

    a. use of isolation, hand restraints, and tranquilizing drugs

    b. violated the Fourteenth Amendment right to due process and Eighth Amendment

7. *Ralston v. Robinson*

    a. dangerousness outweighed the possible effects of rehabilitation

    b. legitimate exercise of state authority to incarcerate juveniles solely to protect society

B. Struggle for basic civil rights

    1. state-sponsored brutality has been outlawed

    2. corporal punishment in any form violates standards of decency and human dignity

    3. Civil Rights of Institutionalized Persons Act (CRIPA)

    4. CRIPA does not create any new substantive rights

    5. 25% of cases involve juvenile detention and correctional facilities

        a. addressed life-threatening conditions

        b. juveniles committing and attempting suicide without staff intervention

        c. widespread infection-control problems caused by rats and other vermin

        d. defective plumbing that forced juveniles to drink from their toilet bowls

VIII. Juvenile Aftercare
    A. Concept
        1. equivalent of parole in the adult criminal justice system
        2. institutionalized youth not simply returned to the community without assistance
        3. factors considered when recommending a juvenile for release
            a. institutional adjustment
            b. length of stay and general attitude
            c. likelihood of success in the community
            d. prior record
            e. type of offense
    B. Supervision
        1. provide support during the readjustment period following release
        2. community may view the returning minor with a good deal of prejudice
        3. parole caseworkers make sure that a corrections plan is followed
        4. Intensive Aftercare Program (IAP) Model
            a. offers a continuum of intervention
            b. geared for serious juvenile offenders returning community
            c. prepare youth for progressively increased responsibility and freedom
            d. facilitate youth-community interaction and involvement
            e. working with both the offender and targeted community support
            f. developing new resources and supports where needed
            g. monitor youth and community on ability to deal with each other
    C. Aftercare revocation procedures
        1. adhere to a reasonable curfew set by youth worker or parent
        2. refrain from associating with persons whose influence would be detrimental
        3. attend school in accordance with the law
        4. abstain from drugs and alcohol
        5. report to the youth worker when required
        6. refrain from acts that would be crimes if committed by an adult
        7. refrain from operating an automobile without permission
        8. refrain from being habitually disobedient
        9. refrain from running away from the lawful custody of parent

CHAPTER SUMMARY

Community treatment encompasses efforts to keep offenders in the community and spare them the stigma of incarceration. The primary purpose is to provide a non-restrictive or home setting, employing educational, vocational, counseling, and employment services. Institutional treatment encompasses provision of these services but in more restrictive and sometimes secure facilities. The most widely used community treatment method is probation. Behavior is monitored by probation officers. If rules are violated, youths may have their probation revoked. It is now common to enhance probation with more restrictive forms of treatment, such as intensive supervision and house arrest with electronic monitoring. Restitution programs involve having juvenile offenders either reimburse their victims or do community service.

Residential community treatment programs allow youths to live at home while receiving treatment. There are also residential programs that require that youths reside in group homes while receiving treatment. The secure juvenile institution was developed in the mid-nineteenth century as an alternative to placing youths in adult prisons. Youth institutions evolved from large, closed institutions to cottage-based education- and rehabilitation-oriented institutions. The juvenile institutional population appears to have stabilized in recent years, but an increasing number of youths are "hidden" in private medical centers and drug treatment clinics.

A disproportionate number of minorities are incarcerated in more secure, state-run youth facilities. Most juvenile institutions maintain intensive treatment programs featuring individual or group therapy. Little evidence has been found that any single method is effective in reducing recidivism, yet rehabilitation remains an important goal of juvenile practitioners. The right to treatment is an important issue in juvenile justice. Legal decisions have mandated that a juvenile cannot simply be warehoused in a correctional center, but must receive proper care and treatment to aid rehabilitation. What constitutes proper care is still being debated, however. Juveniles released from institutions are often placed on parole, or aftercare. There is little evidence that community supervision is more beneficial than simply releasing youths. Many jurisdictions are experiencing success with halfway houses and reintegration centers.

KEY TERMS

Community treatment: Using nonsecure and noninstitutional residences, counseling services, victim restitution programs, and other community services to treat juveniles in their own communities.

Suppression effect: A reduction of the number of arrests per year for youths who have been incarcerated or otherwise punished.

Probation: Nonpunitive, legal disposition of juveniles emphasizing community treatment in which the juvenile is closely supervised by an officer of the court and must adhere to a strict set of rules to avoid incarceration.

Juvenile probation officer: Officer of the court involved in all four stages of the court process—intake, predisposition, postadjudication, and postdisposition—who assists the court and supervises juveniles placed on probation.

Social investigation report (also known as predisposition report): Developed by the juvenile probation officer, this report includes clinical diagnosis of the juvenile and the need for court assistance, relevant environmental and personality factors, and other information to assist the court in developing a treatment plan.

Conditions of probation: Rules and regulations mandating that a juvenile on probation behave in a particular way.

Juvenile intensive probation supervision (JIPS): A true alternative to incarceration that involves almost daily supervision of the juvenile by the probation officer assigned to the case.

Juvenile intensive probation supervision (JIPS): involves treating offenders who would normally have been sent to a secure treatment facility as part of a very small probation caseload that receives almost daily scrutiny.

House arrest: Offender is required to stay home during specific periods of time; monitoring is done by random phone calls and visits or by electronic devices.

Electronic monitoring: Active monitoring systems consist of a radio transmitter worn by the offender that sends a continuous signal to the probation department computer; passive systems employ computer-generated random phone calls that must be answered in a certain period of time from a particular phone.

Balanced probation: Programs that integrate community protection, accountability of the juvenile offender, competency, and individualized attention to the juvenile offender; based on the principle that juvenile offenders must accept responsibility for their behavior.

Monetary restitution: Offenders compensate crime victims for out-of-pocket losses caused by the crime, including property damage, lost wages, and medical expenses.

Victim service restitution: Offenders provide some service directly to the crime victim.

Community service restitution: Offenders assist some worthwhile community organization for a period of time.

Residential programs: Residential, nonsecure facilities such as a group home, foster home, family group home, or rural home where the juvenile can be closely monitored and develop close relationships with staff members.

Group homes: Nonsecured, structured residences that provide counseling, education, job training, and family living.

Foster care programs: Placement with families who provide attention, guidance, and care.

Family group homes: A combination of foster care and group home; they are run by a single family rather than by professional staff.

Rural programs: Specific recreational and work opportunities provided for juveniles in a rural setting such as a forestry camp, a farm, or a ranch.

Reform schools: Institutions in which educational and psychological services are used in an effort to improve the conduct of juveniles who are forcibly detained.

Cottage system: Housing in a compound of small cottages, each of which accommodates twenty to forty children.

Least restrictive alternative: A program with the least restrictive or secure setting that will benefit the child.

Individual counseling: Counselors help juveniles understand and solve their current adjustment problems.

Psychotherapy: Highly structured counseling in which a therapist helps a juvenile solve conflicts and make a more positive adjustment to society.

Reality therapy: A form of counseling that emphasizes current behavior and requires the individual to accept responsibility for all of his or her actions.

Behavior modification: A technique for shaping desired behaviors through a system of rewards and punishments.

Group therapy: Counseling several individuals together in a group session.

Guided group interaction (GGI): Through group interactions a delinquent can acknowledge and solve personal problems with support from other group members.

Positive peer culture (PPC): Counseling program in which peer leaders encourage other group members to modify their behavior and peers help reinforce acceptable behaviors.

Milieu therapy: All aspects of the environment are part of the treatment, and meaningful change, increased growth, and satisfactory adjustment are encouraged.

Wilderness probation: Programs involving outdoor expeditions that provide opportunities for juveniles to confront the difficulties of their lives while achieving positive personal satisfaction.

Boot camps: Programs that combine get-tough elements with education, substance abuse treatment, and social skills training.

Meta-analysis: An analysis technique that synthesizes results and integrates findings across many programs over time.

Right to treatment: Philosophy espoused by many courts that juvenile offenders have a statutory right to treatment while under the jurisdiction of the courts.

Aftercare: Transitional assistance to juveniles equivalent to adult parole to help youths adjust to community life.

Reentry: The process and experience of the transition of juveniles from juvenile and adult correctional settings back into schools, families, communities, and society at large

Intensive Aftercare Program (IAP): A balanced, highly structured, comprehensive continuum of intervention for serious and violent juvenile offenders returning to the community.

SELF TEST QUESTIONS

MULTIPLE CHOICE

1. _____ is(are) defined as using non-secure and non-institutional residences, counseling services, victim restitution programs, and other community services to treat juveniles in their own communities.
    A. community treatment   C. radical non-intervention
    B. residential programs   D. diversion

2. A _____ screens juveniles and assign them to the appropriate facility.
    A. training school   C. ranch facility
    B. reception center   D. reformatory

3. _____ uncovered what they called a suppression effect which is a reduction in the number of arrests per year, following release from a secure treatment facility.
    A. Beccaria and Bentham   C. Sheldon and Eleanor Glueck
    B. Murray and Cox   D. Sampson and Laub

4. Correctional _____ combine the get-tough elements of adult programs with education, substance-abuse treatment, and social skills training.
    A. boot camps   C. group counseling
    B. wilderness camps   D. diagnostic center

5. _____ is a non-punitive legal disposition for youths, emphasizing treatment without incarceration; the primary form of community treatment used by the juvenile justice system.
    A. probation   C. dismissal
    B. parole   D. counseling

6. Which of the following is false concerning community treatment?
    A. maximizes liberty of the individual while at the same time protecting the public
    B. promotes rehabilitation by maintaining normal community contacts
    C. greatly reduces the cost to the public
    D. maintains a high level of stigma to facilitate a deterrent effect on other potential offenders

7. A common group treatment approach, _____ seeks to make all aspects of the inmates' environment part of their treatment and to minimize differences between custodial staff and treatment personnel.
    A. positive peer culture   C. guided group interaction
    B. milieu therapy   D. behavior modification therapy

8. About 385,400 juveniles were placed on probation in 2002, which accounts for about _____ percent of all juvenile dispositions.
    A. 20   C. 62
    B. 40   D. 85

9. A _____ implies a contract between the court and the juvenile; the court promises to hold a period of institutionalization in abeyance and the juvenile promises to adhere to a set of rules mandated by the court.

    A. probation sentence

    B. release on recognizance

    C. shock incarceration sentence

    D. release on bail

10. A version of Guided Group Interaction, called _____, uses groups in which peer leaders encourage other youths to conform to conventional behaviors; the rationale is that if negative peer influence can encourage youths to engage in delinquent behavior then positive peer influence can help them conform.

    A. positive peer culture

    B. milieu therapy

    C. the circle of pain

    D. behavior modification therapy

11. _____ are involved at four stages of the court process: intake, pre-disposition, post-adjudication, and post-disposition.

    A. police officers

    B. probation officers

    C. correctional treatment staff

    D. district attorney

12. The _____ is a clinical diagnosis of the child's problems and of the need for court assistance based on an evaluation of social functioning, personality, and environmental issues; it is prepared by the probation officer.

    A. petition

    B. predisposition report

    C. case study

    D. retrospective reinterpretation

13. The _____ are the rules and regulations mandating that a juvenile on probation behave in a particular way.

    A. conditions of confinement

    B. honor code

    C. conditions of probation

    D. terms of delivery

14. _____ is considered a true alternative to incarceration that involves almost daily supervision of the juvenile by the probation officer assigned to the case.

    A. foster home placement

    B. juvenile intensive probation supervision

    C. work release

    D. alternative school placement

15. Which of the following was not noted as a goal of Juvenile Intensive Probation Supervision?

    A. decarceration

    B. control

    C. reintegration

    D. retribution

16. _____ is when an offender is required to stay at home during specific periods of time; monitoring is done by random phone calls and visits or by electronic devices.

    A. grounding

    B. house arrest

    C. secure care

    D. private corrections

17. According to the authors, which of the following juveniles are the most likely clients of Juvenile Intensive Probation Supervision?
> A. juveniles who would normally be sent to secure facilities
> B. first time property offenders
> C. status offenders
> D. juveniles who would normally be waived to the adult system

18. Murray and Cox identified a _____, a reduction in the number of arrests per year, following release from a secure treatment facility.
> A. sensitizing effect
> B. brutalization effect
> C. resiliency effect
> D. suppression effect

19. _____ is defined as counseling several individuals together in a group session; individuals can obtain support from other group members as they work through similar problems.
> A. reality therapy
> B. psychotherapy
> C. group therapy
> D. behavior modification

20. _____ integrate community protection, the accountability of the juvenile offender, and individualized attention to the offender.
> A. balanced probation systems
> B. active systems
> C. passive systems
> D. intensive probation supervision

21. Reliance on incarceration became costly to states: inflation-controlled juvenile corrections expenditures for public facilities grew to more than $2 billion in 1995, an increase of _____ percent from 1982.
> A. 10 percent
> B. 20 percent
> C. 30 percent
> D 40 percent

22. _____ requires that juvenile offenders compensate crime victims for out of pocket losses caused by the crime, including property damage, lost wages, and medical expenses.
> A. monetary restitution
> B. community service restitution
> C. court cost fees
> D. fines

23. _____ are non-secured, structured residences that provide counseling, education, job training, and family living; they generally house 12-15 youths and the institutional quality of the environment is minimized.
> A. group homes
> B. foster care programs
> C. family group homes
> D. rural programs

24. _____ are designed for juveniles who are orphans or whose parents cannot care for them. Juveniles are placed with families who provide the attention, guidance, and care they did not receive at home; they usually involve one or two juveniles who live with a family usually a husband and wife who serve as surrogate parents.
> A. group homes
> B. foster care programs
> C. family group homes
> D. rural programs

25. _____ include forestry camps, ranches, and farms that provide recreational activities or work for juveniles; these programs typically handle between 30 and 50 youths.
  A. group homes
  B. foster care programs
  C. family group homes
  D. rural programs

26. _____ emphasizes current, rather than past, behavior by stressing that offenders are completely responsible for their own actions; this is accomplished by giving youths confidence through developing their ability to follow a set of expectations as closely as possible.
  A. reality therapy
  B. psychotherapy
  C. electric shock therapy
  D. behavior modification

27. Massachusetts was the first state to establish reform schools, opening the _____ in Westborough in 1846.
  A. Lyman School for Boys
  B. Center for Social Adjustment
  C. Westborough House of Corrections
  D. Westborough Helping Hands Center

28. _____ is based on the theory that all behavior is learned and that current behavior can be shaped through rewards and punishments.
  A. reality therapy
  B. psychotherapy
  C. electric shock therapy
  D. behavior modification

29. A policy known as _____ mandates that a youth should not be put in a secure institution if a community based program is available.
  A. least restrictive alternative
  B. net widening effect
  C. funneling process
  D. coddling tendency

30. Which of the following is not one of the characteristics of the inmate value system identified by Bartollas and his associates?
  A. exploit whomever you can
  B. drop a dime, stop a crime
  C. don't play up to staff
  D. don't rat on your peers

TRUE FALSE

1. Probation and other forms of community treatment generally refer to non-punitive legal disposition for delinquent youths, emphasizing treatment without incarceration.
  A. True
  B. False

2. About 385,400 juveniles are currently being placed on formal probation each year, which accounts for about 62 percent of all juvenile dispositions.
  A. True
  B. False

3. In 2003, there were almost 97000 youth confined in public and private facilities.
    A. True
    B. False

4. Research has found that the traditional big house model is most effective for rehabilitating juveniles.
    A. True
    B. False

5. From 1991 until 2003, the number of female delinquents in custody more than doubled.
    A. True
    B. False

6. An interview survey conducted by the National Council on Crime and Delinquency found that incidents of abuse of female offenders were minimal.
    A. True
    B. False

7. Probation officers are involved at four stages of the court process: intake, predisposition stage, and post disposition.
    A. True
    B. False

8. The authors note that community based programs have lower costs and are especially appropriate for large numbers of non-violent juveniles.
    A. True
    B. False

9. The decarceration policy mandates that courts use the least restrictive alternative in providing services for status offenders; a non-criminal youth should not be put in a secure facility if a community based program is available.
    A. True
    B. False

10. The decarceration policy mandates that courts use the most restrictive alternative in providing services for status offenders; a non-criminal youth should be put in a secure facility if a bed is available.
    A. True
    B. False

11. Juvenile Intensive Probation Supervision (JIPS) involves treating offenders who would have normally have been diverted out of the formal system.
    A. True
    B. False

12. The authors note that community corrections has traditionally emphasized offender rehabilitation.
 A. True
 B. False

13. The authors note that over the years, the number of females held in public institutions has declined; this represents the continuation of a long-term trend to remove girls, many of whom are non-serious offenders, from closed institutions and place them in private or community-based facilities.
 A. True
 B. False

14. The authors note that at last count, there were almost 12,000 juveniles being held in public and private facilities in the United States.
 A. True
 B. False

15. The authors note that although there are more coed institutions for juveniles than in the past, most girls remain incarcerated in single-sex institutions that are isolated in rural areas and rarely offer adequate rehabilitative services.
 A. True
 B. False

16. The authors note that in light of the concept of the right to treatment as determined by case law, if incarcerated, juveniles are entitled to the appropriate social services that will promote their rehabilitation.
 A. True
 B. False

17. Washington DC has more than twice the national juvenile custody rate.
 A. True
 B. False

18. The authors note that females are more likely than boys to be incarcerated for status offenses; institutions for females are generally more restrictive than those for boys, and they have fewer educational and vocational programs and fewer services.
 A. True
 B. False

19. Milieu therapy seeks to make all aspects of the inmates' environment part of their treatment and to minimize differences between custodial staff and treatment personnel.
 A. True
 B. False

20. A recent meta-analysis of the effects of juvenile boot camps on recidivism found this to be an ineffective correctional approach; from the seventeen different program samples, control groups had, on average, lower recidivism rates than treatment groups (boot camps).
    A. True
    B. False

21. Reality therapy is based on the theory that all behavior is learned and that current behavior can be shaped through rewards and punishments.
    A. True
    B. False

22. Behavior modification therapy is based on the theory that all behavior is learned and that current behavior can be shaped through rewards and punishments.
    A. True
    B. False

23. Reality therapy emphasizes current, rather than past, behavior by stressing that offenders are completely responsible for their own actions; this is accomplished by giving youths confidence through developing their ability to follow a set of expectations as closely as possible.
    A. True
    B. False

24. Psychotherapy emphasizes current, rather than past, behavior by stressing that offenders are completely responsible for their own actions; this is accomplished by giving youths confidence through developing their ability to follow a set of expectations as closely as possible.
    A. True
    B. False

25. Group therapy is defined as counseling several individuals together in a group session; individuals can obtain support from other group members as they work through similar problems.
    A. True
    B. False

FILL IN

1. _____ treatment is defined as using non-secure and non-institutional residences, counseling services, victim restitution programs, and other community services to treat juveniles in their own communities.

2. _____ is a non-punitive legal disposition for youths, emphasizing treatment without incarceration; it is the primary form of community treatment used by the juvenile justice system.

3. _____ programs include forestry camps, ranches, and farms that provide recreational activities or work for juveniles; these programs typically handle between 30 and 50 youths.

4. _____ are rules mandating that a juvenile on probation behave in a particular way; they can include restitution, participation in an educational program, refraining from associating with certain types of people, and remain in a particular area unless they have permission to leave.

5. _____ are involved at four stages of the court process: intake, predispositional, post-adjudication, and post-disposition.

6. The social investigation report, or _____ report, is a clinical diagnosis of the child's problems and of the need for court assistance based on an evaluation of social functioning, personality, and environmental issues; it is prepared by the probation officer.

7. Juvenile _____ is considered a true alternative to incarceration that involves almost daily supervision of the juvenile by the probation officer assigned to the case.

8. _____ requires an offender to stay at home during specific periods of time; monitoring is done by random phone calls and visits or by electronic devices.

9. _____ is an analysis technique that synthesizes results across many programs over time.

10. The _____ was based on housing juveniles in a compound containing a series of small cottages, each of which accommodates twenty to forty children and is run by a set of cottage parents who create a home-like atmosphere.

11. _____ integrates community protection, the accountability of the juvenile offender, and individualized attention to the offender.

12. Most of today's _____ are relatively small facilities holding fewer than 30 youths.

13. Monetary _____-___ is a requirement that juvenile offenders compensate crime victims for out of pocket losses caused by the crime, including property damage, lost wages, and medical expenses.

14. _____ are non-secured, structured residences that provide counseling, education, job training, and family living; they generally house 12-15 youths and the institutional quality of the environment is minimized.

15. _____ are designed for juveniles who are orphans or whose parents cannot care for them. Juveniles are placed with families who provide the attention, guidance, and care they did not receive at home; they usually involve one or two juveniles who live with a family usually a husband and wife who serve as surrogate parents.

ESSAY

1. Identify and discuss the various roles and duties of a juvenile probation officer. Are there any inherent contradictions in these duties?

2. Discuss the goals of Juvenile Intensive Probation Supervision.

3. Identify and discuss the various theoretical models of group treatment.

4. Discuss the role and significance of juvenile probation services.

5. Identify and discuss the importance of juvenile aftercare programs. What are characteristics of successful programs?

ANSWER KEY

MULTIPLE CHOICE

1. A	11. B	21. B
2. B	12. B	22. A
3. B	13. C	23. A
4. A	14. B	24. B
5. A	15. D	25. D
6. D	16. B	26. A
7. B	17. A	27. A
8. C	18. D	28. D
9. A	19. C	29. A
10. A	20. A	30. B

TRUE FALSE

1. T	11. F	21. F
2. T	12. T	22. T
3. T	13. T	23. T
4. F	14. F	24. F
5. F	15. T	25. T
6. F	16. T	
7. T	17. T	
8. T	18. T	
9. T	19. T	
10. F	20. T	

FILL IN

1. community
2. probation
3. rural
4. probation conditions
5. probation officers
6. predisposition
7. intensive probation supervision
8. house arrest
9. meta-analysis
10. cottage system
11. balanced probation
12. private institutions
13. restitution
14. group homes
15. foster care programs

Multiple Choice

1. Today what ratio of those in custody for a violent offence belongs to a minority?
   A. 4 in 10
   B. 5 in 10
   C. 6 in 10
   D. 7 in 10

2. Community treatment is based on the idea that
   A. it is cheaper than incarceration.
   B. the juvenile offender is not a danger to the community and has a better chance of being rehabilitated in the community.
   C. by placing as many offenders in intensive community treatment, it is possible to place more serious ones in prison.
   D. even if there is a greater chance of recidivism while the offender is in the community, since the objective of the court is to act in the best interest of the youth, community treatment is the preferred choice.

3. What percentage of adult prison inmates had prior experience with the juvenile court?
   A. 10-20
   B. 20-30
   C. 30-40
   D. 40-50

4. Approximately how many youth were placed on probation in 2002?
   A. 385,400
   B. 425,400
   C. 485,400
   D. 585,400

5. A social investigation or predisposition report
   A. contains the charge and age of the offender.
   B. contains the psychologists assessment of the juvenile.
   C. contains a clinical diagnosis of the child's problem as well his or her capacity to change and environmental influences that can help resolve the problem.
   D. contains a detailed prediction of the presumed chances of recidivism of the child based upon risk assessment, sentencing guidelines, and diagnostic tools of psychologists.

6. Juvenile intensive probation supervision
   A. prevents inmates from committing suicide and taking drugs while confined.
   B. was designed to divert at-risk youth in the schools to community treatment.
   C. involves high caseloads for probation officers and electronic monitoring in the community.
   D. is a strategy employed to effectuate decarceration.

7. In a recent study in California it was found that juvenile intensive probation efforts
    A. lead to similar recidivism rates as regular probation.
    B. have higher recidivism rates as regular probation.
    C. lead to lower recidivism rates than regular probation.
    D. usually to higher suicide and drug abuse rates than regular probation.

8. Renseman and Evan Mayo-Wilson's evaluation of house arrest programs
    A. found that they produce no greater recidivism than other traditional programs.
    B. found that they result in lower recidivism rather than other traditional programs.
    C. found that program evaluations were inconclusive.
    D. found that house arrest programs reduced drug abuse and suicide among probationers.

9. In their research on restorative justice program, Strang and Sherman found that the most effective programs had face-to-face conferences characterized by
    A. quasi-legal negotiations in front of non-judicial magistrates.
    B. sensitivity training and when necessary crisis intervention.
    C. the victim describing the harm, the offender listening, and all participating in deliberations about actions to be taken to restore balance.
    D. confrontational approaches in which the parties were able to release their pent up frustrations and in so doing restore justice.

10. According to the text, the least restrictive alternative policy in reference to status offenders concerns
    A. providing them with sight and sound separation when confined with adult prisoners
    B. placing status offenders in juvenile secure facilities with no adult inmates
    C. providing them with sight, sound separation when confined with juvenile delinquents.
    D. not putting status offenders in a secure facility

True False
1. According to the House Committee on Government Reform, about 25,000 youth with psychiatric disorders were awaiting mental health services while improperly incarcerated in secure detention facilities in 2003. T   F

2 Research suggests that 65 percent of youths in the juvenile justice system suffer from mental health problems.   T   F

3. From 1991 until 2003 the number of female juvenile offenders in custody increased by more than one half T   F

4. William Glaser's reality therapy includes a strict regimen of rewards and punishments and usually calls for behaviour modification schedules and a contract with the clients. T F

5. Guided Group Interaction stresses individualized therapy within the milieu of the group therapy T F

Multiple Choice
1. D
2. B
3. C
4. A
5. C
6. D
7. A
8. C
9. C
10. D

True False
1. F
2. T
3. T
4. F
5. F